Being, Essence, and Substance in Plato and Aristotle

Being, Essence, and Substance in Plato and Aristotle

Paul Ricoeur

Course taught at the University of Strasbourg in 1953–1954
Text verified and annotated by Jean-Louis Schlegel
Translated by David Pellauer and John Starkey

polity

First published in French as *Être, essence et substance chez Platon et Aristote* © Editions du Seuil, 2011

This English edition © Polity Press, 2013

Polity Press
65 Bridge Street
Cambridge CB2 1UR, UK

Polity Press
350 Main Street
Malden, MA 02148, USA

ISBN-13: 978-0-7456-6054-7
ISBN-13: 978-0-7456-6055-4 (pb)

A catalogue record for this book is available from the British Library.

Typeset in 11 on 13 pt Sabon by
Servis Filmsetting Ltd, Stockport, Cheshire

The publisher has used its best endeavours to ensure that the URLs for external websites referred to in this book are correct and active at the time of going to press. However, the publisher has no responsibility for the websites and can make no guarantee that a site will remain live or that the content is or will remain appropriate.

Every effort has been made to trace all copyright holders, but if any have been inadvertently overlooked the publisher will be pleased to include any necessary credits in any subsequent reprint or edition.

For further information on Polity, visit our website: www.politybooks.com

Contents

Editor's Introduction   vii

    The Goal and Plan of the Course   1

I Plato
Part I "True Being" or the Idea

  1 The Meaning of Platonic "*Eidos*"   8
  2 Essence and Language   13
  3 Science and Essence   20
      I "Opinion" as the Negative of Science
  4 Science and Essence   29
      II Right Opinion as "Intermediary"
  5 Science and Essence   34
      III The Mathematical "Intermediary"
  6 Science and Essence (Conclusion)   47
      IV The "Terminus" of Science: Contemplation

Part II The Idea of Being and Non-Being

  7 The Question of Being in the *Parmenides*   74
  8 The Success and Failures of Platonism in the *Sophist*   90
  9 The Genesis of the Sensible in the *Timaeus*   102

Part III Being and the "Divine"

10 The Problem of the "Divine" and Presocratic Philosophy 117
11 The "Divine" in Plato   128

II Aristotle
    Introduction   145

Part I Being as Being

12 The "Genetic" Interpretation of Aristotle's *Metaphysics* 151
13 Philosophy: Its Intention and its Memory   161
14 Philosophy and its "Aporias"   175
15 The Object of "First Philosophy"   182

Part II Being and Substance

    Introduction   195
16 Sensible Substance: Substance as Substrate   198
17 Sensible Substance (continued): Substance as Form   215
18 Substance and the Individual   223
19 "Separate" Substance   237

Index   254
Index of Passages Cited in Plato and Aristotle   262

Editor's Introduction

First taught and distributed in mimeographed form in Strasbourg during the 1953–1954 academic year, this *Course* (as we shall designate it for the rest of this book) certainly had been thought about and in preparation since 1949, if not earlier, as the documents now in the Ricoeur Archive in Paris attest. In 1949, Ricoeur had taught a course on "Plato and the Problem of the Soul." There are two sets of handwritten documents from this time in the archive titled "Problems of the Soul in Plato's Philosophy" (125 pages) and "Plato and the Divine" (45 pages). They include abbreviated words and things crossed out. The folder for the 1953–1954 course now in the archive is composed in part of a notebook entirely and carefully handwritten. It contains sections titled "I. Essence and Being in Plato" (96 pages) and "II. Aristotle" (100 pages). This latter portion includes a good number of pages that appear in the later mimeographed copy of the *Course*, but does not yet represent the definitive state of the text on Aristotle. Beyond this, there is an incomplete copy of the mimeographed course (59 pages) on whose cover is written: "Paul Ricoeur/Being, Essence, and Substance in Plato and Aristotle/Course taught at the University of Strasbourg in 1953–1954."

In establishing this edition of the *Course*, beyond the first complete version from 1954, I have made use of the mimeographed version from the Sorbonne dated 1957 and especially the paperback edition from 1982. On their title pages all of them have the subheading "Course taught at Strasbourg in 1953–1954." Hence in preparing this edition I had at my disposal three "editions" of the same document that was duplicated for student use in 1954, 1957, and 1982. The first one, from Strasbourg, which Ricoeur did not change in any way thereafter, clearly bears the signs of that day and its technology. Its quality is not very good – letters are sometimes run into one another in order to correct a typing mistake, ancient Greek is typewritten without accents and with many errors, and the Greek transcriptions are quite often wrong. The second, Paris version, put out by the CDU, the Centre de documentation universitaire, corrects some of the faults of the earlier one, in particular through a systematic and precise rewriting, by hand, of the quotations from ancient Greek. But apart from this – which is valuable because of the corrections it makes to numerous faults in the first typed version – the course "edited" in Paris in 1957 is identical to the one from Strasbourg. The edition put out in 1982 by the CDU and SEDES (the Société d'édition d'enseignement supérieur) reprints in bound paperback form the mimeographed version from the CDU at the Sorbonne. Its great merit is the publication of a clean version, the ancient Greek this time being set in typographical letters with their diacritical marks. But the text is wholly that of the two earlier "editions" from Strasbourg and Paris (whose typographical errors and other mistakes, such as faulty references, it retains).[1]

Ricoeur never chose to rework this material, even though he was quite aware, particularly over the years, of its limits, perhaps because of the numerous works of high quality on Plato and Aristotle that had been published since 1953 and also because of the appearance of new translations, some of which included important differences. Like many of his subsequent works, this course is the fruit of a careful reading of the texts of Plato and Aristotle, but also of many articles and commentaries on their works. Rather than taking up this course again, at the price of considerable work, Ricoeur preferred to let it lie, as it were, in its original form, despite any dissatisfaction he may have felt about it, and to let it continue its career as a "Course from the Sorbonne."

The basic text published here remains unchanged, but it has been prepared following today's criteria for such an edition and has been annotated in order to assist today's readers.

---

[1] I thank Stéphane Bureau for having shared his own corrections of this edition.

This work turned out to be more complex than I first assumed it would be. Allow me to indicate the interventions and corrections, and the very few modifications I have introduced. It is likely that some of the initial imperfections were due to the passage from a handwritten to a typed manuscript. It is also possible that in the beginning the publication of a mimeographed "course" took place without any proofreading or corrections being made – something Ricoeur would later be much stricter about if one can believe the corrected proofs of other mimeographed courses now in the Ricoeur archive.

– For the present edition, the typographical errors and mistakes in spelling, which are numerous, have been removed. However, the principal things requiring correction were the incomplete or mistaken references to Plato's and Aristotle's works. I have corrected them without always indicating this, so as not to overload the text, using both older and new translations – and in a few cases it may well be that the corrected references do correspond to the translations Ricoeur used. Beyond these corrections to more or less important errors, the text itself remains unchanged. I have left as they first appeared expressions or grammatical phrases that may appear to be incorrect; for example, in the body of the text, the frequent references to passages to Plato or Aristotle that appear with the preposition "at" (e.g., "the *Philebus* at 17c," rather than "*Philebus* 17c"). I have also left unchanged the inconsistent use of capital and lower case letters for important words (Idea, God, Being, and others as well).

– Punctuation, which was often faulty, even incoherent or absent, or which failed to correspond to current standards, has been revised. But, beyond the necessary corrections, changes have been made solely to improve readability, avoiding every arbitrary or unneeded correction. So as not to appear heavy-handed or overly pedantic, I have not indicated those modifications which make no difference in the text's meaning (and if – rarely – there is a difference, it has been indicated).

– The course includes numerous words and expressions in ancient Greek, with or without their transcription. In many cases, there is a transcription but only that; in others, they are written only in Greek letters. I have preserved, correcting if necessary, the ancient Greek spelling and given (as a note) a transcription using the current way of writing them out. The Greek transcriptions (those in the course and those added) have been brought into a unified form. When Ricoeur gives the word in ancient Greek and his transcription, I have indicated this by an equal sign. More generally, given that many readers today do not know ancient Greek, I have sought to restore it with as much clarity as possible and with the necessary clarifications for readers who have not studied the language.

– Citations: (a) I have left in the body of the text references to quotations from Plato and Aristotle, along with references to other ancient authors. As already indicated, all these references have been verified, completed, or re-established when they were inexact. In several cases I have not been able to locate the precise or exact reference; (b) I have taken references to the works of modern commentators that were found originally in the body of the text and placed them in footnotes, again completing or correcting these references as necessary. This is indicated by AC (meaning: author cited in the text, but now in a note); (c) The course as originally published included footnotes by Ricoeur, which I indicate by PR; (d) All notes without these indications were added by me, and I assume the responsibility for them.

– In preparing this work, as already indicated, I found important differences among different existing translations both for Plato and for Aristotle (particularly for the latter, whose texts – especially the *Metaphysics* – present well-known intrinsic difficulties), but I have naturally retained the translations Ricoeur used, which date essentially from the first half of the twentieth century. In general, those he cites come, for Plato, from the "Guillaume Budé" collection issued by the Éditions des Belles Lettres, which began to publish a translation of Plato's collected works in the 1920s and 1930s, and, for Aristotle, from Tricot's translations published by Vrin. Yet it appears that Ricoeur consulted and sometimes combined several translations (some of which go back to the nineteenth century). In any case, for this course, the quotations (in particular Tricot's translation of Aristotle's *Metaphysics*) are not always cited literally by Ricoeur – and sometimes he summarizes or abridges them. This may surprise us, but at that time, unlike ours, no one was expected to cite a translation strictly for an ancient text that was known to many. The stakes for his interpretation may appear to be great, however – and Ricoeur was quite aware of this afterwards. As an example of this, I sometimes cite in the notes particularly divergent translations – where the divergences may perhaps be due to the choice of a different version of the Greek text. But verifying this, which would have required looking at all the critical editions, hardly made sense for what was required for this edition.

The "Course taught at Strasbourg in 1953–1954" certainly did not require these improvements, useful as they might be or even necessary as they may be today, to be what it is: one of the most perspicuous analyses of two monuments – nearly contemporary and yet so very different – of the metaphysical tradition. To have brought together Plato *and* Aristotle, in terms of the breaks *and* continuities of the latter with the former, in already insisting on the function and the critique of the language of metaphysics, is not the least of its original contributions.

Jean-Louis Schlegel

The Goal and Plan of the Course

The long-term goal of this course is to work out the ontological foundations of our Western philosophy, so as to understand its intention by way of the history of its beginning.

Its more immediate goal is to understand the import of the debate between Plato and Aristotle, to grasp there the origin of a rhythm of our philosophy. It is banal to say that this rhythm is that of a philosophy of essence and a philosophy of substance. That is true in part. But the true contribution of Plato and Aristotle to metaphysics lies beyond that. Plato is not solely the theoretician of Forms or Ideas, but rather the one who has most vigorously refuted an elementary and naïve Platonism which could be invoked in the name of the theory of Ideas; beginning with the *Parmenides*, a second-degree ontology is constructed that is Plato's true contribution to ontology. Still, it will be necessary to come to a solid understanding of what we shall call the first-degree ontology and to recover the very strong reasons behind the theory of Ideas, since the meditation on the ideas of being and non-being does not constitute a repudiation of the first ontology, but rather a putting into question of its very foundations. This is why we will begin by lingering over this first ontology, whose rationale we will seek in a justification drawn from human speech more than in an explication of reality. It is on this plane that the idea of a "true being" (*ontos on* = ὄντως ὄν)[1] is constituted, which is precisely the Idea. The more radical ontology proceeds from a redoubling of the question of being: What is the being of these beings, of these genuine be-ings [*etants*] which we have called forms? Under what condition is being thinkable? It is this critical ontology that will occupy us in the second part of the lectures on Plato.

But Aristotle is no less difficult and complex: the apparent symmetric counterpart of Platonic essence is Aristotelian substance, and yet this philosophy of substance, which we too quickly reduce to that of sensible, physical substance, is itself also caught up in an investigation of "being as being." The *Metaphysics* broaches the topic of sensible, physical substance only in starting from this radical problematic, which we will study in the first part of the course devoted to Aristotle. What is more, the object of physics is introduced in the *Metaphysics* only as one step between the clarification of "being as being" and the determination of a supreme substance, an excellent, first substance. It is this latter doctrine that will present itself as the realization of the program of the *Metaphysics*. We shall study this doctrine in the second part of the lectures on Aristotle. In brief, Aristotelian ontology is not a simple antithesis to Platonism; the radical ontology of Aristotle stands in a far more subtle relation of continuity and of opposition to that of Plato; it is this relation we have to understand as giving the true import of an all too simple opposition between a philosophy of essence and a philosophy of substance.

---

[1] Recall what was said in the Editor's Introduction: when Ricoeur gives two ways of writing Greek – ancient Greek and its transcription, or vice versa, the transcription followed by the word in ancient Greek – their equivalence is indicated by the = sign. When just the Greek form exists in the text, the transcription is given in a footnote.

I
Plato

First Part

"True Being" or the Idea

The theme of this first part of my lectures on Plato is the *ontological status* that Plato has accorded to the Ideas or Forms. It is difficult to get back to the origin of the Platonic problem; to do so it is necessary to forget Aristotle's critique, which was carried out from the point of view of his own philosophy. From that point of view, Plato attributed to the Ideas, which were after all only the possible *attributes* of things, the dignity of being that belongs by right to the *subjects* of such attributions, existing things themselves. If one begins in this way, Platonism immediately appears as a great absurdity which can no longer be repeated on its own terms. We must also forget, even beyond Aristotle's critique, Aristotle's question, which is to understand the "why" (the *dioti* = διότι) of existing things, and thereby to make sense of the real such as it is. What we need to do is to allow ourselves to be grasped by Plato's properly Socratic style of posing the question, in order to understand the question that *he* poses to us, in order to unfold all that is implied in his specific question.

Chapter 1

The Meaning of Platonic
"*Eidos*"

The question of essence is born from a question formulated in the following terms: "What is X?" – for example: What is courage? What is virtue? (Cf., for example, *Laches* 190c ff.)

First comment

What does a question formulated in this way put *in* question? This question arises with such virulent force only for those who find within themselves a particular species of *malaise*; not one that is a matter of life or death, obviously, but rather one that has to do with knowing. The mind is no longer satisfied by responses that take the form of enumerating examples and then of coordinating them: *Laches* 191d ("not only . . . but also"; "but also . . . and . . . and . . ."). Having been deceived by the "completely natural" feel of initial definitions, and then overwhelmed by the endless task of coordinating characteristics or species, the mind requires that these be subordinated to a dominant character, to a sovereign kind.

Second comment

Essence will be defined by means of a *function of unity and of identity* (*Laches* 191e). The Idea is *one* (*mia* = μία) and the same (*to auto* = τὸ αὐτό). In the place of multiple cases we now have *one* idea (cf. *Hippias Major* 288a: *auto to kalon* = αὐτὸ τὸ καλόν, translated as "beautiful in itself," which points to the permanence of the meaning of our words). There has to be a shift in levels, a mental leap, if we are to get from the level of enumeration to the level of the "same," from extension to understanding. It is this function that the word *eidos* = εἶδος or "idea" signifies (cf. *Euthyphro* 5d: "what is the idea of . . ."). According to Taylor, the term had a geometric origin and pointed to the shape of a geometric figure. Ross shows that Plato has taken the word from popular vocabulary; the word is already over-determined at this point; it indicates the external contour but also the internal structure (*Beschaffenheit*) of a figure. The word "*eidos*" already has a semi-logical sense (the place of a species within a classification); it is the "look" taken on by anything whatever.[1]

Vision lies at the origin of all the senses of the word: the *eidos* is the visible form (cf. the Latin *forma*). For Diès, what we have is a visualization of the intelligible and the beginning of a series of successive sublimations of seeing (contemplation), a Platonic transcription from the visible to the intelligible. The word *eidos* is itself "capable" of this transposition.

Third comment

From the start the question of *being* underlies the function of identity that essence provides. The verb "to be" is already there: "What is . . . ?" "What has the capacity to be . . . ?" (*Laches* 190e). The question always involves the verb "to be" (cf. *Hippias Major* 288a); the verb "to be" is affirmed two times; things *are* beautiful and they *are*: "If there *exists* a beauty in itself," translates Croiset, "the things that you say *to be* beautiful *are* so in fact."[2] Being as existence, then, already appears as the foundation of being as the copula: this *is* beautiful, if the beautiful itself *is*. It is true that *Hippias Major* 292c-e omits the verb "to be" employed

---

[1] Cf. W. D. Ross, *Plato's Theory of Ideas* (Oxford: Clarendon Press, 1951) (AC). [Remember the addition AC, meaning "author cited," means Ricoeur's own references to modern commentators on Plato and Aristotle have been changed to notes, often with the details of the reference filled in.]

[2] Alfred Croiset's translation of *Hippias Major* appeared in the Belles Lettres series in 1920.

in an absolute sense. The question of the being of essence will in the end be something like a doubling of the original question about it. The final question of Plato's philosophy is already posed at the beginning, implied in the two uses of the word "to be." We catch a glimpse of the difficult problem: What are the connections between the two uses of the verb "to be," as copula and as absolute existence? The whole of Platonism consists in sliding from the verb "to be," with very little emphasis (and employed with person and tense), to a participle (*on* = ὤνὄν) that Latin translates as *ens*, then to the substantive participle (we pass from *ti on* to *to on*), and finally to *ousia* (which Gilson translates by *étance*). It appears that this series of equivalences is present from the very origin of Platonism (*ousia* already appeared in *Cratylus* 401c). It is in fact possible to run permutations on all the functions of the word "to be," as we see for example in *Sophist* 246a (*esti, on, to on, einai, ousia* = ἔστι, ὤν, τὸ ὄν, εἶναι, οὐσία).

Fourth comment

What is the *relation of essence to things*? The Platonic vocabulary is quite supple at the outset. From the *Laches* on, the relation of essence to things is a relation of *inherence* (192a); essence is *in* things. Enumeration is taken up again from a higher standpoint and founded in the definition. Essence wins out over things so as to gather them together, to collect them. Here the ontological intention does not yet separate essence from things: in the early dialogues, the relation of inherence is employed but not reflected upon; this is why the Platonic vocabulary remains hesitant: essence is located within, "en," or throughout, *dia*. Identity is present "in" variation, unity circulates *throughout* the cases (*Meno* 74a, 77a: Plato is led to say there that essence is the *all* of multiple things, which will become the Aristotelian "universal"). In any case, at this point we still have nothing to do with a relation of *imitation*. The relation of imitation, dominated by the mathematical model, will make its appearance in reflection on the mathematical forms as well as on the inadequation of the copy to the model in the moral order; then this relation of imitation will substitute itself for participation, for *methexis*, which at the beginning designates the inverse connection, that of things to their essence.

In the early dialogues, in fact, essence *is* in the things, and the things inversely *have* essence (*Meno* 72a) (the French translation does not respect the construction of the word *methexis*, "participation," which signifies "having a part in"); this is a dialectical relation between being and having. The being of essence is what things have. *Meno* 72c draws the two verbs together; that by which the virtues *are* is what they *have*. Their instrument of existence (that "by which" they are) is their essential having. At the beginning of Platonism, the possible is the possibility *of* the real, and not the possible *as* real. The interest of Platonism is initially absorbed *by the function of essence in connection to things*; that is why the verb "to be" is not accentuated at first. Plato will insist on being in itself only when he begins to emphasize the imperfection of the relation of essence to things, at the moment when he will want to begin to clarify that the things *are only* resemblances. Then he will insist on the split and no longer on the joint possession between particular things and their essences. The sensible, "not having" the intelligible, will not be able to give it, nor will the sensible be able even to "recall" it, to evoke it by "reminiscence." There will be solidarity between reminiscence as distant resemblance (and so no longer an implication) and knowledge of the intelligible.

Fifth comment

The Idea contains a certain *many* from the beginning of Platonism: although a unity, it lets itself be *analyzed*. This is the very condition of definition, which presupposes that, if the Idea is *one* with respect to its examples, it is nonetheless divisible with respect to its characteristics (*Laches* 192b). Definition, as a substitution for the defined items (many) by the defined (simple), presupposes from the beginning that the Idea must be an articulated plurality: the *Sophist*, therefore, presents no innovation in this regard. In the early dialogues we find the common source of the Platonic problem of the "interconnection of kinds" and the Aristotelian problem of the genus–species hierarchy. The interconnection of kinds signifies that certain notions fit together with each other, and it is this fitting together that is attested by the copula. A definition is an attribution where the copula is omitted: defining is attribution without the verb to be. This will be the other side of the same difficulties that will appear with respect to definition and the interconnection of kinds.

Sixth comment

From the beginning, the problem of definition is attached to the problem of *language*, by the *name*. What is it that by rights this word belongs to? The function of unity and identity is inscribed in the name. The problem of essence is the problem of the justification of language; it is the problem of the critique of language,[3] which will be taken up in the following chapter.

---

[3] Cf. Brice Parain, *Essai sur la nature et la fonction du langage* (Paris: Gallimard, "Bibliothèque des Idées," 1943) (AC).

Chapter 2

Essence and Language

The problem of essence is identical to that of language, of naming. The question "What is virtue, courage?" is equivalent to "What is it that we *call* virtue, courage?" The Platonic problem is a problem of a foundation, of the critique of language.

1   In what respect is essence the foundation of the word?
2   What is it that the act of naming tells us about essence?

1   Analysis of the *Cratylus*

In the *Cratylus*, the theses are put forward in the vocabulary of the conflict of that period, between "nature" and "convention." These theses are presented by Cratylus and Hermogenes, the one affirming that naming is "right" by nature, the other that naming is a "convention" that has become customary. The solution is ambiguous: the two theses are both accepted and rejected. The question of knowing whether language is "by nature" or "by convention" is a problem of Sophistic origin. Socrates confronts the two positions but accepts neither the one nor the other.

Socrates, however, is going to transpose the problem from a question of fact into a question of what is correct: What is the *destinatio* of language? It is that of signifying reality. Signification is the foundation of *right* naming. If language were right, it would be the vehicle of essence. In fact, language is not faithful to the nature of things: according to the myth of the *Cratylus* (439c), it has been instituted by a "drunken legislator,"[1] an aberrant one, and bears the mark of this original sin. This turnabout, this balancing between the two theses, is an attempt to express the very situation of language: on the one side it is a *sign* of reality, but at the same time it risks being a false knowing. Language situates itself on the plane of equivocity. Etymology cannot be dialectic, cannot be science. This complex relation of fidelity and treachery is of the very essence of language. Philosophy does not consist of interrogating the words, but the things themselves. It is important to note that it is here that the term dialectic makes its initial appearance in Platonism (439a).[2] True knowledge summons us from the words to the reality. The good dialectician is the one who goes from the words to the reality; he is the good legislator. To do a philosophy of essence is to assign language to the essence that judges it.

2 What new features does this ambiguous relation of word and essence make appear in the essence itself?

a) First feature

Essence is what keeps everything in language from being arbitrary invention.

Plato draws support from the opposition, classic in his time, between what is "by nature" and what is "by convention." If language is convention, it has a history as a human work. But we cannot shut it up in history: essence is what keeps everything in language from being convention. Language comes to man without his being able to bend it to his will arbitrarily. The passage from *legein* to "logos" signifies that one cannot say just anything at all. The thesis of convention, of a temporal slippage of sig-

---

[1] The translation by Émile Chambry (Paris: GF-Flammarion, 1967), 471, does not have the word "drunken." Words have fallen "into a kind of whirlwind" and have gotten "all mixed together" there. [The same applies to the translations of the *Cratylus* into English by Benjamin Jowett in *The Collected Dialogues of Plato*, ed. Edith Hamilton and Huntington Cairns (New York: Pantheon, 1961) and C. D. C. Reeve in *Plato: The Complete Works*, ed. John M. Cooper (Indianapolis: Hackett, 1997). – Trans.]

[2] The "dialectical legislator" does not appear here, but rather in *Cratylus* 390c.

nifications, appears in constant connection with the ontological thesis of universal becoming. That is why, before the *Theaetetus* but like it, the *Cratylus* in its opening section attacks Protagoras' thesis concerning "man as the measure of all things," replacing his thesis with *ousia* as the measure of language. This is one of the first times (along with *Euthyphro* 11a) that being is named under the substantive form of *ousia*; the intention of the substantive is anti-subjectivist: "Do you believe that *ousia* is proper to each one?" But man would be "the measure of all things" if language were nothing but convention (385c). *Ousia* is the measure of language: man, generator of significations, is himself measured by the being of the significations (383d). The sociological nature–convention debate becomes the ontological being–appearing debate. It is *dokein* that is the measure of the human, of convention (cf. the connection of language and appearance in 386a-c). Further on, at 386e, Plato defines a being for itself, a realism of significations. *The problem of essence* is the problem of an absolute language, of a "right" language.[3] We would be faced with the "name in itself" if we could "see" the significations (*Cratylus* 389d); it is this that the legislator of true language does, "eyes fixed on that which is the name in itself" (ibid.); this ideal legislator would be, precisely, the dialectician.

We are thus at the root of the *realism of significations* (articulated at 386e). In effect, one of the sources of the ontology of essences is the refusal of subjectivism and historicism with regard to language. Essence is identified with being, convention is reduced to appearing. Conventional language is therefore seeming. Ross claims that Plato takes no interest in absolute existence except with regard to mathematical essences, by reason of the dissimilarity introduced between the model and the copy with respect to those. But the reality of essence appears from the beginning – because of the problem of language. If Plato was led to say that essence presides over things (*Phaedo*), it is because of having said that essence presides over words (*Cratylus* 439a). If Plato says that things imitate essences, it is because language imitates realities. The problem of imitation was first posed with respect to language. It was therefore necessary to go to the things themselves, dodging

---

[3] Cf. Edmund Husserl, third *Logical Study*: the idea of an absolute grammar that would be logic (AC). [*Logical Investigations*, trans. J. N. Findlay (London: Routledge & Kegan Paul, 1970), 435–89.]

the words, to pass from the "verbal" copy to the "real" model. It is perhaps one of Platonism's weaknesses to present the signs of language as paintings, as imitations, with respect to the realities in themselves that one must try to attain by leaping over the "shadows," of which words are one species. This is the path whose trajectory leads to the cave: the first shadow is the word. Because Plato starts from language, his entire philosophy of essence is marked by that beginning. Meaning pre-exists the word; meaning is thus the initial pre-existence, the initial transcendence of appearing by being. We can add that the problem of the contemplation of the model and of imitation has its origin in the problem of the foundation of language, since the ideal legislator "looks at" things in order to "imitate" them in words (*Cratylus* 439a). From there comes the idea, no doubt chimerical, of ourselves considering the models directly as well, without the copies, and thus going *to the things themselves, without words* (439b). How does the philosophy of essences bear the mark of this linguistic starting point?

b) Second feature

This approach to the problem of essence through language has a converse consequence; the entire philosophy of essence bears the mark of this linguistic starting point (Aristotle in *Metaphysics*, Book A, names Cratylus as Plato's first teacher).[4]

The fundamental act of speaking for Plato is not the act of putting things in relation, but the act of *naming*, the act of discriminating reality, which consists in affixing a verbal contour to things. At its origin, Platonic reflection bears not on the judgment, but on the concept. What is more, to speak is to want to say something to someone: language implies intersubjectivity. Language is therefore at the same time both an instructive and a discriminating instrument; in 388b it is said that through language "we instruct others, and we distinguish things according to their nature"; but naming, that is, discrimination, takes that step through instructing the other at 387c; thus, language can be addressed to another only because it first connects to things. We first distinguish things by their "nature" (*Cratylus* 387c and 388c). Speaking is a "praxis" which connects to things (πράγματα

---

4 Aristotle, *Metaphysics*, 987a30.

387c),[5] and what gives "things" a "nature" is their *ousia*. The consequence is important for all Platonic ontology. Being is *essentially* discontinuous; it gives itself straight away in multiple realities, in beings. On account of this reflection on language, Plato here distances himself from Parmenides, for whom non-being is unthinkable because being is *one*. For Plato it is immediately a plural.[6] The Platonic ontology is a pluralist ontology: because there *are many* words, there *many* beings (*ta onta*). At the same time Platonism is a philosophy engaged in a reflection on the relations of things among themselves. Each being is what it is, but it is not all the rest. Being and non-being are two categories which imply each other: being is what it *is* and at the same time it is not the other beings. Parmenides, on the contrary, has affirmed the identity of Being and of One. Plato is from the start more down to earth. A pluralist ontology is a relational ontology. According to Diès, Parmenides' philosophy would lead to one unique summit, whereas with Plato's we discern "a series of discontinuous peaks" (the Beautiful, the True, etc.): the "true be-ings." Platonism is thus the investigation of a pluralized field of significations: ontology is defined as an exploration of a countryside where there are things to see, a "plain of truths." The laws of essence are implied in this pluralism:

- Law of distinct determination: To think is first to *separate*, to dissociate, to recognize one thing as not being other realities. To philosophize is to recognize the contour of one act of knowing insofar as it is not another. Platonism, in this sense, goes against Kantianism, for which to think is to join, to seize again the unity of a multiplicity of appearances. To think, for Plato, is to separate prior to joining. The Platonic problem is analogous in this sense to the Cartesian one, of the clarity that is achieved only through distinction, which involves pluralizing a field that is initially confused (cf. *Cratylus* 386e). It is a question of "each being": naming is the distributive act which brings it about that there is an "each," that each reality has its nature. Cf. *Phaedo* 78d, *Republic* VI 490b, VII 532a, VI 476a.
- Second law: The problem of being, in the singular, is no longer

---

[5] *pragmata.*
[6] Cf. Auguste Diès, *Autour de Platon: Essais de critique et d'histoire*, Bibliothèque des Archives de Philosophie (Paris: Beauchesne, 1927), 2: 476 (AC).

susceptible of definition. Platonism situates itself initially at the
level of determinate being, and then at the level of an organized
plurality of significations. Ideas are grasped as beings; hence
one must ask oneself, what is the being of these ideas, of these
be-ings? Being is indefinable, the problem of being is the most
obscure of all. What Parmenides claimed as evident primarily at
the beginning, for Plato, becomes evident only at the end. The
equal obscurity of being and of non-being is the counterpart of
this principle of distinction. Being (in the singular) is that which
cannot be pluralized, which is participated in by the ideas, by
the supreme beings which circulate across the kinds. No longer
will there be being *as* idea, but the being *of* the idea.

Conclusions to chapters 1 and 2

1 The idea's function of unity and identity is finally the corollary
of a more fundamental principle, the principle of the determination of essences. In Platonism this final principle confers a
sort of individuality on essences. The *auto* is the *ipse*, the in-
person, that makes each essence have a contour which justifies
its title of *eidos*.

2 The epistemological opposition of being-appearing and the
physical opposition of being-becoming coincide from the start,
because they coincide in language: the appearing of words is
the becoming of language. To say "things are as they appear to
me" and to say "things are flowing" are the same thing. Plato
always made one and the same case against Protagoras and
Heraclitus. It is the "drunken legislator" who makes "man, the
measure of all things" and "all things pass" coincide; it is this
legislator who gives the false measure of man to the appearance
of being, because the legislator is himself errant and aberrant.
That is why essence, in return, will be a function of unity and of
identity: vis-à-vis Heraclitus, essence introduces a stop; it prevents things from flowing (*Cratylus* 439d-e). Heracliteanism
is for Plato the philosophy of the "runny nose," of the cold
(440d), a philosophy of snot. Things escape change because
they have a distinct determination.

3 Language holds in reserve another line of reflection: that on
relations. It is the investigation of language that makes a unity
out of what one had believed were two different philoso-

phies. Speaking is naming, but also the sentence (noun–verb). Language is the initial "interlacing" (*Sophist* 262c) of noun and verb. An investigation of relations is implied in the investigation of language. The pluralism of significations entails a reflection on the principle of distinct determination: in return the noun–verb relation calls for a reflection on *implications* and *exclusions*.

In his initial phase, Plato has above all emphasized the discrimination among significations, the link of the sensible to the homonymous essence: how do the beautiful things change while the Beautiful remains? The relations of things among themselves will arise next as a more important problem. But a shift in attention is sufficient to make the problem of the relation to essences spring to the foreground, because the investigation of language holds together the two faces of Platonism.

Chapter 3

Science and Essence

1 Opinion as the negative of science

The goal of the following four chapters will be to elucidate the relationships among science (*episteme* = ἐπιστήμη), truth (*aletheia* = ἀλήθεια), and being. This comes down to discovering by what acts of the soul and by what methods of knowing essence and being are apprehended. At first glance, this line of inquiry ought not teach us anything, since, according to Plato, science is never defined by subjective criteria (criteria of certitude, efficacy, duration, resistance to doubt, etc.), but always by its object (the Cartesian problem of certitude does not figure in Platonism). Subjective criteria never take priority: because the object remains, science remains (cf. *Meno* 98a, *Phaedo* 66a, 98a, on the necessity and permanence of science in the soul). Psychological criteria for science are nothing but the shadow cast within the soul by the most important characteristics pertaining to the essence. What is more, there is no epistemological criterion: the definition of science does not begin from reflection on the existing sciences; on the contrary, the sciences of the day are measured by an absolute standard, Science (cf. *Theaetetus* 146d). There is a difficulty in attaining unity, "that which is in itself science." Plato treats the problem of the unity of science as he has treated that of the unity of virtue. In the same way that human words have of referring to words in themselves, Science is defined by the purity of its object (*Phaedo* 66a–67b: "to be pure" is "to know" and to grasp what is "pure" – here pure signifies "without mixture"). Science is defined by being, not the converse. The clearest text in this regard is *Republic* V 476d–end:[1] "Science, which has to do with being, has for its object that which is." And yet inspection of the acts by which science gives itself will teach us about being in an unexpected way, given these declarations about principles.

First surprise

Plato spends a great deal of time saying that there is no science. The structure of failure, the aporetic form of a dialogue like the *Theaetetus*, seems to indicate that science is what is missing from the human acts of knowing considered in this dialogue (sensation and opinion, right opinion, and opinion accompanied by reasoning). The Platonic inquiry into essences always takes a critical turn: the "hunt" for essences is one that seems not to succeed. It is the same with Kant, where being is what we would see *if* we had originary intuition. This feature gives us an initial group of analyses: an entirely negative approach to science by way of critique and failure.

Second surprise

Seen from the side of the object, science seems to have but one contrary: ignorance. But, if ontology forces us to think in terms of contraries, science forces us to posit intermediaries; science gives itself to us only through these intermediaries that constitute the actual condition of the soul in movement between two limits which it never reaches, ignorance and total knowledge. Yet there is an intermediary *that does not belong to science* and that has a particular status: right opinion. The question is whether there is an object for right opinion.

Third surprise

Another intermediary, which is *in* science, without for all that being *the* absolute science, is mathematics. What is the ontological status of mathematics? According to Books VI and VII of the

---

[1] This should be Book V 477b–end.

Republic, mathematics is an obligatory stage in the purification of the philosopher, without its object being itself a true intermediary between being and non-being.

Fourth surprise

To pose the problem of the end of science is to pose the problem of contemplation (*theoria*). Is this an act really given to man? Is it anything more than a simple limit, a sort of horizon for the ascesis of knowing? The problem of the transcendence of essence in Platonism is that of the link between essence and death.

Science as what falls short in human acts of knowing: analysis of Letter VII *and* Theaetetus

a) Letter VII, whose authenticity is no longer in doubt, proposes a scale of knowing that quite clearly differs from that proposed in the *Theaetetus* and Books VI and VII of the *Republic*. What matters most in this letter is the powerful warning that accompanies this analysis of the degrees of knowledge: it is a strong caution against the pretensions of the tyrant philosopher who takes himself to be the philosopher in power. Dionysius of Syracuse had written a vaguely Platonizing catechism. Plato writes this letter in order to denounce the imposture of Dionysius' approach, which consists in making believe that to be a philosopher it is sufficient to chat about essence, to Platonize. The meaning of *Letter VII* is to denounce a potential pitfall in the philosophy of essences: philosophy is not anti-Heraclitean chatter about essences. Philosophy is difficult; it always requires an effort, a sacrifice. Essence is not what lies nearest, but what is farthest away. This letter, which implies a morality of knowing, bears the same accent as the final *scolium* of Spinoza's *Ethics*: "Everything beautiful is as difficult as it is rare." The time of truth is a time that has its own maturation period, its own rhythm, and that is therefore quite different from the time of industry, where one always can shorten a manufacturing process. The Sophists had let it be believed that a philosophic education was a technique like any other, a technique that one can rush and make easy. But in fact philosophy involves a discipline more closely akin to the purification of the mysteries than to the technique of the artisans; essence always involves the long "way." The Platonic language is here the same as that of the Pythagoreans, of Parmenides: philosophy is a way, a voyage. That truth lies at a distance is an initial reason for multiplying the degrees of knowledge: the theme of intermediaries is introduced under the heading of an ascetic progression. No stage ever arrives except in a negative way: none is ever yet the truth.

Letter VII (342a–344d) enumerates four stages, four degrees of knowing: the name, the definition, the image, science. *Ousia* comes only in fifth place; it is "something of a fifth." The *Cratylus* had put us on guard against the pretensions of etymology, which is a pseudo-science: definition, which figures here as the second degree of knowing, is not what the Socratic dialogues inquire about. When science is found in a textbook, definition falls very low, becoming nothing but the paraphrase of the name. Definition cannot fulfill its potential when it begins from verbalism, within a merely verbal approach it remains exegesis of a word. Essence is therefore neither a definition nor an image (what Kant would call a "construction"). The "circle in itself" is completely other than the definition or the image of the circle. Science is spoken "in the soul"; it is a pure act of thought and has neither verbal nor figurative (material) support; science is in the *nous*. Here science has an "affinity," a "similitude" with essence, it is co-generated with it (cf. *Phaedo*, the homogeneity of the soul with the ideas). Science is a way of trying to conform to being.[2] Essence is rather that toward which science tends, that by which it reaches a limit. What is in question here is a limit through approximation, a limit by means of ascesis. Essence is therefore pointed to as the end point of the "hunt."

b) It is when we start from *Letter VII* that we can grasp the style of *Theaetetus*, which ends in failure, as the negative form of the ontology of knowledge.[3] Why is science defined here indirectly, by everything that it is not? In the *Theaetetus*, science is first of all the art of refuting every false science. Science presents itself in this way as a limit or as the positing of a limit, a "Halt!" addressed to every philosophy of the immediate. This is why it is presented sketchily,

---

[2] Ricoeur says "*se faire conformer à*" which is certainly, given the context, the correct reading.

[3] Cf. Goldschmidt (AC). The reference is undoubtedly to Victor Goldschmidt, *Les Dialogues de Platon, structure et méthode dialectique* (Paris: Presses Universitaires de France, 1935), cited below.

present–absent throughout the dialogue. Science is the critique of initial immediacy, of the "wholly natural," in the Husserlian sense, which covers sensation, opinion, and even "true opinion accompanied by reason." The longest discussion bears on sensation, which is made the object of an enormous critique: all of this plays out in the first part of the *Theaetetus*. Truth must always be reconquered by means of a critique, by means of a refutation of empiricism. This is a way of always beginning again by means of doubt which draws Plato even closer to Descartes. "That which is sure is not sure." It is necessary to recover being by a critique of the phenomenon and of phenomenalism. And what is the *pièce de résistance* of phenomenalism? It is the same formula as that of the *Cratylus*, which is attributed to Protagoras: "Man is the measure of all things."

But the angle of attack is no longer the same: whereas, in the *Cratylus*, Plato attacks the subjective side, the "to each his own truth" or "the truth appropriate to each," in the *Theaetetus* he critiques the evidence of seeming, the evidence of the sensation of perception ("the one who knows senses what he knows," 151e). It is the *aisthanomai* that is attacked.[4] The principle of the refutation rests on the identity of three theses: man the measure of all things (Protagoras), ontological mobility (Heraclitus), science = sensation (Theaetetus). So far as the movement of this refutation is concerned, Plato employs a strategy of discussion that consists in profusely developing everything that is wrapped up in the empiricist thesis and in radicalizing that thesis up to the point at which it becomes untenable. This process of self-destruction consists in leading the empiricist thesis to the constant change hypothesis and then leading this latter to its foundation, which is indetermination, the absence of a contour to truth, which means there will no longer be an *eidos*.

If one says: "What I think is true," it must be said that the sensation is of the moment; it is defined by its very upsurge, by the "here-now" (*lebendige Gegenwart* in Husserlian language).[5] We have a variable present for an ever new subject. But, for Plato, a philosophy of the now is not possible. The encounter, itself a shifting one, of the now of the object and the now of the subject renders fundamental human acts impossible, bringing them to ruin in indetermination. And so discussion is rendered impossible: how

---

[4] *aisthanomai*: to perceive through the senses or the understanding.
[5] Literally "living present."

are we to discuss, to contest matters, if all appearances are given equal rights? More than that, one cannot legislate: there is an indetermination with respect to the just and the unjust (177c–179d). The most critical moment is found in the critique of the "impression": the pathos, "that which I undergo each time in the present" (179d). If one takes the impression seriously, one catches sight of the fact that it is a not-thought. The principal argument is posed in 181c–183c: indetermination sinks into the unthought, and the clue to this impossibility of thinking is the impossibility of an act of naming: a more ruinous impossibility than that with respect to discussion or legislation. I cannot even say any longer that science is sensation, because the indetermination of thought allows me to affirm the contrary at the same time, 183a-b: sensation is "so and not-so," "science and not-science." This means that empiricism is necessarily a mute philosophy. The goal of *legein* is the goal of *logos*. For Plato, thought about the moving of what is moving is an absurdity enunciated in a not-word, a not-thought. And so we find in this discussion the negative version of the principle of distinct determination to which we have reduced the philosophy of essences. It is this principle that is understood in the argument which identifies indetermination with a not-word and a not-thought. A purely sociological critique which limits itself to criticizing the fixity of language with respect to its social and pragmatic utility remains at the surface of the problem. For there to be "something," it is necessary that it be determined: for us to be able to think, it is necessary that there be a discursivity about the real that permits us to determine a something (this is what Kant calls the synthesis of identification, *erkennen, wiederkennen,* the recognition of a meaning that subsists even in its own flowing away. So too with Husserl).

The cunning, the irony, of Plato is not to say the final word.[6] The dialogue unfolds up to the end in this setting of opinion, right opinion, and opinion in agreement with reason. The rest of the dialogue will consist in applying a "going beyond by apposition" (one just adds the epithet "right," and then "reasonable") and not a "going beyond by conversion." What is this reason that gets added to opinion? In attacking true opinion accompanied by reason at the end of the *Theaetetus*, Plato takes aim at the logical positivism

---

6 Cf. Victor Goldschmidt, *Les Dialogues de Platon, structure et méthode dialectique* (Paris: Presses Universitaires de France, 1935) (AC).

that sees in reason a formal function of synthesis: this would be a sort of reason tucked away in perception. What is missing in this thesis is the very presence of being (187a) – for "the soul is in labor concerning the subject of being."[7] There is a kind of rationality that is not yet science. It is the same as with Spinoza's criticism of the second kind of knowing: it still remains a knowing by means of a general idea, and not by a singular essence. It is not, as the *Short Treatise* puts it, "the enjoyment of the thing itself."

Thus the truth of being is pursued vainly throughout the *Theaetetus*. However, the defeat in the *Theaetetus* is not total: curiously, it is in the middle of the dialogue (185a–187a) that Plato hands us the key: the soul's true knowing is the knowing of the *koina*, of the *communs*.[8] These common things take us back to the essence with its *ontological weight*, because they bear the "this is" inasmuch as the *esti* and the *ouk esti* is essentially present in them.[9] "You want to speak of *ousia*[10] and of *not being*, of similarity and dissimilarity, of identity and of difference, finally of unity and of every other number conceivable on their subject . . ." (185c). And one asks: "Can he reach truth who never reaches as far as *ousia*?" (186c). "And where one never reaches truth, can one ever have science?" (ibid.). Thus the act in which science realizes both itself and science's truth is "the act by which the soul applies itself solely and directly to the being of beings" (187b). As for "being, it is that which has the greatest extension[11] among all the kinds" (186a, cf. *Sophist*). Being is not a determination, but that which circulates among all the essences, all the determinations. But is this an answer? The truth-being identity is proposed here as a *task* of knowing, it pertains to those things "which the soul tries to attain itself and without intermediary" (186a). This is why the *Theaetetus* is not pressed to a conclusion (cf. 186c). Festugière says: "The *Theaetetus* presents us not with the joy of being, but rather its tragedy."[12]

---

7   The reference to 187a and the passage cited does not seem correct.
8   In Diès' translation (AC).
9   *esti*: "is"; *ouk esti*: "is not."
10   In this context, the translation of *ousia* is therefore "being."
11   Chambry's translation in GF-Flammarion: being "is what is most common to all things" (127). [F. M. Cornford (*Collected Dialogues*): "a thing that belongs to everything"; Levett, rev. Myles F. Burnyeat (*Plato: Complete Works*): "something that accompanies everything." – Trans.]
12   No reference is given at this point in the *Course*. No doubt it is the book cited further on: *Contemplation et vie contemplative selon Platon*.

Why does the *Theaetetus* not press further to a conclusion? The key lies in the portrait of the philosopher (172c–177c) which is produced by means of the praise of Protagoras, in which this portrait can be seen out of the corner of one's eye: this is an existential answer and not a dialectical one, where the theme of defeat is introduced as being of the very essence of philosophy.

This portrait of the philosopher constitutes a sort of assumed pose at the center of the dialogue, and, at the same time, it gives us the dialogue's real intention. It comes through the portrayal of Protagoras, which characterizes not only a thesis but a philosophic style as well: the sophist is the one who finds things easy, who delights in absurdity, who "fishes in troubled waters"; the sophist is at ease amid universal change; where there is no longer any difference between the true and the false, the sophist will be content with a criterion of sanity and utility. He will not change opinions, all of which are valid; he will overturn all noxious "states," like a physician whose discourses are supposed to be remedies.

The true refutation of Protagoras lies in the praise of the philosopher and not in the refutational argument, [a] sort of "testimony" that links up with the tone of *Letter VII*. The tone of this portrayal of the philosopher is largely pessimistic, of a great bitterness. This is the trial of the mundane. The sophist is at ease here below, the man of the moment, like the politician (172e). The philosopher, on the contrary, is the man of patience, of the long detour; but, by the same token, the philosopher is out of place, maladapted, when it comes to human affairs (cf. *Gorgias*, the philosopher "who needs a poke in the ribs").[13] *Optimism about truth is linked to pessimism about life*: "It is impossible that evil should disappear, Theodorus" (176a). This is why philosophy is not only a "way," an "ascent," as the *Republic* will say, but also a "flight," an "evasion." "One should as quickly as possible escape upward from here below." Evasion consists in "making oneself as similar to God insofar as possible." But one becomes similar by becoming just and holy in the clarity of the mind (*meta phroneseos*). Philosophic success on the level of the ideas is therefore linked to a defeat on the level of life: we must not forget that philosophy is linked to a kind of failure. Is Plato really that far from Kant's negative ontology? For, with Kant too, the unconditional is that which reason posits in order to limit the pretensions of sensibility; the

---

13 Quotation marks added.

critique of Protagoras announces the same move. An important and double problem poses itself in this regard:

- concerning *Plato*: does Plato present any trace of a genuine intuition in this life? Is there a second immediacy, or does *theoria* remain only the most distant hope, linked to the double "cipher" of reminiscence and death?
- concerning *Platonism*: Platonism has come down through history as a philosophy of contemplation. But it is neo-Platonism that posited the idea that the soul can make itself *nous* and find its apotheosis in union with essence. This apotheosis of the soul in the truth of essence – is this the true Platonism?

Chapter 4

Science and Essence

2 Right opinion as "intermediary"

Right opinion – is it an intermediary in the direction of true knowledge for Plato? *Meno* is, *par excellence*, the dialogue concerned with right opinion. The question whether right opinion constitutes an intermediary between non-science and science comes down to asking whether *Meno* is an aporetic dialogue or one that reaches its goal. As we shall see, despite the dialogue's positive response with regard to right opinion, it is a dialogue that fails with respect to science.

a) Introduction to the notion of right opinion in Meno, through the "aporia"

One must always take up a Platonic dialogue in its dramatic unity. At the end of the first third of *Meno*, the notion of right opinion is brought forward as a response to a long inquiry that has failed: right opinion appears as the soul's riposte to failure. The initial question in *Meno* is this: Can virtue be taught? This is a characteristic problem of the period. It leads one to ask: Is there a morality that takes the form of a transmissible knowledge? (cf. *Meno* 72c, 74a, 77a). There are three attempts to respond, which end up in three failures. The third is an attempt to define virtue by justice. It is at this moment that Socrates is compared to a torpedo fish that numbs all that it touches (80a-c). But Socrates at this point declares: If I perplex others, it is only because I am myself perplexed. It is in connection with this dead end in the discussion that the question of right opinion appears.

b) The turn from "aporia" to "investigation"

Right opinion appears for the first time in connection with the idea of investigation. "How do you investigate something when you don't at all know what it is – and supposing that you do come upon it, by what do you recognize it?" (80d). The analysis starts with a perplexity, an *aporia*, which is not an inert ignorance. An *aporia* is an oriented ignorance, a charged ignorance. In this perplexity, there is something like a presentiment about what is being investigated (cf. the expression "I had it on the tip of my tongue": it is like a "negative recognition" of what one is investigating). The problem posed is that of a pre-knowing, a pre-science. Plato always attaches two attributes to the soul, perplexity and investigation (corresponding to the verbs *aporein* and *zetein*). The theme of reminiscence appears for the first time in *Meno*. Its precise function is to elucidate in mythic fashion that state of the soul that is *visited* by the presentiment of the truth. Plato wants to emphasize the state of fervor, of enthusiasm within the soul, that discovers the truth without yet being able to give a reason for it. Right opinion is much more than a "hypothesis" (in the modern sense of the word), a hypothesis that one will subsequently verify. For Plato, a hypothesis comes to birth wreathed in an irrational and quasi-mystical atmosphere. For Plato, the problem of right opinion corresponds to the problem of the beginning of the advent of truth in a soul, the problem of the "growth" of the truth, which begins and ends subjectively although in itself it neither begins nor grows. The third verb is *manthanein*, to learn: it is this that Plato calls reminiscence. Even before reminiscence is a revelation of the anteriority of the soul to its body (81d), it represents the upwelling (*Ursprung*) of truth in a soul. With this notion of the soul's labor, we are faced with an ambiguous psychological intermediary between knowing and not-knowing.

c) Recognition of the true

But right opinion is more than that: it will be shown to be the power to *recognize* the true before proving it: this is the meaning of the famous episode of the slave, whose meaning gets distorted if one says that the slave, like the child Pascal, rediscovers geometry all by himself and without help resolves the problem of the doubling of the square. If one examines the questioning of the slave closely, one discovers that the result is much more modest. How does this questioning proceed? We must note that the slave does not do geometry. The point of the passage is to show that the slave is capable of participating in the questioning and of responding correctly without the use of an argument from authority (82b). It is a way of learning on one's own somewhat comparable to the natural light in Descartes. When the slave makes a mistake a first time in 82e, Socrates remarks to Meno: "You note that I am limiting myself to asking him questions," "I'm teaching him nothing." Right opinion is participation in such questioning, the capacity to come up with answers: right opinion is essentially linked to dialogue. The slave is treated as a disciple and not as a thing, and under this rubric he takes part in a process of questioning that includes attempts and errors. That is why the investigation includes two pseudo-solutions, suggested by the encouragement of the words (the "double," or "half-way"). At 84a-b the slave is perplexed, but this perplexity is not simply a negative matter: Socrates says with regard to the slave that, if he does not know, at least he does not believe that he knows.

But it is Socrates and not the slave who indicates the means of finding the solution, which is to divide each square by its diagonal. Right opinion is not capable of doing mathematics, but permits participation through questioning in the resolution of a problem. The problem raised here is that of the *spontaneity* of the discovery (85d) in the sense that the slave recognizes the truth as a dimension of his own soul – as "internal" to himself – and not as the fruit of an "external" teaching. Plato connects this spontaneity with the notion of "investigation" (86b-c) one last time: "the existence of truth in the 'soul'" (86b) signifies that it is "possible to investigate"; furthermore, Socrates speaks here of a "duty to investigate" (*dein zetein* = δεῖν ζετεῖν) which should incite us to leave idleness behind. Plato himself reduces his myth of reminiscence to an encouraging of effort: one can find (*heurein* = εὑρεῖν) the truth, because one possesses it in oneself. Right opinion is the truth as a "lucky find."

We have now come to a place where we can answer our initial question: In what sense is right opinion an intermediary leading to science?

d) Connections between right opinion and science

Three features characterize right opinion in relation to science.

- Right opinion is not a degree of knowledge to which a degree of being would correspond; rather, right opinion is only a *psychological* intermediary whose full meaning appears if one considers that the soul is itself is an intermediary. This notion of right opinion pertains not to an epistemology, but rather to a pedagogy or a "psychagogy," as Robin says. Right opinion is science's coming to be in the soul (85c).
- A new function will appear when we return to the problem left in suspense, i.e., the question of knowing whether virtue can be taught. At that point, a *pragmatic* function of right opinion will appear on the plane of ethics. This function could not appear in the analysis of mathematics, where right opinion is absorbed into science by the very progress of knowledge, but on the plane of morality and politics, where right opinion stabilizes, to become a level of the soul for itself. The right opinion of the politicians is the problem of those who have succeeded, Pericles, the Sage Solon. But these latter figures are not at the level of science, they were incapable of forming disciples. They were not teachers, which means that there is no science of politics. (The Greek links these three in a single root: the teacher, the student, knowledge; the teaching, the taught, and the one who is teachable: "a thing where there is neither 'teaching,' nor 'taught,' is not 'teachable'" [96c].) It is in this pragmatic function that opinion is right, ὀρθῶς (= *orthos*, 97a-b); this rightness is compared to the quality of a guide who leads somewhere, but, without being capable of rendering an account for his being right by means of science, he will possess a "rightness for the purpose of action" (97b). It is in this sense that right opinion is a good guide, perhaps better than science: in politics, for example, where urgency requires foregoing the long detour (98c), "science does not figure as a guide in political action" (99b).
- In connection with true knowledge, right opinion is an unstable and fleeting state of the soul, an *Einfall*,[1] a fleeting impression of truth. "Right opinions escape our soul so long as one has not

---

[1] The French in the *Course* has a feminine indefinite article, but *Einfall* in German is masculine.

chained them down by reasoning in terms of causality" (99a). This instability is confirmed by comparison to the words of the poets (99c), the diviners, the prophets, who "often speak the truth, but without knowledge of the things about which they speak": their truth is the oracle's truth. They deserve to be called "diviners" (θεíους),[2] but are without real understanding. Their truth is the truth as a lie (*onar* = ὄναρ), as a divine favor, as grace (*theia moira*), as a visitation. They are qualified as diviners, but this word for Plato indicates at once both praise and condemnation. Right opinion is divine inspiration, truth as grace and not as demonstration.

Conclusion

So this psychological and pragmatic intermediary is finally excluded from science. This is why *Meno*, in spite of its positive result, is an "aporetic" dialogue. Socrates ends it, in fact, with a Parthian shot (100b): virtue, "divine favor," is not knowledge, as long as we do not *know* "what virtue is *itself in itself.*" Right opinion is at the same time a beginning and a snare: it sets the slave on the path to mathematical truth; but it keeps the best statesman outside true philosophy. This is why the ambiguous result of *Meno* does not contradict the intransigent tone of *Gorgias*, which makes no concession to the relative and the pragmatic.

---

[2] *theious.*

Chapter 5

Science and Essence

3 The mathematical "intermediary"

The problem: Platonism rests on an *ontological opposition* of two terms: being and appearing, or being and becoming. The critique in *Cratylus* and *Theaetetus* shows the solidarity between *dokein* (= δοκεῖν) according to Protagoras and *genesthai* (= γενέσθαι) according to Heraclitus. What is, then, the import of an epistemological theory of intermediaries? To answer that, it is necessary to see in what sense mathematics has an intermediary function. Are mathematical objects themselves intermediary beings, or is it perhaps only mathematical knowing that holds an intermediary position, with, for example, the mathematical object itself in no way a lesser being than the ethical object?

a) Mathematical and ethical beings on the same plane.
b) The unification through the Good in *Republic*.
c) The allegory of the straight line.[1]

a) Mathematical and ethical beings on the same plane

In dialogues other than *Republic*, mathematical beings, ethical beings, and the other examples of Ideas are treated on exactly the

---

[1] Below in (c) it is a question of "the allegory of the divided line."

same footing: the mathematical Ideas are Ideas like the others, and nothing authorizes us to say that they are any less Ideas than the others. If in the early dialogues the examples for the most part belong to the ethical order, that is above all for circumstantial reasons pertaining to the actual object of inquiry (courage, etc.). But there are also aesthetic objects such as the Beautiful in the *Hippias Major* (*auto to kalon* = αυτο το καλόν). It is striking that the *Phaedo* gives arithmetic or mathematical examples as the typical example of ideas: the Odd, the Even, the Dyad, the Triad (75c-d, 76d, 78d, 100b). Actually, it is a dialogue with a strongly ethical and even mystical cast, where even the quality of the soul, as being related to the Ideas, appears in a reflection on mathematical objects. What is more, the weight of mathematical examples will increase in Platonism: it will make a new relation spring up between sensible objects and their Idea, a relation no longer of immanence and possession (*methexis*), but of a model and an inadequate imitation (*mimesis*); we shall return to this with respect to the problem of the pre-existence of the Idea. Not only do the mathematical examples weigh quite heavily, they also tend to swallow up the moral examples;[2] for instance, Justice in the *Republic* is a mathematical relation of proportionality between parts, parts of the soul and parts of the city. And finally, if Aristotle is to be believed, at Platonism's end all the Ideas would have been numbers, which would have turned it into a meta-mathematics. What, then, can the pejorative attitude relative to the mathematical beings mean in *Republic* Books VI and VII?

Theaetetus at 185c gives, pell-mell,[3] as specific objects of the soul, when it reasons "alone, by itself," essential qualities (heat, cold), determinations that Aristotle will later call categories (being and non-being, the same and the other, which will be kinds of being), formal relations such as resemblance and difference, mathematical structures such as the One and the numbers, then also the Beautiful, the Ugly, the Good, the Evil (186a-b). At the same time, Plato mysteriously reserves to being (*ousia*) a broader extension: being extends across all the other essences. This text gives us a presentiment that there are two points of view possible on Ideas:

---

[2] Cf. Joseph Moreau, *La Construction de l'idéalisme platonicien* (Paris: les Belles Lettres, 1936) (AC).

[3] In fact, that passage opposes seeing and hearing, then sound and color, salty and unsalted . . .

- The first, which would be the point of view of enumeration, where the Ideas, considered "each time" in themselves, that is to say, in relation to the sensibles of the same name that they represent, are no less Ideas, any one no less than the others. This point of view is tied to the principle of "distinct determination," which appeared to us to be the origin of the Idea; the Triad is in relation to concrete groups of three objects, in the same relation that Courage has in connection to courageous acts. From this point of view, there would be, it seems, a privileging of the mathematical example over the ethical one (cf. *Letter VII*: the Circle in itself). As sheer multiplicity, the world of Ideas is a flat world,[4] or rather this is not a "cosmos." There is each time, each Idea; this point of view of "each one each time" (ἕκαστος ἑκάστοτε) – *hekastos hekastote* – is the one where mathematical beings are as much beings as are ethical beings. But this is not the only point of view possible.

- As soon as one passes from *enumeration to order*, Ideas are no longer all of the same rank: the privileging of *ousia* in the *Theaetetus* warns us of that. This point of view of order – which will require Plato to offset the principle of distinction through a principle of "communication" – that is to say, of compossibility – is just as primitive as the first one; it depends on discourse itself, which not only *names* but *links, attributes, compares*. It is therefore from a perspective of order and no longer one of distinction that the problem of the hierarchizing of beings poses itself.

b) Unification by the Good in Republic

The place given to mathematics in Books VI and VII cannot be understood if one does not keep in mind the overall context: it is a question of establishing "in what manner, and with the aid of what sciences and of what exercises the guardians of the constitution will be trained, and at what age they will apply themselves to each study" (502d). It is, therefore, in the course of a political project, within the framework of an *education* in view of government by philosophers, that a reflection on the sciences gets inserted. The proposed hierarchy is therefore a *pedagogical* hierarchy, in view

---

4   The original French text has an error in that it says *monde plane* rather than *plan*.

of a practical politics. This is to say that the problem is taken up from the side not of being but of knowing. This is why afterwards the degrees of knowledge will be taken up on the side solely of the subject and not of the object (one will oppose the visible [ὁρατός] and the intelligible [νοητός]).[5]

What is more, before broaching the division of the sciences, *Republic* turns straight away to the *ultimate terminus of science*: the Good: "as you have often heard me say, the Idea of the Good is the object of the highest science" (505a). It is important not to jump past this text on the Idea of the Good (504e to 509c) in order to go directly to the famous division of the line (509c).[6] One cannot go directly to the allegory of the cave that opens Book VII at 514a. The three texts – the Good-Sun, the division of the line, the cave – form a totality that must be taken *en bloc*, and a triple introduction to the detailed examination of the sciences proper to the training of the philosopher: an examination that constitutes the essential matter of Book VII. In addition, the conclusion of Book VII[7] itself belongs to this long introduction, which in looking back anticipates the conclusion of the whole.

We will not exhaust this problem of the Idea of the Good according to Plato today;[8] we will take it solely as an introduction to a possible hierarchy of the sciences and their object, in brief as a principle for a *final unification*. So, from this point on, the problem of distinct determination which puts all Ideas on the same footing is offset by a problem of final unification. Let us therefore set aside the question of knowing whether this Good is a religious reality, a God – and the properly dialectical question of knowing whether this is the Being of the *Theaetetus*, the One of the *Philebus*, or one of the "kinds of being" in the *Sophist*.[9]

In this text, the function of the Good is more than epistemological: it is that which "every soul pursues" (505d). Therefore it unifies theoretical and practical research, love and knowing, and it

---

[5] *horatos* and *noetos*.

[6] In fact, 509d.

[7] It looks as though on the basis of what follows this should be the end of *Republic* Book VI.

[8] Cf. Part III, chapter 2; and Part II, chapter 4, 3 – PR.

[9] Cf. on this subject Paul Shorey, "On the Idea of Good in Plato's Republic," *Chicago Studies in Classical Philology* (Chicago, 1895) (AC). [*The Idea of the Good in Plato's Republic: A Study in the Logic of Speculative Ethics* (Chicago: University of Chicago Press, 1895).]

is right away presented as the supreme *aporia*, at the same time as the supreme foundation: *Grund* and *Abgrund* (505e). That which is compared to the sun is at the same time shadow (506a). This is why one does not say what the Good is, but instead speaks of that which it resembles, "its offshoot that most resembles it."[10] It is the light that mediates between the color of things and the vision of the soul, which makes objects visible and eyes able to see (507e: the light is like a γένος τρίτον = *genos triton*, a third kind). In the same way, "that which communicates truth to knowable objects and the faculty of knowing to the mind, is assuredly the Idea of the Good" (508e). So the Idea of the Good is neither on the side of the soul nor on the side of the Ideas, however much it may be spoken of as *tou agathou idea*, but as a *third* between them, as the cause, *aitia*, in the sense of a final cause. The Idea is, as it were, an all-encompassing kind, a final cause of the encounter of the object and the subject. It is in this sense that Plato says that it is necessary "to transfer even higher" than the truth (of each Idea) and of science, "the nature, ἕξις (= *hexis*),[11] of the Good" (509a). And, to finish, the most mysterious text of all: in the same way the sun gives things not only to be seen, but increase and nourishment, in the same way the Idea of the Good confers on the Ideas, beyond the faculty of being seen, "existence and essence" (*to einai te kai ten ousian*). "Although the Good is not in any way essence, but something which far surpasses it in majesty[12] and in power" (509b).

The Idea of the Good therefore poses the problem of the foundation of the determination of each Idea at the same time as it poses the foundation of the act of knowing as an act common to the intelligible and the intelligence. It is this foundation of the many Ideas in the One of the Good that introduces a possible principle of hierarchy among beings. (This principle of distinct multiplicity is recalled at 507b, πολλά, ἕκαστα = *polla, hekasta*, and joined with the possibility of speaking and defining.) The whole problem of hierarchy that we are going to find in the passage on the "division of the line" will be governed by a principle of final unification.

---

[10] 506e.

[11] Pachet's translation has "mode of being."

[12] Pachet, *id.*: "by right of primogeniture." [Paul Shorey (*Collected Dialogues*): "in dignity and surpassing power"; G. M. A. Grube, rev. C. D. C. Reeve (*Collected Works*): "in rank and power." – Trans.]

Conclusion

If, therefore, the decisive text is the division of the line, the point is contained in this first passage; one can already grasp that the mathematical beings as such are not deficient in comparison to the other (principally ethical) beings; it is mathematical *knowing* that must be seen as having a defect belonging to it that prevents it from participating fully in the dynamism of the world of Ideas and of *pointing* toward the Idea of the Good.

c) The allegory of the divided line: hierarchizing the intelligible

The principal text for our investigation is that of the division of the line into two parts, AC and CB, representing respectively the "visible" and the "invisible," each being in its turn divided according to the same rationale.

	VISIBLE		INVISIBLE	
A		C		B

	D		E	
Images (conjectures)	Real things (world of belief) Faith	Mathematical objects (world of discursive knowledge) DIANOETIC	True science or dialectic (world of comprehension) NOETIC	

$$\frac{AD}{DC} = \frac{AC}{CB} = \frac{CE}{EB} = \frac{1}{n}$$

First comment

We do not have a hierarchy of objects here, but rather a hierarchy of modes of knowing: the analysis is taken up from the side of knowing: conjecture, faith, discursive knowing, comprehension [*intelligence*].

Second comment

The visible portion (AC) is to the invisible (CB) what, in the visible, images (AD) are to real things (DC). What does this division of the visible into two sections indicate? It is fiction with respect to reality, but at the interior of the visible world: it is the world of a dream, of hallucination, of simulacra, presented in order to suggest symbolically the value of the division of the line within the intelligible world. Plato certainly does not interest himself in this world below the level of perception: he suggests rather two important connections, namely, the division of the line itself into two parts, and the division of the right-hand section into two parts. Opinion falls short of the truth, as illusion does the sensible itself. Just as the sun is a parable of the True, a relationship of proportionality at the interior of the visible world is a parable of the division of the invisible one.

Third comment

The division of the intelligible takes place in turn according to the same proportion: the mathematical section is to the dialectical section what images are to things: it is this new proportion that alone is important, because the dianoetic[13] section is the only one that Plato calls *intermediary* (511d). What characterizes this intermediary status? It is that there are two deficits in mathematical knowing: it is dependent on figures, on the one hand, and uncriticized hypotheses, on the other. *Republic* 510b: "The soul, treating the things which formerly were those one imitated as copies, is obliged in its inquiry to start from hypotheses, on the way not toward a first principle, but rather toward a terminal point."[14] Plato therefore addresses this double reproach to mathematics:

- making use of real objects "as images";
- this investigation is carried out starting from hypotheses and moves in the direction not of the *arche* (principle) but of the *teleute* (terminus).

The first reproach – in addition to being sharply subordinated to the second, as we shall see – has to do with the function of figures in geometry and at the same time the function of arithmetic symbolism, since arithmetic is mentioned further on at 510c (cf. Aristotle, *Metaphysics*, Book Theta 1051a22). It is the problem we meet throughout the whole history of philosophy, with Descartes (mathematics = understanding + imagination), with Malebranche (sensible reasoning), and above all with Kant, who will seek his

---

13 *dianoetikos*: "having to do with the intellect," *dianoema*: "comprehension" [*intelligence*].

14 Robin's translation (AC). [Ricoeur refers to the translation of *Republic* by Léon Robin, published in the Bibliothèque de la Pléiade (Paris: Gallimard, 1950).]

way between empiricism and logicism by his theory of *a priori* intuition and of the demonstration of concepts by construction. We should not to register this disavowal by Plato too quickly, since it seems to contradict a number of features of Plato's own geometric work. Indeed, this reproach carries more weight in that Plato did his utmost to exclude the sensible from mathematical definitions and from the material manipulations of demonstration. With respect to the first point, Mugler[15] has shown that Plato's work as a geometrician was to expel the sensible from the definitions of space, the line, the surface, and solids. As for the second point, the struggle against *constructions* is attested to by Plato himself in the long examination of geometry in Book VII 526c, where he argues against pragmatic geometries that manipulate figures (527a) and proclaims a break between the stability of the mathematical object ("Geometry is the knowledge of what always is," 527b) and the order of that which is born and perishes. It is in this sense that geometry "draws the soul away from that which is born to that which is" (521d). Mathematical objects are, therefore, unchanging beings that pre-exist every construction (521d and also *Phaedo* 101c). But Plato, precisely, recognized the limit of this purification of definition and of mathematical demonstration. The example of the *Meno* is instructive in this regard. At what moment do the constructions intervene and what is their function? Three constructions, two false (a square of side 4, then 3) and one correct (the square constructed on the diagonal): the three constructions are done by Socrates himself, and so do not make up part of the reminiscence of the slave, who *sees* using the figure once it has been traced, in an isolated and unchanging intuition. The construction does not make up a part of science as remembering. By the same token, the slave's intuition "jumps" from one moment to the next: the definition of the square, *then* the equality of the diagonals, *then* the division into two by the diagonal, *then* the successful doubling. The intervals between the intuitions, which correspond precisely to the constructions, are thus "attempts" by Socrates, at first false, then true: it is for the moment of *investigation* that it is necessary to have "good courage" (86b-c). In the same way at 81d: "all of nature being homogeneous and the soul having learned everything, nothing stands in the way of a single act of remembering (it is this that humans call knowledge) making

---

[15] See below.

him recover all the others, if one is tenacious and courageous in investigation, because investigating and knowing are nothing at all but reminiscence." The slave's reminiscence is an unchanging vision that responds to the movement of Socrates' construction. In this way, the figures, in their sensible texture and in the movement of the construction that is born and dies, adhere to mathematics in the moment of investigation, even if it is possible to exclude them from the moment of *truth*, which is a moment of static "vision." Plato does not think, therefore, that the mathematical objects *are* the figures themselves, but rather that the figure is an element in geometric *work*. This is the sense of *Republic* 510d-e: the geometricians "construct reasons, without having in mind these figures themselves, but the perfect figures of which these are here images, reasoning in view of the square in itself, of its diagonal in itself, but not in view of the diagonal that he traces; and the same for all the other figures." It should be noted that all the words of this text are important: one makes *use* of the images (the idea of a geometric praxis) in order "to carry out" the reasoning, but the mathematical object in itself is the true object; whence the final opposition between "investigating" (*zetein*) and "seeing" (*idein* = ἰδεῖν). The figure can be excluded from the *seeing*, it cannot be excluded from the *investigating*.

This leads us to the *second reproach*. Mathematics "is forced to begin from hypotheses in order to direct itself not toward the principle, but toward the conclusion." Dialectic alone goes from the hypothesis toward the *arche*. This is both the first discovery and the first critique of hypothetical-deductive reasoning. The first discovery: "treating as things known" and "passing through all the steps, they end up as a result at the demonstration that they went to work to find" (510c-d).[16] Cf. *Meno* 86c–87a. What does this reproach mean? It gets its full meaning only if one connects the non-hypothetical of this passage and the Idea of the Good in the preceding passage: as a result, if one carries the argument to the metaphysical plane. Nonetheless, the attempt has been made to see an epistemological critique here (Mugler) bearing on a procedure of demonstration, "synthetic" demonstration, which goes from propositions already demonstrated to propositions to be demonstrated. For how to

---

[16] Regarding all this, see Charles Mugler, *Platon et la recherche mathématique de son temps* (Strasbourg[: Heitz], 1948) (AC).

choose a starting point among the known theorems? This will be the way of Euclidean demonstration, which hides the moment of discovery, which is linked precisely to the figures and changes in the figure. We have seen that in the questioning in *Meno*, which advances only gropingly, by trial and error; the regressive moment remains in the order of anticipation, precisely owing to the positing of the uncritiqued hypothesis. The decisive moment of the proof in the questioning in *Meno* is the moment when one leaps from the quadruple square to find the doubled square; it is easier to divide in two than to double: one goes then from the complex to the simple. Does Plato allow us to think through this that he was on the way to discovering the analytic method? Mugler notes precisely that Proclus and Diogenes attribute the invention of the analytic method to him, but recognizes the silence of Plato's successors, and the rare use of this method by Euclid. In any case, Mugler looks for the possibility of discursive thinking, of constructions and analysis, in the discovery of monodromic time in the *Timaeus*.

But the reproach against the mathematical method has no meaning outside the perspective of the Good, which was posited in the allegory of the Good-Sun; this makes no sense as purely methodological, but is rather essentially metaphysical; do not proceed on the non-hypothetical principle, do not "give reasons" for hypotheses taken as "evident" (*phaneros*). Mathematical beings are beings by supposition, beings that in a way close in on themselves through their own evidence, uncriticized hypotheses which thus break off the ascending movement, since they propose only the descending movement toward the theorem to be demonstrated or the problem to be resolved, here called the "terminus" (*teleute* = τελευτή).

Rodier expresses this connection of hypothetical knowledge to non-hypothetical knowledge in another way:[17] mathematical beings are *possibles*, and mathematical reasoning necessarily remains within the possible; indeed, not being attached to the problem of the Good, they are cut off from the radical origin of things; only dialectic is the science of *final realities*. This interpretation is even attested to in the *Republic* (533a–535a), which expressly identifies *logon didonai*, "giving reason" (λόγον διδόναι,

---

[17] Georges Rodier, *Études de Philosophie grecque* (Paris: Vrin, 1926), 43–44 (AC).

535c), and access to the supreme Idea: the Idea of the Good. Mathematics wavers like a "dream" (533c); whereas it is only true knowledge of the Good that cuts off the dream, the slumber here-below (534c). Thus Plato no longer says, as in *Phaedo*, that it is necessary to have recourse to "something sufficient," but rather to the non-hypothetical.

What then can be meant by this attaching of Ideas to the Idea of the Good by a regressive and no longer by a progressive path? This immense program remains highly enigmatic (511b). It evidently belongs to a dimension other than investigation into "each" essence and introduces a structure, or rather a structuration, into the world of Ideas, the lineaments of which were first disclosed by the dialogues called metaphysical (*Parmenides, Sophist, Statesman*). Plato initially took himself back to the ἀρχή[18] that gives its "aim" to this investigation before filling the interval between a conception of the "discrete" Ideas and this recourse to the *arche*.

We can in any case say one thing: to attach Ideas to the Good is to make them enter into *suitable relations*, that is, into *relations of compossibility* in which finality prevails over the mere implication of the possible by the possible. That must be why the supreme Idea is called the Good and not just the One: the ethical or axiological aspect of the Good. It is this aspect that Rodier emphasizes in his celebrated article. Two texts confirm his interpretation:

- *Statesman* (283c–285a): there are two arts of measure, says the *Statesman*: "we will put on one side all the arts for which number, lengths, depths, widths, thicknesses are measured by reference to their contraries, and on the other side all those which refer to the *just measure* – to what is suitable, τὸ πρέπον (*to prepon*); timely, καιρόν (*kairon*); requisite, δέον (*deon*), to all that holds the mean between the extremes" (284e). In this way, just measure introduces a principle of critical evaluation, an optimum, a better, in reference to which there is excess or defect. But mathematics remains a relative matter, without a greater or lesser end, a reciprocal relation that ignores just *measure* and hence also *disproportion*. This text is quite illuminating, because it brings together these reflections on the two arts of measuring with *politics*: what one seeks to define is the political or royal art (on the paradigm of weaving). But we must

---

[18] *arche*.

not lose sight of the fact that the movement of the *Republic* also has a political concern: it is a question of educating the ruler-philosophers. The inadequacy of mathematics lies in its remaining within the relativity of pure quantity and of not acceding to the relations of appropriateness without which there is neither art in general, nor politics in particular (284d). This analysis is of the highest importance for locating the Justice that lies at the center of the *Republic*: it is a mathematical relation in one sense – a proportion – but it is a *just* measure between the parts of the soul and of the city.

• *Philebus*, 64e–65a, 66b: The text of the *Philebus* goes even further: the context is different here: it is a question of appropriateness in the "mixtures"; every mixture requires the confrontation of a principle of determination and a principle of indetermination (*peras* and *apeiron*),[19] beyond this there must be a principle of value ("the cause which makes for the mixture's eminent value or its absolute lack of value"): this is the *metron* or rather the *symmetron*, which is expressly called "the power of the Good." Thus the order of the "better" overflows mathematical order, which is simply logical and not axiological. This is why, in the final order of dignity, measure comes at the head, then "proportion, beauty, perfection," then intellect and wisdom, only then the sciences (66a-b).

Conclusions

So we are in a position to answer the question: in what sense are the mathematical disciplines intermediaries?

1) This privileging of axiological relations of suitability over merely logical relations of mathematical reasoning is therefore the probable meaning of this text on the division of the line. This first conclusion is supported by the confrontation with the allegory of the cave, which places the ethical and ascetic accent on the "anabasis" of the truth. It is necessary in particular to connect this whole methodological study of the line to the two passages where Plato gives the key to the allegory: [*Republic* VII,] 517a-c, where the Good is expressly identified with the terminus of the intelligible world, with "the universal cause of all that there is of good and of beauty," and 532a-d, where Plato says that it is necessary to go from the essence of "each" Idea to the essence of the Good,

---

[19] *peras*: terminus, end; *apeiron*: infinity.

"all the way to the contemplation of the most excellent of all the beings."

2) There is, therefore, no place to conclude that mathematical objects as such should be intermediaries, in spite of what Aristotle says (*Metaphysics* 987b).[20] The line is a division as a function not of objects, but of ways of knowing, and that from the start (509d). The Ideas of the *dianoia* are mathematical because they have recourse to images and to hypotheses that restrain the ascending movement and access to the relations of suitability and of the optimal: the ethical ideas have a privilege not owing to their greater *determination*, but owing to their more transparent *relation* to the supreme principal. Yet in principle all the Ideas are susceptible to this communion with the Good (511d): "Without a doubt those who study the objects of the sciences are constrained to do so by thinking, not by the senses; but because they examine them without going back to principles, but by starting from hypotheses, they do not seem to you to have real comprehension [*intelligence*] of these objects, even though they are comprehensible with a principle." Hence beings have no other hierarchy than their aptitude to *"make the Idea of the Good more easily seen"* (526e).

---

20 *Metaphysics*, A VI 987b15.

Chapter 6

Science and Essence (Conclusion)

4 The "terminus" of science: contemplation

Everything in Platonism – the critique of opinion and the "aporetic" style of a great number of approaches, the suggestive power but final deception of "right opinion," the propaedeutic value and ultimate failure of mathematics – points toward a fulfillment of science that would be *noesis*, that is, the moment when the intellect (*nous*), no longer requiring development, time, and effort, would therefore be vision: simple, instantaneous, fully at rest. It is this theme, through neo-Platonism, that has made the historical fortune of Platonism. Every resurgence of Platonism is something like an apology for *intellectual contemplation*, a celebration of the mystique of reason. And yet, for all that, this contemplation in which one attains the height of clarity is the point where the greatest difficulties of Platonism are concentrated.

Let us consider these difficulties as a block before stopping to look at each one separately:

1) The theme of contemplation first appears connected to the myth of the pre-empirical existence of the soul; the initial vision, or the original vision, if one may put it this way, is behind us, in such a manner that it does not belong to the history of human knowledge. Here, for a first time, we have the supreme clarity of science linked to the enigma of myth in general and to the

enigma of a myth of time in particular. But this initial difficulty is not so much a single difficulty as a packet of them: the
status of the Idea as *reality*, as a separate reality, seems quite
inseparable from the pre-empirical existence of the soul; the
myth of the time of the soul, of an epoch of the soul, and that
of the "place" of the Ideas seem quite inseparable from one
another.

2) This difficulty has its symmetric opposite in a second difficulty:
my vision appears as a quality of the soul to be restored – but
the term of this restoration seems inseparable from that crisis
of existence, death. For a second time vision is outside history:
ahead and no longer behind. A second time vision is connected
to the double myth of time and of space, no longer as a myth of
birth but as a myth of death.

3) If, trying to go beyond this level of myth, we now seek to
surprise *the object* of contemplation, in the *movement of investigation*, it appears that this object is not just any Idea whatever, but rather the terminus of the world of Ideas, the Idea
of the Good according to the *Republic*, of the One according
to the *Philebus*. At the same time, contemplation leads us back
to the problem of the *surpassing of language* and its determinations and, if one has spoken of a myth of birth and of death, to
a myth of silence.

4) This will bring us to the problem of the *methodological* function of *theoria*, which will appear to us in contrast less like the
abolition of discourse than like its *founding* beyond discourse:
intuition will then be the principle of a new discourse. In this
way, we will be brought again to the connection of vision
and dialectic. We will then have circumscribed from above
that well-known "dialectic" that we perceived from below in
coming from mathematics. However, when taken up beyond
myth, intuition has its meaning held in suspense so long as
we have not penetrated the difficult problem of the one-and-
many structure of each Idea and of the totality of Ideas in their
dependence on the One. Intuition would be that blind vision
that is never finished recovering itself in the structuring of an
intelligible *dialectic*.

We are therefore going to follow a dialectical recovery of the
content of myth. This movement will bring us to the threshold of
the second part of this course, concerning the *dialectic of Being*.

1) *The myth of pre-empirical vision*

It may seem disconcerting that, as the end *to be attained,* vision is always presented by Plato as an awakening, as the restoration of a *previous* vision that does not belong to current experience. For example, the fulfillment of science is linked to the myth of the beginning of science in the soul, to *Reminiscence.*

This link appears in the two dialogues that have Platonic "Eros" for their central theme: the *Symposium* and the *Phaedrus.*

a) The *Symposium* does not yet make apparent the connection with previous existence, but situates the problem in its mythic atmosphere. That is why we will take it as a transition between *Republic* VI–VII and the *Phaedrus.* The ascending dialectic of the *Republic* appeared as a purely epistemological one, but the fulfillment of this dialectic refers us back not to its degrees – the degrees of knowledge – but to its dynamism, to its *élan.* This is the dynamism that the Platonic "erotics" clarifies. It does so in mythic language: in the *Symposium,* it is not Socrates who speaks, but rather an inspired woman who tells the story of the birth of Eros, child of Resource and Poverty, "mid-way between knowledge and ignorance" (203e–end). In *daemonic* terms he is the "intermediary," just as mathematics was in epistemological terms. It is "the desire for eternity" at work in all investigation, in *philosophizing.* That it is the same dialectic in the *Republic* and in the *Symposium* is beyond doubt. Plato has taken pains to repeat *Republic*'s *intellectual* ascension toward the Good by a *sensual* ascension toward the Beautiful: from beautiful bodies to beautiful souls, to beautiful virtues, with many steps in each degree, toward the Idea purified of all that is sensory.

This ascension of feeling is itself expressed in religious terms characteristic of initiation. Hence intuition is compared to a "revelation," at the end of an initiation into beauty in itself (210c–211: *auto to kalon,* 211d; *auto . . . ho esti kalon,* 211c).

But this intuition:

- is said to be sudden (*exaiphnes* = ἐξαίφνης, 210c), the reason for the difficulties, but itself no longer difficult;
- is expressed in a language of contact: "touch the goal" (211b–end);
- is enunciated in the language of a negative mysticism: in twenty

lines there are twenty negations: *neither* genesis, *nor* destruction, *nor* increase, *nor* decrease, *neither* beautiful in this point,
nor ugly in that other, *nor* beautiful in that respect, etc., *not*
accessible to perception like a facial appearance, *not discourse,
not science* (211a–end).

This last point is of capital importance, for it announces a suspen-
sion of the discourse of science, as we will see in the third section.
It is striking that this accumulation of negations frames the highest
affirmation, precisely the one that up until now has characterized
essence: ἀλλ' αὐτὸ καθ' αὐτὸ μεθ' αὑτοῦ μονοειδὲς ἀεὶ ὄν = *all'auto
kath'auto meth'autou monoeides aei on:* "but (it will rather present itself) in itself, and by itself, eternally joined to itself by the
unicity of the form" (211b). There is a suggestion here that this
must not be just any idea whatever, but a definite root of Ideas, the
Good of *Republic* VI–VII; the use of the word *mathema* assures us
of this (211c–end): starting from the sciences one arrives in the end
at this science about which I have spoken . . ., etc.

We thus have the suggestion that the problem of reasonable
discourse is that of *determinations* and *relations*, but that the
problem of the foundation of rationality plunges into an irrationality that requires this subversion of language; that is, both the
accomplishment and the shattering of language in the myth: this is
why Socrates *lets* Diotima *speak.* But it is not said that the fulfill-
ing of this nostalgia for vision might be a possibility for present
human knowledge.

b) The *Phaedrus* pushes the myth to its limit: in order to see, it is
necessary *to have seen.* "Having seen" appears here as the mythic
foundation of "knowledge." It is here that the myth is enriched by
its many harmonics:

• It is, first of all, the myth of a "place" of the Ideas, a supra-
celestial place, which is to the heavens what fulfilled science is
to astronomy, a mathematical science. Plato even speaks of a
"plane of truth." This mythic spatialization of the "world" of
Ideas governs the "naïve" realism developed in 247c-e:
• "the essence become really manifest";
• vision as contact, as spiritual touching;
• vision is also envisaged as *nourishment;* the association of
"seeing" and "eating" signifies the end of the distance from the

object.[1] The theme of sustenance returns further on with the "wing" nourished by nectar (248c);

- the soul nourishes itself on the Ideas and at first sight what is in question are Ideas in the plural: justice, wisdom. We shall see that by this plurality we are to understand the dialectical relation of each idea to every other Idea and to the principle of the Ideas (both at 250b);
- next there is the myth of the loss of vision, of the fall of the souls, hence of the establishing that situation of *mixture* described in the myth of Eros in the *Symposium*. The fall is here the myth of composition, that is, of the ambiguous intermediate situation of the soul, which is its current situation;
- there is finally the third myth, that of awakening, of restoration: love appears then as compensation for a fall (249c).

Conclusions

The myth of pre-empirical vision can be understood only by starting from and in relation to an all-encompassing mythic structure. Plato wants to suggest to us that rationality is intermingled with a threefold irrationality that is not its contrary.

a) An irrational something about the *foundation*. Determinations must be founded in the indeterminate just as the totality of the conditioned refers back to the unconditioned. Time appears here as the chronological anteriority that serves as a cipher for a logical anteriority, or rather as an anteriority in relation to logic. Time is a figure here for the radical beginning in the *ontological* order.

b) This first irrational aspect calls for a second one: every philosophical itinerary starts from a scandal, from an initial distress as a cipher of the human condition. This "before" constituted by the fall is prior in a sense other than that of being a foundation: it is a question of giving an account of a situation of prior confusion that is presupposed by every philosophy that begins from the *aporia* (just as, in Kant, the dialectical situation of reason results from sensibility's *claim* to set itself up as absolute).

c) The third irrational aspect is that of an *élan*: the "delirium" irreducible to a method. Everything propaedeutic, as for example

---

[1] Cf. Pradines (AC). [The work in question is not spelled out. It may be a reference to Maurice Pradines, *Philosophie de la sensation*, vol. 1: *Les Sens du besoin*; vol. 2: *Les Sens de la défense* (Paris: Les Belles Lettres, 1932 and 1934).]

mathematics, is possible only through a certain movement of desire. The ontological restoration occurs through a "rapture," an "enchantment." This should be compared to Cartesian "generosity," to Kant's "respect" and "sublime," to Bergson's "emotion," to Faustian *Streben*. Even in the most rationalist philosophies, there is some recourse to the irrationality proper to the becoming of the soul, an irrationality that is both feeling and action. This is the existential side of the intellectual progression: the mediation by the work. Plato adopts the word "Beauty" in order to speak of this *affective dynamic* that underlies the truth. It is what Fouillé calls the "splendor of the true."[2] The *Philebus*, at 64b and 65a, speaks of the "power of the Good that takes refuge in the nature of the Beautiful."[3] It is this threefold irrational, constituting a sort of Pythic structure at the root of science, that gets concentrated in the theme of Reminiscence.

2) Intuition and death

Intuition is first linked to myth through the theme of pre-empirical intuition. It is linked to myth a second time by the theme of immortality: the fulfillment of desire passes through death. In this sense, philosophic existence is only an approximation of *theoria*, and this latter is the upper limit of this approximation.

It is principally the *Phaedo* that underlines this aspect, which one could call the nocturnal side of intuition. The "night of death" coincides with the "light of the understanding," for which the sun is the myth, accompanied by the figure of Apollo throughout Plato's works from the oracle of the Python and the voice of the *Daimonion* up to the allegory of the *Republic*. Vision is the defeat of life.

We shall take up the example of the *Phaedo*, not for the immortality of the soul, but rather for the progression of the argument in the direction of *theoria*, hence to disentangle the properly epistemological implications of the doctrine of the *Phaedo*. In effect,

[2] Cited by Léon Robin, *La Théorie platonicienne de l'Amour* (Paris: Alcan, 1933), p. 224 (AC).

[3] The exact reference for this citation is *Philebus* 64e; it does not appear as such in 65. Chambry translates "power" as "essence." [R. Hackworth (*Collected Dialogues*): "the good has taken refuge in the character of the beautiful"; Dorothea Frede (*Collected Works*): "the good has taken refuge in an alliance with the nature of the beautiful." – Trans.]

the *Phaedo* in its own way presents an ascending dialectic, but one that terminates not in vision but in death. All our analysis will therefore rest on this remarkable structure that Guéroult has brought to light.[4]

a) The level of exhortation and right opinion
The *Phaedo* does not take place on just one level, but rather develops through different stages of knowledge. It begins with an exhortation at the level of true opinion. The soul that reaches this level is itself a power of forming opinion (cf. *Theaetetus*: on the soul which comes to opinion in the spontaneous posing of objects "itself by itself"; αυτη καθ' αὐτην = *aute kath'auten*, 185e, 187a).

The soul's degree of knowledge and the soul's degree of existence are thus suited to each other. So the *Phaedo* begins with right opinion about the soul that has the power of forming opinions. This is why the entire first part is an eloquent discourse, in a tone of conviction and of hope. The conviction that philosophy is an exercise of release from the body; the hope that the soul, after death, will come close to the true εὔελπις (*euelpis*, 64a);[5] this hope is deliberately situated at the margin of philosophical autonomy, of proof properly speaking, and clearly attached to an ancient tradition: *hosper palai legetai*.[6]

Certainly, this is an experience that gives accounts, "gives reasons," like the "faith seeking understanding" of Saint Anselm's *Proslogion*. But this is a hope that dips into belief, particularly into Orphic belief. Philosophy is here reflection on religion. "There is a chance that those who instituted the initiations were not without merit, that they spoke in hidden words yet about reality." The underlying conviction is that the religious is ready for this philosophic reprise, [that it][7] has a grandeur that is not alien or inadmissible to philosophy. Here Plato announces the position of Spinoza, of Hegel, with regard to religion as the *organon* of philosophy.

The whole effort of the *Phaedo* is to bring this conviction, born in the sphere of the sacred, to philosophical clarity, that to

---

[4] Martial Guéroult, "La Méditation de l'âme sur l'âme dans le *Phédon*," *Revue de métaphysique et de morale* [33] (1926)[: 469–91] (AC).

[5] In the French text of the *Course* it says *du vrai*, but *euelpis* (literally, "good hope") is feminine in Greek.

[6] *hosper palai legetai*: "as one said of old."

[7] A word is missing. Editor's conjecture.

philosophize is to get ready to die, better: "to be dead" τεθνάναι
(= *tethnanai*). To what point does the *Phaedo* succeed in philosophically recuperating the content of the myth and transforming it into something that is intellectually evident? Or succeed in
carrying out the philosophic transposition, to speak like Diès and
Festugière?

What is at stake, from the beginning, is a quality of the soul that
is not irrational, in the manner of Orphic and Dionysiac ecstasies
but, rather, lucid. From the opening section of the *Phaedo*, the
fruit of the rupture with the body (64e) is called *phronesis*[8] (65a);
by means of it, the soul "touches" the true (ἅπτεται)[9] or at least the
desire to be, ορεγηται τοῦ οντος (= *oregetai tou ontos*). Even more
strongly: "what is really a being becomes evident to the soul." The
first level already belongs, therefore, to philosophy, and no longer
to the religious mysteries. It comes down to the soul attaining to
the purity of its object by means of its own purity, that the "for
itself" (*auto kath' auto*) of the soul should be of the same degree
as the for-itself of being; in this way, the pure will be for the pure,
desire will turn into seeing as a possessive contact, κτήσασαι τὸ
εἰδέναι, 66e; ἐφάπτεσθαι, 67b).[10] But even if from the first argument
the reflection on the Orphic mysteries is directed toward philosophical autonomy, is this an autonomy that can be achieved?

b) The level of hypothetical reasoning

At the second level, the soul meditating on the soul brings itself
to reasoning. The "true opinion accompanied by reason" of the
Theaetetus corresponds to this level of the *Phaedo*; this is also, in
the language of the *Republic*, the *dianoia* represented by the third
part of the line. Let us set aside the two initial arguments of this
second episode to consider the most philosophical among them,
the third one (78b), the one that establishes that the soul is that
which resembles the idea, because it is simple, "non-composed"
(*axuntheton*), "one and by itself," "identical," "accessible to the
reckonings of thought alone" (*to tes dianoias logismo*), and "itself
invisible" (80a-b). In brief, the philosopher attempts to reason
about the reasoning soul just as a while earlier he had opined
about the opining soul. But has he in so doing reached a con-

---

[8] *phronesis*: thought, reason, wisdom.
[9] *haptetai*.
[10] *ktesasthai to eidenai* and *ephaptesthai*.

templating soul? No, not yet. This soul capable of the intelligible is still *only* similar to the idea, "that which most resembles the idea," "of the same race as the idea." We understand the point of disappointment that attaches to this expression, if we compare it with Parmenides' axiom "To think and to be are the same thing" (fragment 3: *to gar auto noun estin te kai einai*).

Contemplation would be realized in this life if we could go beyond the resemblance between the soul and the Idea to their identity, which the myth of the *Phaedrus* "realizes" in the metaphor of "touching" and of "eating." But, precisely, the soul only resembles the idea. This gap subsisting between the soul and being explains why the proof of its immortality should be so difficult to produce (this aspect of the problem does not interest us here) and that the dialogue at this spot results in a sort of crisis: for resembling the indivisible and unchangeable idea is to be only a similitude of the indivisible and the unchangeable (*e engus ti toutou*): moreover, the *Republic* and the *Timaeus* will not hesitate to call the soul composed, at least up to a certain point.

The problem, therefore, is that the soul reasoning on the reasoning soul is still subjected to what the *Republic* calls hypotheses; it is therefore not only in mathematics that we find thought proceeding by uncriticized hypotheses; here, it is the simplicity of the soul that is the uncriticized hypothesis. This is why corrosive doubt is introduced by Cebes and Simmias: even supposing the soul to be simple, is it not susceptible to an annihilation which, in agreement with M. Guéroult's expression in his article, has to do with its very existence and no longer the destruction of an essence? ("When one is speaking about the soul, what matters concerning an assurance of indissolubility is not its essence, but its existence.") Therefore, we have here the possibility of an extinction that concerns "the qualitative subjective intensity of the soul" (*idem*), the possibility of an existential [*existentielle*] diminution: "this diminution is the wearing away of the soul, this intensity is its existence."[11] It is necessary therefore to rise to a higher level where the soul will no longer meditate on the ideas in general, but on that very Idea that structures its own existence, in brief, its own *ti esti*.

---

[11]　Guéroult, *op. cit.*, pp. 486 and 487 (AC).

c) The level of dialectic

Does the dialogue in its third part get to *theoria*?

The third level of arguments rests, as we know, on the participation of the soul in a specific Idea, Life, which excludes death. The demonstration rests therefore on a dialectical structure of implication and exclusions among Ideas: Soul implies Life as an inseparable attribute and Life excludes Death. Therefore Soul excludes Death. Soul–Death is as unsustainable a contradiction as Hot Snow.

Is this an exercise in *theoria*? Not yet. Why not?

One cannot get this long dialectic to correspond completely to what the *Republic* calls recourse to the *non-hypothetical*; to do that, it would be necessary to place this system of Ideas in the light of the Good: but that the *Phaedo* does not do. This is why in the celebrated passage *Phaedo* 101d, which corresponds to the texts of *Republic* on the hypothetical and the non-hypothetical, it is a question not of an "absolute principle" (ἀρχὴν ἀνυπόθετον,[12] *Republic* 510b [and] 511b) but solely of a recourse to "something sufficient" (*ti hikanon*). In fact, the argument shifts among a plurality of Ideas which are called "first hypotheses" (*Phaedo* 107b). Festugière, who, as we shall see, insists perhaps too much on the mystical presence of the Good and of the Ideas illuminated by the Good, agrees that the absolute being of the Idea, on the level of the third argument of the *Phaedo*, remains "in a certain sense an object of faith."[13] This is why Cebes and Simmias hold them solely as "sure" (*pistai*); one finds them "suitable" (107b), all the while declaring that hypotheses demand a more certain examination (along the same line 74a-b, 77a, 100b-c); the *necessity* which is so often insisted upon (72e, 73a, 76c–77a, 77b-c, 92c-e) occurs within the interior of a sphere of truth which is more accepted *en bloc* than founded in a radical way. 99e–100b: "To take refuge on the side of the ideas in order to find the truth of the beings . . . that there exists a Beautiful in itself, a Good, a Large. So if you agree with me, then I hope, beginning from there, to show that the soul is immortal . . .."

---

[12] *archen anhupotheton*. Pierre Pachet in his translation of this text (Paris: Gallimard, "Folio-Essais,"1993), p. 353, has "not hypothetical." [Shorey (*Collected Dialogues*): "a beginning or principle that transcends assumption"; Grube, rev. Reeve (*Complete Works*): "*not* a hypothesis." – Trans.]

[13] Paul Festugière, *Contemplation et vie contemplative selon Platon* (Paris: Vrin, 1936[, 1975]), p. 100 (AC).

The absence of a reference to a final terminus has as its counterpart not just the overall hypothetical character of the argument, but its *composed* character. The argument moves among the *Ideas*: from this point of view, the *Phaedo* is important moreover in that it announces the composition of the Ideas in the *Sophist*. In this sense, *Phaedo* stakes out the dialectical path that goes from *Cratylus* to *Theaetetus–Sophist–Statesman*; it announces the opening of a new way, beyond the blunt alternative that opposes the changeability of opinion and the absolute unchangeability of logical being; it announces a technology of essential relations (what Plato calls the "communication of kinds"); that is, no longer the vertical participation of the sensible in an intelligible homonym, but a sort of lateral participation of essence with essence. Yet the hierarchy of essences in the *Phaedo* still seems truncated: one finds in it nothing corresponding to the "synoptic intuition" about which we are going to speak.

d) The end of the Phaedo
Platonic *theoria* remains dependent in the end on its starting point in the religious mystery: instead of an ultimate passage from dialectic to intuition, it involves a double ending, the one spoken, the other mute.

The first ending is the last great eschatological mystery: in this the dialogue has no difficulty linking the most rational argument to a mythical narrative placed on the same level as the latter. The indestructibility attained by the argument is straight away identified with existence by Plato (107a). Belief is therefore quite close to the most logical argument. It seems that the argument is inside belief in order to rationalize it but does not truly substitute for it.

What this means is that the figurative representation of a landscape as the image of the purified soul, as a *myth of the future*, corresponds to the representation of a previous existence. The dialectic thus is a logical episode stretched between two mythical moments, the first playing the role of origin, the second that of the limit of effort.

But there is a second conclusion, which is precisely the death of Socrates as recounted by Echecrates, which is not a simple appendix to the dialogue but, in a certain way, its fulfillment. Socrates' "death" fulfills Plato's "logos." His proposal – "to philosophize is to die and to be dead" – is fulfilled in silence. The equivalent of *theoria* is here the very quality of Socrates' dying, for Socrates does

not die like Jesus, in distress and abandonment by God, burdened
by the sin of the world, but rather in serenity and certitude, like a
man who is completing his meditation.

It is in this sense that one can say that *theoria is inseparable from
the cipher of death.* Death, which in the first part was a theme for
preaching, for exhortation (*apologia*), has become a non-discursive
event. Only at this moment is the soul purely *nous* and adequate
to the ideas. Here lies the great difference from Plotinus, who in
place of the soul's *resemblance* to the Idea substituted the *identity*
of the *nous* and being. The *nous is* the beings. The soul, in making
itself *nous*, is itself an intelligible that knows the intelligibles by a
sort of self-unfolding (*Enneads* V). Thus contemplation is actual,
and no longer hoped for. Correlatively, the fulfillment by death is
eliminated in favor of an eternal present.[14] But Plato himself did
not take this step: it is in death that *theoria* breaks through.

3) Intuition and the idea of the Good

If intuition is fundamentally linked to the double myth of pre-
existence and survival, if therefore it is the end prior to all philosophy and the end linked to death, the question arises: What is the
status of intuition in real philosophical life?

Let us break the question down:

- With respect to what is there intuition? (§3)
- Does this intuition realize itself wholly by means of dialectic?
  (§4)

With respect to what is there intuition?
a) At first glance, every Idea can be intuited: intuition is linked
to "each" of the ideas (see the opening lectures on the principle
of distinct determination of the Ideas). There is each time a sort
of "presence" of the pure Idea to the pure soul for each Idea. It is
probable that the "friends" of the Forms, criticized in the *Sophist*,
have so interpreted Platonism on the basis of an equivocal teaching for which the well-known text of the *Symposium* on intuition

---

[14] Cf. Volkmann-Schluck: *Plotin et la théorie platonicienne des Idées* (AC). [We
have been unable to locate this translation, which probably should be a reference to Karl-Heinz Volkmann-Schluck, *Plotin als Interpret der Ontologie
Platos* (Frankfurt: Vittorio Klostermann, 1941).]

is the witness: intuition would be the vision of the *unity* of the Idea beyond its multiple instances and sensible matter. If this were so, the unity of signification would not be simply presumed, constructed, posited, but rather encountered "in flesh and blood" and the Idea would be an intelligible image [*statue*].

What seems to justify this interpretation is that intuition is beyond discourse, like a resting of the mind in vision, beyond the articulated movement of thought (*Symposium* 210c–211a; *Letter VII* 341a).[15]

b) And yet Festugière shows with a great deal of force that intuition has a specific object, the Good or the ONE. The consequence, as we will see in §4, is that intuition does not exclude dialectic, but on the contrary implies it.

Indeed, it is not necessary to separate intuition from the terminal point of the ascending dialectic; rather, it is just this terminal point that is beyond discourse. Two fundamental texts illuminate, obliquely, the *Symposium* text (which seems to link intuition to any Idea whatsoever): they are Books VI–VII of the *Republic*, already examined from the point of view of the mathematical intermediary, and the *Philebus* text on the One (13c–27e), to which Festugière grants even more value (because it dissipates an equivocity that remains attached to the Good and that arises in substituting the One for the Good). We recall that *Republic* VI 508e–509c granted to the Good the power of rendering the subject knowing and beings known, and furthermore to confer essence and existence on the Ideas; the Good appeared therefore as the principle determining essential beings. But it was the Good alone that was indefinable and beyond all intelligibility. It was in this sense that the ancient commentators interpreted the One of the *Philebus* as what *confers* being on the Idea (cf. the text of Olympiodorus, *In Philebum*: ην δε αν άμεινον το μεν εν [the one form] πάντων [of all the singulars] αίτιον ποιειν, ἐνώσεως δε το πέρας = *en de an ameinon, to men hen panton aition poiein, enoseos de to peras*).[16] The Good therefore clarifies the *One* of the *Philebus*

---

15 Letter VII, 341c-d, would better correspond to the content of the text.

16 Cited by Festugière, *op. cit.*, p. 202 n. 2 (AC). [This commentary on the *Philebus* is no longer attributed to Olympiodorus, a neo-Platonic philosopher from the sixth century AD, but to Damascius Damascenus (who died c. AD 544), Plato's last successor as the head of the Academy, closed by the emperor Justinian in AD 529.]

by allowing it to present a composition of a system of Ideas starting from the power of the "non-hypothetical principle" (no doubt
in passing through the highest "kinds," about which we will say
more later, which are in turn equally one and many).

But, in return, the One of the *Philebus* resolves the equivocity of
this Good which is an Idea (for it has the power of determining the
Ideas) and beyond the Idea; and it is therefore the true unknowable, the determining indeterminable, the unconditioned that Kant
says is required by the series of conditions (a premonition of this
correction by the *Philebus* would thus be found in several allusions
in the *Republic*, 506d and 517b-c). Rodier[17] already interpreted
the *Philebus* in this sense as a rectification of *Republic* VI (the
Good regressing to a role of "sovereign good" for humans and the
universe).

If we allow ourselves to be guided by these two texts, it would
appear that intuition has for its privileged terminus this Good-
One-Cause beyond essential determinations ("cause," that is, a
foundation that makes Ideas beings; *Phaedo* is met up with again,
which confers on the Idea the function of "cause": *Philebus* 58a,
65e, 67a-b). So the object of contemplation is not the Ideas as
such, but the Ideas *under the determination of the ONE*. Hence,
to ask if man is capable of intuition is to ask if he is capable of
acceding to the ascetic terminus of every ascending dialectic – to
see the Good – next, if he is capable of that "synthetic"[18] intuition,
that is, that "direct and global apperception of the entire hierarchy
of the intelligibles"[19] – of that intuition that would grasp "in one
and the same act the Ideas and their relations" starting from their
unifying and founding root.

Festugière does not doubt that Plato had this *feeling of presence, of contact*, to which he compares intuition, rather "than
the apperception that is explicated by means of an Idea."[20] This
presupposes that one should take the terms of the *Symposium*,
the *Republic*, and the *Philebus* literally, in the fashion of the neo-
Platonists: "These conclusions, I admit, could have been obtained
only by interpreting certain texts of the *Symposium*, the *Republic*,
and the *Philebus* in their literal sense: this was the method of the

---

[17] *Op. cit.*, pp. 130–31 (AC).
[18] Festugière, *op. cit.*, p. 208 (AC).
[19] *Id.* (AC).
[20] *Id.*, p. 209 (AC).

neo-Platonists and our results agree with theirs."[21] But is this not to "psychologize" what Plato's whole dialectic tends to "logicize"? Festugière indicates this, by invoking "a fact of psychological experience that I cannot define any better than by calling it mystical";[22] he sees something more here than a synopsis like a definition, a true face-to-face encounter with the Good of the *Republic* and the One of the *Philebus*, a union higher than the production of a concept, an "inexpressible union," an "ecstasy where the mind belongs to the Idea,"[23] following the analogy of being bedazzled by the sun.

But:

- the negative mysticism of the *Symposium* comes from the mouth of Diotima, not Socrates; there is reason to be scrupulous here;
- access to the Good is not attested to as an actual success;
- above all the intuition of the Good cannot be actual if it is not at the same time an intuition of the Ideas in their "principle," if therefore "synopsis" and *theoria* do not coincide. Festugière himself speaks of this "vision of the realities in their being and in their order";[24] it is therefore necessary to go all the way to the end: the intuition of the "principle" is not possible without *the completion of the system*, without the success of the dialectic. But has Plato shown, in demonstrating this, the One's foundational power with respect to the whole system of Ideas?

4) Intuition and dialectic

It is therefore now necessary to make sense of the fundamental connection between intuition and dialectic, rest and movement, contemplation and discourse. *Republic* VII 537c brings together these two functions of truth in a daring combined expression: the synoptic dialectician, ὁ μὲν γὰρ συνοπτικὸς διαλεκτικός = *ho men gar sunoptikos dialektikos*. This consists in seeing all the beings in a single being, the multiplicity of the Ideas in the One of the Good. "This synthetic vision of the One and of the All in the One is the

---

[21] *Id.*, p. 234 (AC).
[22] *Id.*, p. 217 (AC).
[23] *Id.*, p. 224 (AC).
[24] *Id.*, p. 233 (AC).

peak of contemplation and of science."[25] We are going to see that this joining of intuition and dialectic appears fully only in the *descending dialectic*, whereas the ascending dialectic is a movement that looks beyond discourse.

a) One finds an initial approximation to this synthesis of intuition and dialectic in *Phaedrus* (265d–266c; 270a–272c; 277b). The Idea appears there not as an image of truth, but as implicated in a double movement:

- of implication in a diversity that Plato identifies with definition and that he assimilates to a unifying vision (*sunoronta*). This unification bears upon *one* idea as such; it is therefore implicitly linked to the segregation of the ideas, to the *hekaston*, to "each" of the ideas; it is a question therefore of a discriminating unification, if we may put it this way. Moreover, this initial unifying movement (συναγωγή)[26] is therefore linked to the disjunction of the field of significations; it is unifying uniquely with respect to the sensible.
- "division" (διαίρεσις)[27] is thus the constructive moment in making connections: the Idea appears as an organic Whole to be disarticulated; an organic vision succeeds the discriminating unification; the ideas found along this path are thus constituted by the very work of division (here the division is dichotomous or apparently at least dichotomous, since one always takes the left side and leaves all the rest on the right).

So *sunagoge* is linked to the disjointed vision of the Idea, each time "one"; *diairesis* has an ordered vision of the "world" of the Ideas; it is to *diairesis* and not to *sunagoge* that an articulated conception of the Ideas, or even a *regulated multiplicity* of Ideas, gets attached. Socrates concludes this movement of thought concerning the "dialectician" at 266b: "Concerning this, Phaedrus, I for my part am indeed deeply amorous – these divisions and these collections that are made so we can be capable of speech and thought. Beyond this, if I believe I see in someone else an aptitude to direct his attention in the direction of a unity, and one that would be the natural unity of a

---

[25] *Id.*, p. 189 (AC).

[26] *sunagoge.*

[27] *diairesis.*

multiplicity . . ., etc. Men who have the aptitude to do this . . . I call dialecticians." Thus, as Rodier forcefully puts it, it is the descending movement that "alone is purely rational: it alone reaches the Ideas and no longer empirical generalizations";[28] this interpretation is confirmed by *Republic* (Book VI 511a-d; VII 532a).

b) The *Sophist* (253b–254b) is better at making the hierarchic character of this rule-governed structure appear: "The one who is capable of doing this has a gaze that is penetrating enough to perceive:

1) a) one unique form deployed in every direction across a plurality of forms, each of which remains distinct;
   b) a plurality of naturally differing forms, which one unique form externally envelops;
2) a) one unique form spread across a multiplicity of wholes without thereby breaking its unity;
   b) finally, numerous absolutely solitary forms."[29]

There are two levels of this multiplicity: a level of "kinds," a level of "transcendentals." That at least is Festugière's interpretation of this extraordinarily obscure text (in particular 253d5-9, as Festugière structures it).[30]

1) *the level of "kinds":*
   a) a universal form present as a kind to its species;
   b) a universal form present as a species to a higher kind.
   The kind is said to envelop its species "extensively."
   This level, the highest attained in this direction, still leaves us faced with "a plurality of the whole."
2) *the level of transcendentals:*
   a) each highest kind functions analogically like a genus in respect to its species; this form is said to be spread out within the "whole" without breaking its unity. For example, the "same" is participated in by everything that is identical, and each "highest kind" or "transcendental" joins itself to such kinds as the Equal, the Just;

---

28 Rodier, *op. cit.*, p. 57 (AC).
29 Diès' translation (AC).
30 *Op. cit.*, pp. 193–95 (AC).

b) but this process leaves us faced with a with a multiplicity of kinds which are each "solitary."[31]

Such a text in no way puts an end to all suspicion about a final unity attained through the One and leaves one quite skeptical about the systematic character of Platonism; does not dialectic taken seriously and attempted in practice make the constantly adjourned total synthesis of all the kinds in a unity vanish like a dream? Does not the appearance of the problem of the transcendentals, which we will look at in the second part of the course, make a new difficulty appear, one which gets inserted as a wedge between the *ideas* and *the* Good, since one sees a new dialectic being constituted, no longer the dialectic of the Ideas as beings, but of Being itself as one of the transcendentals: "As for the philosopher, it is the form of Being to which he continually applies his reasonings" (*dia logismon, Sophist* 254a)? I am not convinced by the confident declaration of Festugière, who finds this text in agreement with the "sun" of the *Republic* and who makes it the type for the continuity from dialectic to contemplation; in the ascending order, he says, dialectic prepares for contemplation; in the descending order, it is the inverse "when one systematically reconstructs the real,"[32] "dialectic is founded, then, on a vision of being"[33] – the vision guaranteeing the deduction.

Nothing in the *Sophist* justifies this view that the form of Being permits a deduction of all the forms and an overall vision of the totality of all the forms in the principle that engenders them.

Not only does this text remain quite *programmatic*, but the principal dialectical exercise of the *Sophist* – the one that elaborates the five kinds of Being – remains a partial execution, "a little like Leibniz tried to constitute one part of the universal Characteristic."[34] Plato recognizes this quite clearly: the five kinds

---

[31] Cf. Apelt, who sees three species of generic notions; Zeller's critique in ["Bericht über die deutsche Litteratur der sokratischen, platonischen und aristotelischen Philosophie 1886, 1887. Zweiter Artikel: Plato"], *Archiv für Geschichte der Philosophie* 1 [1888]: 600; Rodier claims to find the two movements of the *Phaedrus* reconciled in 253b-c (AC). [Otto Apelt was one of the German translators of Plato's dialogues in the nineteenth century, particularly of the *Sophist*; Eduard Zeller was the founder, in 1888, of the journal cited.]

[32] *Op. cit.*, p. 195 (AC).

[33] *Id.* (AC).

[34] Rodier, *op. cit.*, p. 64 (AC).

are kinds among the others, and it would be necessary to carry out the same work for all the other Ideas. A gigantic task!

Perhaps even Plato was not satisfied with this construction by means of the implication of one kind in another, through necessary attribution.[35] In any case, the *Philebus* shows that another method might perhaps permit realization of the great dialectical work, different than the one that [was] applied in the *Sophist* during the construction of the series of the five greatest kinds (movement, rest, being, same, other).

c) The *Philebus* contains a page on dialectic (16c–17a) that at first glance covers again, fairly precisely, the two texts of the *Phaedrus* and the *Sophist*; but there is a new accent that announces the arithmology to which Aristotle bears witness. It seems as though Plato, faced with the difficulty of finding the laws of exclusion and compatibility required by the principle of the communication of kinds according to the *Sophist*, finds himself returning to an interpretation in the Pythagorean style. We know that for the Pythagoreans a number is born from the encounter of unity with a sort of indefinitely numeric matter (in the same way that a figure is born from the limitation of an indefinite space, number repeats itself in the indefinite and carves out there the series of numbers). This transposition to a pure arithmetic is interpreted in two ways:

- in the first place, the *Philebus* accentuates the dialectical character not only of the ideas in relation to one another, but even in their texture; each idea is a fragment of a relational system; one finds in it something of the unlimited and the limited (16c end); hence dynamism invades the idea itself: Rodier speaks of a "rational reconstruction of essence."[36]
- on the other hand – and this point interests us more here, in relation to the intuition of a radical principle – what appears most to interest Plato in the dialectical exercise is the *entre-deux*, the rule-governed multiplicity that extends between the higher unity and the indefinite variety of concretes cases. 16d–17a proposes the following schema:

---

[35] Rodier, *op. cit.*, p. 66, is harsher than necessary with respect to this construction (AC).

[36] *Id.*, p. 56 (AC).

For the one idea – divide into species, as far as the *infima species* (which assumes that the division stops somewhere, at an *atomon eidos*, for the *infima species* no longer divides into species, but loses itself in the concrete) – "only so are each of the species dispersed in the infinite." There is thus an *intermediary* number of operations and structures between the One and the Infinite.

Here, therefore, the accent is placed less on the mystical terminus of the dialectic than on the "precise quantity," on the "total number that the many realizes in the interval between the Infinite and the One." What is more, Plato underscores this clearly (17a end): "As for intermediaries, they (the bad dialecticians) take no notice of them, whereas in our discussion respecting them is what distinguishes the dialectical from the eristic manner." The accent is placed on this counting of the intermediary units, on the numbering of the species (which thus does not reduce to the dichotomizing division).

Is this to say that Plato falls back on mathematics, which is a degree below dialectic? Not at all: this is the place to recall the opposition of two types of measure, according to the *Statesman* (283c); the counting of the intermediaries that the *Philebus* calls dialectic and what the *Statesman* calls *just* measure are the same thing. We are not, therefore, far from the great principle of distinction between mathematics, which is the "pure possible," and "real" essences, which communicate with the Good and are governed by relations of finality.

For all that, does the *Philebus* go any further than the *Sophist* in the realization of the immense program of dialectic? These "mixed Ideas" like every number – true unities of multiplicities – are not really elaborated; the four "kinds" of the *Philebus* remain points of view under which one can consider a single Idea: it is in one sense one, in one sense many, in one sense mixed, and it requires a cause for the mixture. (Rodier discusses the possibility of superposing the four or five principles of the *Philebus* on the five kinds of the *Sophist*.)[37] So the *Philebus* does not even go as far as the *Sophist* in the direction of constructing the first Ideas: the five kinds of the *Sophist* were the first terms of the series of intelligibles and constituted the debut of a deduction of Being. "The four terms of the *Philebus* designate the four roles that have to be filled" by one or another of these Ideas. "Thus the *Philebus* is not at all, like the *Sophist*, an attempt to realize a part of the dialectic: its goal

---

[37] *Id.*, pp. 70–72 (AC).

is to determine more precisely the conditions for doing so. It indicates the principles and causes with respect to which one must be confident and master, if one wishes to attempt a construction that would have any chance of succeeding."[38]

If one follows Rodier, one is led to say that the recourse to structures of an arithmological type, far from bringing the goal closer, have made it even further off by making one aware of the difficulties of the enterprise. This is why the *Philebus* provides both a more advanced idea about the program to be carried out and less confidence about the possibility of realizing it; at 16c, Plato says, with respect to the way of dialectic: "pointing it out is not at all difficult, but practicing it is very much so." This is an even more striking declaration in that it is the same dialogue that shifts the highest term of the ascending dialectic beyond the Idea of the Good, to the One. What remains to be learned is what Plato's teachings about the Idea-numbers actually include; we shall return to this later on. The written works give us only one example of systematic composition, in the construction of the first elements of the sensible in the *Timaeus*; the world soul, the human soul, the sensible; but, as Rodier remarks, "this dialectic of the sensible is not at all a rational construction."[39]

General conclusion

Contemplation is less contemplation of the Idea as a distinct determination than a contemplation of its principle (GOOD-ONE-BEING) and of the descending hierarchy that proceeds from it. Contemplation and dialectic are therefore inseparably bound together: the incompleteness of the one is likewise the incompleteness of the other.

This is why it seems difficult to systematize these two faces of Platonism as proposed by Festugière, who distinguishes five moments, three moments of contemplation framing two moments of dialectic (pre-empirical vision – ascending dialectic – grasp of Being in itself – descending dialectic – synoptic intuition): "this perfect vision of the many in the One, of the One in the Many, holding the many together, is the peak of contemplation and of science."[40]

---

[38] *Id.*, p. 72 (AC).
[39] *Id.*, pp. 73f. (AC).
[40] Festugière, *op. cit.*, p. 196 (AC).

But:

a) the first moment is mythical;
b) Festugière does not take into account the equivalence of philosophy and death, which postpones the final intuition to an
   eschatological future;
c) the highest principle is not elaborated fully by Plato: is it Being,
   Good, or One?
d) the dialectic of being makes the highest "kinds" spring up,
   whose unity does not appear and which are even spoken of
   expressly as "solitary" (*Sophist* 253d).

What does the *Parmenides* say? Its "laborious game" unfolds
"entirely outside the light of intuition": "In the formulas that the
Parmenides repeats almost without variation where it makes use
of the dichotomizing argument, it is always reflective thought,
dianoia that divides. The word *nous* is absent from the *Parmenides*
and its derivatives appear only in the first part for the rejection of
conceptualism. The laborious game of the contradictions takes
place only in a domain of thought that is not illuminated by the
unifying vision of the intellect."[41]

e) In the end Plato proposes a conception of dialectic that is more
   programmatic than actual. If the system of ideas were wholly
   complete, without images or hypotheses, without lacunae or
   exceptions, the mythic intuition would be entirely recuperated
   in the philosophic act. There would be nothing more in the
   myth of birth and death than in philosophy, and philosophy
   would no longer need the myth of recollection; the synoptic
   intuition would have entirely absorbed it into its light and its
   order. This is why the realization of philosophy in intuition is
   perhaps in the end the very myth of philosophy; this is why, to
   speak of intuition in this life, it was necessary in the *Symposium*
   for the sobriety of Socrates to be replaced by the drunkenness
   of Diotima the prophetess.

---

[41] Diès, Notice du *Parménide*, pp. 47–48 (AC).

Second Part

The Idea of Being and Non-Being

In basing itself on language, Platonic philosophy is immediately situated on a level where there are multiple beings, in the sense that there are distinct significations. It is this initial situation that puts the problem of the mutual participation of the Ideas at the heart of Platonism. Is the problem of Being resolved by a philosophy of *beings*, it being understood that Being is the Idea? Not at all. Why?

The question of being comes up in two different ways: first, what does being mean for an Idea? In Platonic language, being is attributed to *this* or to *that*; therefore there is a problem that belongs to the signification of being taken absolutely, as that in which the Ideas participate. Being is "mixed," as the *Sophist* says, with all the Ideas. Therefore, there is a philosophical problem with regard to knowledge: "What it is to be" as a determination attributed to this or that being. This question, therefore, is the second-degree ontological question.

Socratic inquiry starts from the definition of this or of that. "What is (or what do you call) courage, virtue, etc.?" One has answered that these are determinate beings. This first-degree ontology or ontology of determinations gives impetus to a second-degree ontology; and, just as the question "What is this? What is that?" was born from a difficulty, began with an aporia, the question "What is the *being* attributed to this or to that" too makes its debut from a difficulty: there is an aporia of being. Thus the appearing of this question bears witness not to a revision of Platonism, but rather to a redoubling of the ontological question: in language that has a quite modern appearance but that is in reality properly Platonic, we pass from the question of the "be-ings" (*ta onta*) to the question of being (*to on* or *ousia*). The group of dialogues designated as *metaphysical* bears witness to this question.[1]

---

[1] Let us recall Diès' arguments in favor of the chronological order: *Parmenides, Theaetetus, Sophist, Statesman*, in the *Notice générale*, Paris, Les Belles Lettres, "Guillaume Budé," 1923–1924–1925, vol. VIII/1–3, p. xiii: *Theaetetus*, at 183c, recalls the old encounter with Parmenides, not as a historical recollection but as an allusion to the dialogue based on the fiction of this encounter. The *Theaetetus* in turn ends with the announcement of an encounter

But where is the difficulty, and how to show it? The aporia of the "be-ings" was shown through the questioning of contemporaries, in brief, by the Socratic method of "examination," issuing from the oracle at Delphi; the aporia of being is shown through the *reprise of the history of philosophy*, by a reimmersion in the pre-Socratics. It is *their* history that is aporetic.

How is this recourse to the history of being made manifest?

In diverse ways: first, by means of the fiction of the *Parmenides*, the fiction of a very old dialogue, set fifty years earlier, which has the old Parmenides wrestling with a young and inexperienced Socrates, knocked into a stupor by the old master's dialectic. The fiction of the *archaism* of the debate is essential: the idea of making Zeno, Parmenides, and the young Socrates meet creates an impression of reaching back in time that both gives figurative shape to how old the problem is and invites us to investigate its antinomic structure precisely in terms of its antiquity. This is why it was necessary that Socrates be inexperienced: Socrates' youth is the youth of reflection itself, faced with an archaic problem. And if, in the *Sophist* and the *Theaetetus*, Socrates remains unobtrusive, it is so that Eleatism itself will confess its failure, and not because Plato is changing philosophy. Socrates was meant to have reappeared in the unwritten dialogue: the *Philosopher*. So Aristotle was seeing things correctly when he reproached the *Sophist* (*Metaphysics* N 1088b–1089a) for its "archaic manner of posing the problem" (*to aporesai archaikos*).[2] This applies to the whole discussion, whose archaism is intended.

This interpretation of the fictional archaism of the *Parmenides* is

---

with Theodorus and Theaetetus, which takes place precisely in the *Sophist*. It announces the definition of the sophist, the statesman, and the philosopher. The first definition is taken up in the *Sophist*, and the *Statesman* continues the conversation and makes a reference to the *Sophist* at 284b. "The order *Parmenides, Theaetetus, Sophist, Statesman* is indeed the succession intended by Plato, and we have no reason to claim that this reading order is not the chronological order" (PR). [Auguste Diès (1875–1958) translated Plato's metaphysical dialogues – *Parmenides, Statesman* . . . – for the Budé collection.]

2   One would have expected "the *Parmenides*," which is named in the passage referred to and confirmed by Ricoeur at the start of the next paragraph.

confirmed by the explicit evocation of the history of the problem of Being in the *Sophist*. We grasp there an intention quite different from that of Aristotle the historian: Aristotle wants to show a path in history leading toward him, a progressive construction of Aristotelianism. Plato wants to present an *antinomic* structure, a demonstration of the aporia of being: Ionian pluralism–Eleatic monism (*Theaetetus*), pluralism of Ideas–monism of Being (*Parmenides*), materialist–idealist (*Sophist*). It is a dangerous method from the historical point of view, one that makes no sense except meta-historically, as a dialogue among the dead where the confrontation of the characters *dramatizes* in a single stroke the fundamental oppositions of ontological thought. In this dramatization, the conflict of the ONE–MANY has the leading role; it is an archaic propaedeutic. But the aporia develops in three directions: one–many, movement–rest, same and other (we see the intersection of these three aporias in the *Sophist* at 252a-b).

Chapter 7

The Question of Being in the *Parmenides*

1 The problem of the *Parmenides*: the internal unity of the dialogue and its connection to the *Parmenides–Sophist* series

Our first task is to retrieve the *meaning of the problem of being* posed by this enigmatic dialogue; it is necessary to retrieve this sense by going beyond the external fabrication (on which we have insisted in the introduction) to the radical question that at first glance seems to conceal itself behind a laborious dialectic game. More exactly, on a first reading we find only two halves of an argument, the first appearing to be a ruinous critique and the second a sterile game. To understand the problem is to understand that the *Sophist*, a non-aporetic dialogue, resolves the difficulties of the *Parmenides*, an aporetic dialogue. But, for this, it is necessary to have recognized *the* problem that seems to be split in two, between critique and playing.

a) From the fabrication to the problem

Let us start, then, from the archaizing fabrication: the encounter of Zeno of Elea, Parmenides, and Socrates; the disposition of the characters already has an indicative value with respect to Plato's intentions. In a kind of prelude (127e–130a) Socrates is set to wrestling with Zeno of Elea, a disciple of Parmenides, and triumphs over him easily; then, the ground having been cleared to some degree, Socrates gets put in difficulty by the master himself, who piles up apparently mortal objections to the theory of Ideas (130a–135c). Then, instead of continuing to enumerate objections against the theory of Ideas, Parmenides makes a brusque about-face and indicates that a more extended and more profound science would allow for their resolution, and he announces that he will give an example of the method that would resolve the objections; there then follows an immense exercise, where the consequences are drawn from a series of hypotheses concerning the ONE, depending on whether one does or does not attribute being to it; but this exercise in discussion, with its hypothetical-deductive allure, leaves us thirsty; at first glance we do not see how this exercise sets up the answers to the objections in the first part. It seems to be a purely formal, purely propaedeutic exercise.

It is this apparent discord between a critique without an answer and an exercise without an application that makes up the enigma of the *Parmenides*. We will have to understand, following Brochard's analysis, that "this dialectical section constitutes a new objection against the theory of ideas, the most formidable of them all, an objection that gets added to the preceding ones and completes them," but that at the same time it "poses a new problem, of capital importance, and in doing so prepares the solution, indeed already more than half gives it, without anyone taking notice."[1] If the last word is not yet said, that may be because Plato is still not clear, or because he wants to delay the revelation of the truth, or because he too wishes to play with and like his adversaries.

b) The scheme of incoherence posed by Zeno

We have said that the disposition of characters already has a value indicative of Plato's intentions: the elimination of Zeno of Elea by Socrates is not a *hors-d'oeuvre*; why knock down Zeno to the profit of Parmenides? To dissociate orthodox Eleatic doctrine from what appears here to be just a vain eristic exercise, and so to make the real problem stand out. Zeno wants to demonstrate by absurdity that the many cannot exist because it is incoherent (the one excludes the many); the *incoherent scheme* is therefore from the beginning the One–Many relation. The whole art of the dialogue is going to radi-

---

[1] Victor Brochard, *Études de philosophie ancienne et de philosophie moderne* (Paris: Vrin, 1926), p. 117 (AC).

calize this incoherent scheme in order to make a coherent scheme appear, albeit one of dialectical coherence. But, for that, one must radicalize the scheme. How? At first by carrying it to the very level of the Ideas or the Forms – that is what Socrates does in his response to Zeno (128c–130a); then by transforming it into an *aporia* in the relation of the forms to the sensible (130a–135c); then by transforming it into a *preparatory exercise* to the solution through the dialectical game (the second part of the dialogue). Therefore there is a dramatic progression: positing the One–Many as an incoherent scheme at the level of the sensible by Zeno, transposition of this scheme to the plane of the ideas by Socrates, its radicalization by Parmenides in his riposte to Socrates, and transformation into a solution by means of the "play" in Parmenides' monologue.

c) The incoherent scheme transposed from the sensible to the Forms (128e–130a)

Zeno poses a false problem: how can a thing be similar to one thing and dissimilar to another? This does not prove that the thing does not exist: this proves simply that its meaning is double, or, in Platonic language, that it participates doubly:

- in the Idea of the similar;
- in the Idea of the dissimilar, which is to say that it is thinkable under two rules of intelligibility (for example, Socrates is one among seven, but many in respect to his parts, properties, attributes; the same as well with the example of right–left). But, remarks Socrates, what would be astonishing is that the very Idea of the similar would be dissimilar in some respect: "that the kinds and forms in themselves receive into themselves contrary affections, that would be what one would marvel at"; and, further on: that the forms as such should be capable of "mixing and separating themselves" (129e), that is what calls for wonder. It is a question therefore of transforming what one has naïvely practiced into astonishment.

d) The incoherent scheme transformed into an aporia (130a–135c)

Here begins the critique of the theory of Ideas, a formidable critique that Aristotle in large part simply took up again: it consists in rendering the participation of the sensible realities in the Ideas *unthinkable*. The aporia bears therefore on the relation, in some sense a vertical one, involved in Idea–Sensible participation. This should be emphasized, because Socrates had announced a discussion about the lateral relation involved in the Idea–Idea participation; and the dialectical exercise, led by Parmenides as a model of resolution, unfolds precisely from Idea to Idea; as a result, the unity of the *Parmenides* depends on the unity of two meanings of participation: of the sensible in the Intelligible and of the Intelligible in the Intelligible. Everything invites us to suspect that to resolve the second is to resolve the first and therefore that to radicalize the first is to introduce the second. The aporia serves therefore, if I dare say so, to whet the appetite. The aporia is an aperitif!

2 Situating the critique of the theory of Ideas

Let us look therefore at how Parmenides' objections to the theory of Ideas are able to insert themselves between Socrates' astonishment (that the One should be the Many and vice-versa) and Parmenides' dialectical exercise.

a) Pre-combat

The objections bear essentially on the relation between the form and the object participating in it, but these objections are preceded by a pre-combat. *Of what* is there a form? What is the *breadth* of the world of the forms? There is a form of the One, the Many, the Like, the Unlike, the Beautiful, the Good? – Agreed – Of man, Fire, water? – Socrates hesitates: in effect, the extension of the ethical function, or, in other words, the passage from the "regulative" (or normative) function to the "constitutive" (or causal) function, and from the ideas' mathematical function to their physical function, creates a problem: and yet it is quite necessary to take this step, otherwise the Idea will no longer be the complete reason for things, if it is not at the same time the *best* (ideal) and the *origin* (real). The whole discussion of the *Phaedo* at the beginning of the third part, on the role of the idea as "cause," runs in this direction, and the ideal genesis of the sensible that constitutes the *Timaeus* supposes that this extension ought to be ventured. But then it is necessary to go all the way to the end and to pose an idea for vile objects, hair, mud, filth – that is, for objects that not only are, but also are neither beautiful nor good, which leave out the *kalos kagathos*; Socrates recoils before the ludicrousness of going so far as "to lose ourselves and drown in some abyss of foolishness" (130d); this ludicrousness hides the shame of positing Ideas where the "causal" function seems as though it cannot be coordinated with the "final" function, where *the origin* no longer seems to be *the best.*

This scruple must therefore be connected to the problem of the "errant cause" and of the *ananke* of the *Timaeus*, which marks the lower limit of a genesis of the sensible. Parmenides concludes this first skirmish in these terms (130e1-4): "It is because you are still young, Socrates," Parmenides said, "and not yet seized by philosophy, with that firm hold with which, as I trust, it will seize you some day, *the day when you will no longer distrust all this for no reason.*"

b) Objection to the theory of Forms

All the objections that constitute the centerpiece of the trial of young Socrates by old Parmenides mean to show that participation, admitted as a hypothesis and in some sense employed in the investigation of essence, cannot be reflected upon without suddenly appearing to be unthinkable: participation is a relation *used* prospectively but *unthinkable* reflexively. The difficulties involved in vertical participation are therefore one aspect of the question: What is the *being* of this or that which is? The aporia of being, which will take a different form in the *Sophist*, here takes the following form: If being is being participated in by . . ., the meaning of being is murky, for we do not know what it means to say "participated in by . . ." (any more than we know what it means to say "participate in . . ." after the second part of *Parmenides*). We will therefore attempt, like a set of keys, several possible interpretations of participation.

First we try a somewhat material representation, where the form would be like a whole, wholly spread throughout its parts, or like the day that is everywhere, or like a veil thrown over things. One draws absurd consequences from this participation-sharing.

Next we try a more subtle representation: participation as a relation of resemblance; it is therefore an inner-worldly relation,

like that put in play between a model and a copy. But, in order
for the model and the copy to resemble each other, it is necessary
to connect the two under a third idea; and, as the relation of this
"third" to the initial pair is itself too a relation of resemblance,
it will be necessary to refer the resemblance to a prior model *ad
infinitum*. Aristotle will make this into the argument of the third
man (Socrates and the idea of man resemble each other by participation in a third man). But we need to see that in Plato's eyes
this objection does not ruin participation any more than did the
preceding objection: both objections push participation beyond an
intelligibility constituted by comparisons of one thing to another.

Finally, we are going to put to the test a more subtle relation
involving four terms: (1) a man and (2) the Idea of man; (3) a
science practiced by concrete men and (4) the Idea of science; we
easily see that the man does the science and that the Idea of man
connects to the Idea of science; but we do not see how the pair
man–science, taken on the historical level, enters into relation with
the man–science pair, taken at the level of absolute significations;
the in itself refers to the in itself, the we to us – but the in itself
never comes to be for "us." This argument is more subtle than the
preceding one, for it no longer puts in relation things and their
meaning, but men and the meaning of things. The impossibility
of participation becomes the impossibility of human knowing; the
relation "in itself – for us," a relation we can call an intentional
relation,[2] is impossible. The in itself is closed in on itself, like a
Hinterwelt without relation; in other words, the in itself is the
unknowable. We oscillate therefore between a material relation
and an absence of relation.

But, once again, the failure of the material representation, the
analogical representation, and the intentional representation of
participation signifies not an absolute defeat, but *unthinkability*.
The discussion makes sense only because of the interlocutors'
agreement about the truth of participation; that is why at the
beginning (133b) and at the end (135a) Parmenides lets it be
understood that "a rich experience" and "a nature well endowed"
(133b) will make it possible to come to a conclusion (cf. 135a-b).

---

[2] The following schema helps clarify the reading:
  science in itself   thing in itself
  our science   science for us

Provisional conclusion

1) The difficulties of vertical participation must be *coordinated* with the difficulties of lateral participation.
2) The two must be *subordinated* to the question: What does the *being* of each of these beings that are the Ideas or Forms signify?

3 The aporetic use of dialectic in the second part of the *Parmenides*

Instead of following through on all the objections against the theory of Ideas, Parmenides makes a sudden about-face: he proposes a propaedeutic exercise borrowed from Zeno, an exercise that consists of positing hypotheses and examining them in terms of their consequences. It is understood that this exercise will no longer waste its time with a dialectic of the sensible, in order to show its unreality, but that this gymnastic exercise will instead proceed straightaway on the level of ideas. Parmenides is therefore going to give a sample of this gymnastic exercise with respect to the Idea of the One which is familiar to him, and will "play this laborious game" which consists in elaborating and then wrecking all the hypotheses in succession (137b). But with respect to this game, meant to be propaedeutic, we can make out neither its connection to the preceding difficulties nor its function in preparing a solution. We will thus first present the structure of the argumentation (§3), then sketch the possible various interpretations (§4); we shall retain only what seems to answer our question: the being of Ideas.

First preliminary comment

This argument bears the name dialectic yet does not seem to have any connection to the method that the *Republic* and the *Phaedrus* call dialectic and that reappears in the *Sophist*. Dialectic here presents itself in its most suspect light, as an *eristic*, something Platonism wants to defeat. This fall back into eristic – and even sophistic – is part of the *deliberate archaism* that dominates the new problematic that Parmenides wants to bring forward. In practice, dialectic, at least when projected as a program, calls for a

reflection on its conditions of possibility; the problem of the communication of the ideas is in this respect the second-degree problem
that arises through the use of dialectic. For the "collection" and
"division" of the *Phaedrus* to be possible, it is necessary that the
being of an idea be such that it be the *non-being* of another Idea
as well. In brief, the dialectic of the ideas presupposes a dialectical
structure of the being of the Ideas. It is therefore a reduplicated
dialectic that is, in some manner, put into play in the *Parmenides*.
Just as the most radical problem of being requires that one make
oneself older than Socrates, that one makes oneself pre-Socratic,
in the same way the most radical problem of dialectic requires that
one give oneself over to what is most valid in the eristic of Gorgias,
Protagoras, Euclid, Antisthenes. The "irony" of the *Parmenides*
is to leave us completely disarmed in the face of this triumphant
eristic; in order to pose the problem, it was necessary to make the
truth of sophistic reasoning appear.[3] This truth, which surpasses
sophistic reasoning, is that sophistic reasoning is the ludic enve-
lope of the most basic aporia, the aporia of being and no longer
of the "be-ings." Socratic doubt has led to "be-ings" (*ta onta*);
the reprise of sophistic reasoning puts in question the very being
assigned to the essences.

Second preliminary comment

The "aporetic" function of sophistic reasoning is further
accentuated by the employment of the "hypotheses" that the
Republic, however, seemed to have relegated to the lower level of

---

[3] Jean Wahl, in his *Étude sur le* Parménide *de Platon*, retells the history of this
pre-Socratic dialectic from Anaxagoras to the Sophists (pp. 53–60) and shows
persuasively how "this antilogic, which he had so harshly condemned in the
Republic (Bk. VII), in the *Phaedo* (101c), and in the *Phaedrus* (261c) gets
transmuted into a higher science" (p. 61). Sophistic reasoning has a purify-
ing value, comparable to that of tragedy; it carries the *docta ignorantia* from
the the sensibles to the intelligibles. In this way, there is "a sophistic use of
dianoia that makes us move toward *noesis.*" Jean Wahl even dares the expression: "there is a *doxa* about Ideas" (p. 61). There is, if one may put it this
way, something of opinion in what Parmenides thought to be the truth; what
refutes Socrates even more radically refutes Parmenides. Jean Wahl sees here a
means of making a "beyond *ousia*" appear, in accord with the project of the
Republic, and of placing the Ideas in relation by the movement of implication
of *being* and *non-being*. We shall see whether these two functions are compatible (PR).

mathematics. To ground the dialectic of the beings in a dialectic of being, it is necessary to return to the hypothetical procedure of the Eleatics and Megareans, which plunges the investigation back into a problematic atmosphere.

Third comment

This feature is accentuated further by duplicating each series of positive hypotheses with a *negative series*. Example: If the One is not, what happens? ("It is necessary to make use of Zeno's procedures to convert the ideas into hypothetical judgments on the subject of their very existence, but it must be added that these hypothetical judgments can be affirmative or negative.")[4] At the same time, the *non-positing* of an idea constitutes the content of a hypothesis: this is a way of already introducing *non-being* among the conditions of possibility of ideal beings or, as the *Sophist* will put it, otherness as a "highest kind."

Fourth comment

Finally, the "aporetic" turn of the whole discussion will be crowned by the *destruction* of the hypotheses; the posing and disposing of a series of hypotheses, themselves positive and negative, such will be the aporetic style of the dialectical exercise of the *Parmenides*. Jean Wahl sees in this a sort of "dark night of the understanding" that follows upon thought caught up in images and that provides access to that which is above the intelligible and the hypotheses. But we shall return later to this more "mystical" than "propaedeutic" interpretation of the *Parmenides*, which was fundamentally that of Proclus (Proclus connects the *anhupotheton* of *Republic* VI 510b and 511b and of[5] the destruction of the hypotheses in the *Parmenides*).[6] It is worth noting, further, that this destruction is not obtained by means of a rigorous deduction; the "consequences" of the hypothesis are brought together by an assonance of ideas: dialectic here is a supple method of examining hypotheses, a "flexible world of simple natures that are in

---

[4] Wahl, *id.*, p. 66 (AC).
[5] This "of" (*de*) surely needs to be suppressed for this sentence to make sense (AC).
[6] Cited by Wahl, *id.*, p. 70 (AC).

communication and whose *vincula* are the very movement of the mind."[7] It all constitutes a sort of wandering, of "floating," on the ocean of discourse which Proclus already compared to the voyage of Ulysses.

We can now set forth the schema of the "hypotheses" of the *Parmenides*. The hypothesis "if the One is" is augmented a first time: "If the One is not"; then it is augmented a second time: What results for it? What results for the others (*t'alla*)? Finally, it gets augmented even more subtly in accord with a principle indicated only at the beginning of the second hypothesis (142b-c). What does it mean to say: the One is? We take this hypothesis in two senses, depending on whether we accentuate the One's Unity or its *Reality*, "for if the One *is*, in the full sense of the verb to be, it is not wholly one, since reality gets attached to it; and if the One is *one*, in the full sense of the word one, it is not completely real . . ... It is necessary to abandon being to have the One, or to abandon the one to have being."[8]

So we have a complex field of hypotheses:

1) If we affirm the *Oneness* of the One, what results for it?
2) If we affirm the *Being* of the One, what results for it?
3) If we affirm the *Being* of the One, what results for the other things?
4) If we affirm the *Oneness* of the One, what results for the other things?
5) If we negate the *Being* of the One, what results for the One?
6) If we negate the *Oneness* of the One, what results for the One?
7) If we negate the *Being* of the One, what results for the other things?
8) If we negate the *Oneness* of the One, what results for the other things?

4 The formalist interpretation

The problem of the interpretation of the *Parmenides* was already posed in antiquity just as it arises in our own day. Is what we have

---

[7] Wahl., *id.*, p. 71, who contrasts this passage to Spinoza and Hegel and compares it to Descartes (AC).
[8] Wahl, *id.*, p. 86 (AC).

here a game, or an esoteric dialogue?[9] This question is closely
tied to the question of knowing what the One is here. Is it only
an example, like that of the fisherman in the *Sophist*? Or is it
precisely the Good of the *Republic*, which will become the One
in the *Philebus*? This is what is affirmed by the neo-Platonists,
who thereby privilege the first hypothesis. And the "others" put
in relation with the One, is this the sensible as understood by the
Marburg school? If so, the dialectic would be that of the intelligible and the sensible. Or is this otherness a structure of the intelligible? If so, the dialectic does not at any moment exit the rational
field of the principal elements of representation. What is more,
none of these diverse interpretations takes account of the total
number of hypotheses. Why all these hypotheses? Why any at all
after the first and the second one? Is it necessary to grant the third
one, indeed the fourth one, a key place?

We will take as a guide Brochard,[10] because his interpretation is
the closest to the theory of a pure game, even though he looks for
the serious element in the *form* of the game. Brochard attempts, as
does moreover the entire tradition, to reduce the eight hypotheses
to one alternative. The alternative is not between the affirmative hypothesis and the negative hypothesis (and therefore not
between the first group of four and the second group of four), or
between the consequences "for itself" and "for the others" – but
rather in the separation of Being and the One, which opens up
two possibilities: either the One can only reduplicate itself; or
being can be attributed to the One; there are, then, two sets of
hypotheses, the one guided by the first hypothesis, the other by
the second. What does this splitting of the Parmenidean thesis into
two hypotheses signify? According to Brochard, it is not at all the
theology of the One that is at issue; the One is one example among
others. What is at issue is the attribution of Being to the One. With
the first hypothesis, participation is impossible, with the second, it
is possible. Immediately, everything becomes clear: the *Parmenides*
is an exercise about "participation." But this exercise is "aporetic," precisely because there are just two hypotheses, more or
less hidden – for love of the game (and here, on the "eristic" side,
lies what makes it a game) – under an apparent complication.

---

[9] Cf. the citation of Proclus in Wahl, *id.*, notes, p. 243 (AC).
[10] Brochard, *Études de philosophie ancienne et de philosophie moderne, op. cit.*
(AC).

In what does the aporia consist? Let us look at the conclusion of both series: if the One is, in the sense that one affirms its unity and not its being, then non-participation makes it that the one is neither this nor that, it is perfectly indeterminate; one cannot say anything about it: *nothing is true*. If the One is, in the sense that one affirms its reality, then the being that one attributes to it is understood in so determined a manner that we get lost in all the determinations, and it is anything we want, for every determination fits it; in short, *everything is true*.

Hence the *Parmenides* would be the final and the most formidable objection to the theory of Ideas. The first part showed that the participation of the sensible in the intelligible is unintelligible; the second part will show that the participation of the intelligible in the intelligible is itself unintelligible; since if we do not allow it, nothing is true, if we do allow it, then everything is true. This seems to be what is indicated in 166c, which Brochard summarizes as follows: "We can affirm everything about the One and the other things; we can affirm nothing about the One and the other things."[11] The *Parmenides* would be a virtuoso reprise of the thesis of Protagoras, the Cynics, and the Megarians, who held error and more generally all attribution to be impossible. Brochard summarizes his interpretation in this way: "Posit the participation of any idea whatever in being and everything is true; negate such participation and nothing is true. Participation, in whatever manner one understands it, is therefore entirely impossible, and with this impossibility the theory of Ideas collapses."[12]

This interpretation, which reduces the *Parmenides* to the ruinous alternative: everything is true – nothing is true, has the advantage of showing in a clear way the unity of the *Parmenides* and the *Sophist*; the answer to the enigma will then lie in the *Sophist*, at 251d–252e, where it appears that there are not two solutions (nothing communicates with anything – everything can be affirmed of anything whatsoever) but *three*. The "third solution," that of the *compossibility of some Ideas with some Ideas*, is therefore the solution to the *Parmenides*. The aporia of the *Parmenides* would consist in this, that Plato, whether by ruse or from real ignorance concerning the solution, got locked up in a ruinous alternative with respect to the problem of participation. It may well be, in

---

[11] Brochard, *id.*, p. 128 (AC).
[12] *Id.*, p. 129 (AC).

addition, that in writing the *Parmenides* he did not as yet have the key to the enigma, for the participation of some Ideas with some Ideas presupposes the elaboration of the highest kinds where, in turn, the Ideas of being and non-being participate in one another, that is, they all imply one another at the same time as they stay distinct. And letting Brochard conclude: in the *Parmenides*, Plato sins "solely by omission, he does not point to the solution which he no doubt already had before him. The game consists in discussing just two solutions to the problem, whereas in reality there are three." "The *Parmenides* would be nothing but a tissue of sophisms if its author had not written the *Sophist*."[13]

5 Critical comments: that the meaning of the *Parmenides* is over-determined

In so linking the *Parmenides* and the *Sophist* through the problematic of participation, Brochard brings a helpful simplicity to this extraordinarily complex game. But in treating the One as one example of an Idea among others (something Plato authorizes by saying clearly that he would have been able to do the same thing with the Many, the Like, the Unlike, Movement, Rest, Coming-to-Be, Ceasing-to-Be, Being or Non-Being, and "for anything for which you can claim existence or non-existence or any other determination" [136b]),[14] Brochard lets slip away the other dimensions of the *Parmenides*, a dialogue that Jean Wahl designates as "stereometric" or pluridimensional. Perhaps Plato is pursuing several designs at the same time: already at the level where Brochard situates himself, one can suppose the intent to confound the eristics through the use and abuse of their own dialectic; there would thus be a polemical goal which in large part escapes us, given our ignorance about the scholastic quarrels among the intermingled descendants of the Eleatics and the Socratics.

---

[13] *Id.*, pp. 131 and 132 (AC).

[14] Émile Chambry (Paris: GF-Flammarion, 1967) translates as follows: "anything you may suppose to be or not to be or to sustain any affection whatever." [F. M. Cornford (*Collected Dialogues*): "whenever you suppose that anything whatsoever exists or does not exist or has any other character"; Mary Louise Gill and Paul Ryan (*Collected Works*): "concerning whatever you might ever hypothesize as being or as not being or as having any other property." – Trans.]

Yet it hardly seems contestable that under the cover of the purely *logical* problem of the attribution of Being to whatever may be, Plato at the same time pursues the design of a philosophy of the One along the line of the *Republic* and the *Philebus*. The One is thus more than an example: it is also what is at stake. There would therefore be at least two things at stake: the first, entirely formal, linked to the doubling of the hypothesis about the One (the One-ness of the One, the Being of the One), which is what is at stake in the communication of the kinds, that is, the possibility of attribution; the other, ontological and even theological, linked to the very choice of the One as the theme of the exercise. The first hypothesis would then consist in pushing the idea of the transcendence of the One all the way, to the point of wrecking all discourse; it would be the radicalization of the thesis of the *Republic* (the Good is *epekeina tes ousias* = ἐπέκεινα τῆς οὐσίας) by means of the "dark night of the understanding"; the second hypothesis, on the contrary, would push to the farthest extent the immanence of the One to the determinations of discourse: to save knowledge, one would render it impossible. In this way, the aporia of Platonism that the *Parmenides* brings to light would be far more than the aporia of attribution, it would be the very aporia of a philosophy of discourse, rendered impossible at both poles: the pole of the one without words and the pole of the many, of fugitive and shifting reality, that likewise wrecks all speech. The stake would thus be the equilibrium in Platonism between the *élan* that pushes it beyond the determinations of discourse, toward silence and the night, and the *élan* that pushes it toward the mastery of a discourse that is itself many and changing, which paradoxically makes Heraclitus triumph at the very heart of the intelligible that one had victoriously opposed to him in constructing the theory of the Ideas. That is what study of the *Sophist* will confirm.

Conclusion to chapter 1: from *Parmenides* to the *Sophist*

Let us return to this chapter's initial question, and push it a little further.

What makes for the internal unity of the *Parmenides* is therefore the same as what makes for the unity of the series *Parmenides, Theaetetus, Sophist, Statesman* – namely, the question of "participation," taken up in its two dimensions: participation of the sensibles in the ideas, participation of the ideas among themselves.

How does this problem get attached to the question we have called the *ontological* question of the second degree (no longer: what *is* this, what *is* that? but: what is being?). The question of participation in fact concerns not the unit of signification (First Part, chap. 1), on which denomination depends, but that of relation, on which true or false attribution depends. But, someone will say, we have already dealt with this question within the framework of dialectic; dialectic, under the name of "collection" and "division," had already constrained us to add to the principle of distinct determination a principle of compossibility. What does the problem of the "participation of kinds" add to that of dialectic? Dialectic is participation at work, in labor in a method; participation is reflective dialectic, that is, considered from the angle of its conditions of possibility. That is why it requires an archaizing reprise of the problem, which had initially been dealt with in the style of the methodological investigation in the *Phaedrus*.

But if one places oneself in a realist system of truth, to reflect on the conditions of possibility of the dialectic of ideas is to make new ideas spring up, but ideas which are ideas of the second degree, those that Plato calls "the greatest kinds." Here it is necessary for us to be on guard against Kantianism and treating these supreme kinds as possibles that would have no other rooting than the "I Think." The supreme kinds are themselves forms in which the preceding ones participate; it will be said that they circulate among the other forms: this realist turn of the question explains why the category of non-being, which creates the possibility of attribution in general and error in particular, should be called BEING: the *Sophist* drives thinking toward that thesis which is so difficult to sustain: non-being is. This means, to make attribution *possible*, non-being must be *real*; and to be really non-being, as the *Sophist* will put it, it will have itself to participate in being, that is, in its "other." In this way, the attribution of non-being to being and of being to non-being will be a second-degree structure of participation. For me to be able to say: "Socrates is sitting," there must be a participation between the subject Socrates and the verb to be seated, a participation of a first degree; but for this participation to be possible, I have to be able to say, at a second degree, otherness *is*; this being of otherness is the condition of possibility of attribution. Hence the transcendental attribution of being to non-being and of non-being to being is the second-degree ontological structure that makes attribution possible at the first level of thinking (for example, when I say that the number three *is* odd). One could say the same thing in different terms: the problem of the *Sophist* and the *Parmenides* stems from a reflection on dialectic as *method*, where attribution occurs simply by means of the copula; this reflection reduplicates dialectic, in a foundational dialectic, where being is attributed anew, no longer to essences but to otherness, to identity, to movement, which are all categories brought into play by the first-degree dialectic: in this way the reciprocity of being and non-being is uncovered.

Chapter 8

The Success and Failures of Platonism in the *Sophist*

Bringing together the *Sophist* and the *Parmenides* is quite illuminating in several respects: on the one hand, it constitutes a solution to a number of the fundamental difficulties of Platonism; on the other, it consecrates abandoning certain problems that remain aporetic; finally, it opens up new difficulties at the heart of Platonism. What this comparison makes apparent is the blend of what is resolved and what is left unresolved in Platonism – at least in that of the published dialogues.

Let us begin with the questions that were abandoned, for abandoning them is the price of the partial success of the *Sophist*.

1 Removing the problem of the One and the Many

What is remarkable first of all is how the problem of the One and the Many loses the key position which it had occupied in the *Parmenides*, to the profit of the question *being/non-being*, or, better, *being–other*. What does of this change of emphasis signify?

a) Let us first consider the *Sophist*: the problem of the One is reintegrated with the aporias found in the history of philosophy: what is remarkable is that it is in this grand retrospective consideration of doctrines about being that Parmenides' problem figures as an abandoned question: "How many beings are there, and what are they?" (242c). Here the problem of being is quantified in a way. Whereas in the *Parmenides* the refutation of the One–all proceeds by means of the destruction of hypotheses, in order to arrive at "everything is true – nothing is true" in the *Sophist* the refutation rests on the very operation of naming: to say "the One is" is to say "two," for it is to say "One" and then "Being" (244b-c); furthermore: to say "One" is to posit something *and* its name, therefore again to double the One (244d) (at this point we shall leave aside what follows in the refutation in *Parmenides* that bears on the Idea of "All," something we will meet again in the critique of the Idea of Being).

b) If, starting from the *Sophist*, we return to the *Parmenides* in a kind of retrospective or retroactive way, what does this bring out about the ever-so-vain game of "hypotheses"?

This: the notion of being, in the *Parmenides*, is always taken in a corporeal and even material sense; as if the notion of being had been intentionally degraded by the finally impracticable problematic of the One. It is understood, in the first and the second hypotheses, that such determinations as whole–part, beginning–end, middle, limit, shape, space, time, are the determinations of being; for example, the first hypothesis concludes thusly: to participate in time is to participate in being, under the form of is, was, will be (*Parmenides* 141e). The adherence of the idea of being to spatial and temporal determinations is the implicit postulate of this whole argument. The second hypothesis (the One that is) remains faithful to the same postulate: whole–part, shape, time, etc., are the ontological determinations of the One: in particular it is confirmed that participation in Being is a *methexis ousias meta chronou tou parontos* = μέθεξις οὐσίας μετὰ χρόνου τοῦ παρόντος. The change of emphasis from the *Parmenides* to the *Sophist* suggests the idea that it is possible to rectify the question of being – the question "what is being?" *ti to on* (Sophist 218a, 243d-e, 244b) at the expense of the question "if the One is," *ei on estin*. What does this effacement mean for Platonism overall? This abandoning of the question of the One – a provisional abandonment as the *Philebus* attests – is the abandoning of a genuinely Platonic question, since it is the question of the terminus of the ascending dialectic; here the *Philebus* is quite illuminating (23c–27e): the One is the Good of the *Republic*; but the *Republic* did not speak in an absolutely aporetic way, since the Good was that which makes the subject knowledgeable and the beings known and, beyond that, that which confers essence and existence on the Ideas. The Good is therefore the radical origin. Plato cannot deny a philosophy of the Good and of the One without decapitating his philosophy. But what Plato becomes aware of in the *Parmenides* is that the One, like the many, but at the other extremity of his system, is a sort of nihilation [*neant*], not an absolute nihilation, but a nihilation of determination, and the limit of the philosophy of language; on the contrary the problem of being, as posed in the *Sophist*, remains within the limits of the questionable and the limits of *legein*: does *one say* something in *saying* being? The problem of the One is the end of discourse, whereas the problem of *Ousia*[1] still lies within the kingdom of philosophic speaking.

The *Philebus* does not contradict this interpretation; in ceasing to call Being the end point of the dialectic, it sanctions the affirmation of the *Republic* that *ousia* remains on this side of the "negation of discourse" constituted by the problem of the One, since the Good was said to be "beyond *ousia*." The *Parmenides*, clarified by the *Sophist*, allows us to see that a philosophy of the intelligible, like that of Plato, i.e., a philosophy that has its first basis in naming and in the reality of spoken significations, moves through a *certain interval* that is no longer either the One or the Many. The *Sophist* itself takes place precisely in this interval, closer to the One but falling short of the One. A second comparison with the *Philebus* will make this easier to understand; the *Philebus* is not just the exaltation of the One, it is also a warning about the sobriety of dialectic: in the passage 16c–18d, it is said that the dialectician enumerates the *intermediate ideas* between the One and the Many, whereas eristic on the contrary "too quickly reaches one" or "too quickly many." The *Sophist* is faithful to this rule: it counts the "supreme kinds": "We were in agreement to *count* as five distinct kinds the kinds deduced during our examination ..." Theaetetus answers the Stranger: "It is quite impossible that we should consent to reduce this *number* below the figure just now clearly obtained" (256c).

It is at this price that the philosophy of definition can be radically followed through: by renouncing defining the One, which becomes the upper limit of discourse, and seeking the definition of being on the side of an enumeration of the multiple, but not unlimited, determinations.

---

[1] *Ousia* with a capital here in the *Course*.

2 Explicit resolution of the problem of being: the same and the other

In turn, the question *ti on* – what is being? – is susceptible of *definition* only on the condition of being rendered initially as obscure as the question of non-being. This abandoning of onto-logical dogmatism is the meaning of the long *reprise of the history of philosophy*, which occupies so large a place in the *Sophist*. But this aporia [is]² constructive, if one may put it so, not destructive. For it ends in the affirmation that I do not think being, and there-fore do not define it, except in relation with another idea – which is precisely the idea of the Other. In place of the ruinous dialectic of the One is substituted a definitional dialectic, or, if one prefers, the dialectical definition of Being by means of the Same and the Other: Heraclitus and Parmenides are both saved, after each had been lost separately, the first at the beginning of Socratism, the second at the end of Socratism.

But it is important to understand well how putting forward this unusual Idea of the "Other" saves the question of *ti on* from defeat. The *Parmenides* ceaselessly touches on the ideas of the Same and the Other, but does so without benefit, because these dif-ferent determinations are subordinated to the search for the One. The same notions that serve to solve the problem of the One serve to destroy the problem of the One. In the first hypothesis, both the Same and the Other are refused to the One (139b-e) because they are extraneous, separated "natures" (cf. the words *phusis* and *choris*): "If the One should be affected by a character that would remain distinct from its proper unity, it would by this affection become something more than one, and that is impossible" (146a). The relation "One–many" or "One–other" remains outside the field of all "participation" (cf. the repetition of the word μετέχον = *metechon* at 140a-e). In the second hypothesis, the Same and the Other are affirmed of the One, but completely otherwise than in the *Sophist*: by pure and simple confusion (146b–147a).

In the *Sophist*, the Same and the Other (and the Same is there for the sake of the Other) are not at all some significations among others, which we ask whether we can apply to so radical a principle as the One; they are, rather, higher determinations, obtained through reflection on a primary dialectic, that of Being with Movement and

---

² "is": restored here.

Rest. So the Idea of Being has to have been placed in relation with "two great kinds" so that out of Being's dialectical situation there will arise the two categories that express this dialectical situation itself. In fact, the trilogy Being–Movement–Rest already had been acquired during the discussion with the Friends of the Forms: as soon as an idea is known, its being implies movement and rest: rest since it is what it is, movement since it has come to be known.

Cornford strongly emphasizes the eminent place of the final pair of the five kinds with respect to the preceding ones: Same and Other are "even greater kinds" than Movement, Rest, or Being.

What does this imply for the idea of Being? Two things that we can draw from the place of the idea of Being at the turning point of the five kinds:

On one side, Being is what dominates the Movement–Rest opposition; in Plato's language, these two Ideas "exclude" each other, while Being is "mixed" with the two; Being is participated in by Movement and by Rest. In other words, creating a philosophy of permanence or a philosophy of becoming does not mean one has yet succeeded in thinking Being. Being is neither becoming nor permanence, but what allows grounding their opposition and their alternation in the history of philosophy. To employ a Heideggerian language, I will say that becoming and permanence remain within the *ontic* and are not yet in the *ontological*. This is important to put us on guard against the illusions of a philosophy of permanence: for whether one posits logical atoms in the manner of the Friends of the Forms or physical atoms in the manner of the atomists, it is still *ta onta*, not yet *to on*. The philosophies of becoming and the philosophies of substance are not yet at the level of the problem of Being and are condemned to mutually undercut each other. Being is a *triton ti* (something of a "third"). In all opposition, there is thus an initial stage in the definition of Being, indicated by a *triton ti*, a third term.

Then there is a second stage: the *triton ti* is thinkable in turn only because there is a fourth and, above all, a fifth kind. The notion of Being looks, therefore, in two directions: it is what overcomes the historical oppositions between philosophies of change and philosophies of eternity and hence escapes their sempiternal tipping back and forth; but, on the other side, this notion is thinkable only as dialecticized by two kinds that are in a sense even greater: what Plato expresses in saying: the three kinds Being, Same, and Other are *mutually predicable*, whereas Movement and Rest "participate

in the same and the other" (*Sophist* 255b) without either participating in the other. What does this finally imply for the problem of
Being? This: that the being of this or that should always be defined
both by what is "relative to itself" and by what is "relative to
another." By the same token, the *Other* has a privilege over Being,
just as a moment ago Being was privileged in regard to Movement
and Rest: the Other has the noteworthy trait of being the category
that reflects the relationship among all the categories (for example,
if I say that movement is *other* than rest, or *other* than being): this
category "is spread," says Plato, "across all others; each of them,
in fact, is other than the rest, not in virtue of its own nature, but
in virtue of the fact that it participates in the form of the other"
(*Sophist* 255e). The Other is therefore the category that, in reflecting the mutual relationship of the categories, reiterates itself without referring to any other category. This is why it is the fifth and
final kind (Plato emphasizes the dignity of this great kind: "Among
the series of kinds, the nature of the Other makes each of them
other than Being and, by the same token, even non-Being," *Sophist*
256e; cf. also 258b and d).

Thus Being is the highest notion of philosophy, in contrast to
change and permanence, only if it allows itself to be supplanted by
the most ungraspable category; Being is the "third" only because
there is a "fifth." Being's situation as third is consolidated in this
dialectical manner by the role of the fifth: what this means is that
something is being on condition that it is also non-being: being
by virtue of its identity with itself and non-being by virtue of its
otherness from the rest. "Thus universally for all the kinds, in this
connection, we correctly say that they are nonbeing, and on the
contrary, because they participate in being, we say that they are,
we name them beings" (*Sophist* 256e). It is this dialectical situation of the notion of being that Plato sums up in a scintillating way
at 259a-b (read carefully 259a-b).

We see what comes from the sterile game of the *Parmenides* in
constituting a positive critique of being (259c). But we see also
a dialectical relation that condemns those ontologies that would
base themselves firmly on the *dogmatic* notion of Being, attained
at the level of the third kind through the mutual refutation of
movement and rest. So, an ontology has the double task of getting
beyond the historical contrasts of movement and of rest, of time
and of atemporality, and of allowing itself to be critiqued and
limited by "the Same and the Other."

3 Partial resolution of the difficulties of the first part of the *Parmenides*

The *Sophist* was explicitly oriented toward resolving the problem of attribution in general, and of false attribution in particular, i.e., the problem of error; under this heading, the dialogue first resolves the problem of the *Theaetetus* – the problem of the error of error: the category of the Other is introduced with this goal in mind at the dialogue's conclusion; but, more generally, this category furnishes a solution to the *enigma* at the beginning of the *Parmenides*, a solution that the second half seems not to announce; but it may be that this resolution can only be implicit, like the indication of a direction that one cannot follow all the way to the end.

a) Does the problem of the participation of the sensibles in the intelligible, which lies at the center of the aporias of the first part (129d-e), find an answer, even indirectly, in the dialectic of the five great kinds? Explicitly no, since, speaking absolutely, this problem is not broached in the *Sophist*; implicitly perhaps, to the degree one might suspect that the participation of the ideas among themselves is the clue to the participation of the sensibles in the intelligible. This is what Brochard thinks: "The connections among things and ideas are without doubt the same as those of the ideas among themselves."[3] He refers to the text on the dialectic that we have already discussed (253d): "one single idea spread across the multitude of others." Presence to itself according to the Same and presence to another thing according to the Other will be the universal structure of participation.

This extension of dialectic to the passage from the intelligible to the sensible is very suggestive: indeed, why is it that participation seemed so absurd in the *Parmenides*? Because it was imagined on a material model (the whole that spreads over the parts, the model that allows itself to be imitated by its copy . . .), "Sharing" and "resembling" thus fell short as regards participation. Perhaps it is necessary to think that the relation of "this" to its "meaning," of the sensible to the Idea, is a dialectical relation of the Same and the Other; this would be the dialectical response to the third man argument, which is finally as naïve as the representation of participation itself as a resemblance. ("Aristotle

---

[3] Brochard, *op. cit.*, p. 148 (AC).

would have done well to remember this when he insists com-
placently on the objection of the 'third man.'")[4] Dialectic would
therefore allow us to *correct* all the materialist representations of
participation.

In spite of the interest and the seductiveness of this hypothesis,
it is necessary to acknowledge that Plato here touches on a limit
of his philosophy, a lower limit so to speak. Just as the One is
the upper limit of philosophic discourse, the sensible is the lower
limit of this discourse. It is this, it seems to me, that is to be discerned in the text of the *Philebus* about dialectic: "To grasp what
full number the multitude realizes between the Infinite and the
One; *thus merely to allow each of the unities of this collection to
disperse itself into the infinite*" (16e) (χαίρειν ἐᾶν = *chairein ean*
expressly means "to send on its way," "to say farewell"). The
passage from "meaning" to full and brute "existence" is no longer
an act of dialectical thought. This is what a philosophy of Ideas
admits; there is something scandalous in the relation of even the
most concrete Idea to brute presence; this is the scandal of a "genesis" not entirely reducible to a "dialectic of Ideas."

This scandal, which is the lower limit of discourse, can be staked
out across Plato's work by the quasi-sexual myth of the generation
of the sensible from a pair, one of whose terms is unintelligible;
the three fundamental landmarks are the marriage of *ploutos* and
penia in the *Phaedrus*, the union of the "limit" and the "unlimited" in the *Philebus*, and the role of the *chora* in the *Timaeus*; the
text of the *Philebus* is the most striking because it tries to overcome the myth, and yet the *meixis* of limit and unlimited retains
a sexual resonance. "The result of this union," Diès recalls in his
"Introduction to the *Philebus*," is the generation of a product
(*ekgenen*), the apparition of an existence that is no longer eternal
as the principles are, but composed and engendered (*meikte kai
gege nemene ousia*, 27b)."[5] The *Philebus* speaks of the *apeiron*,
in terms bordering on those of the *Timaeus*, about the *chora*,
which is so much more than just a geometric space, but rather
a "wet nurse," a "womb of existence," something which moves
without order. The justification of Brochard's thesis that participation among ideas is the key to the participation of the sensible

---

4 *Id.*, p. 148 (AC).
5 Diès, *Notice du Philèbe*, Paris: Les Belles Lettres, 1941 (AC).

in the Ideas rests on this conviction, expressed elsewhere,[6] that the *chora* of the *Timaeus* is an Idea, the Idea of the Other. The instability of the *chora*, the qualitative agitation that it gives to "all receiving" and makes it be called an "errant cause," brings it close to the *apeiron* of the *Philebus* – to the "Great–Small" of the *Phaedo*, to the dyad of Great–Small according to Aristotle's *Metaphysics*, therefore, of a principle of indetermination, in brief the Idea of the Other: "There is no essential difference between the Other and this matter of the sensible world that is matter itself."[7] Furthermore, this Other is an Idea, it is the "Idea of the other," according to the *Timaeus* (51a), which calls the *chora* an *eidos*. But then, if matter is itself an Idea, the very Idea of non-Being, does the sensible world differ fundamentally from the intelligible world? "To this question," says Brochard, "it is necessary to reply that the difference between the two worlds is entirely one of degree." In the intelligible, the Ideas would have an aptitude only for participation, "in the world of becoming, on the contrary, this participation takes place."[8] An unsustainable premise, refuted by the dialectic of the five kinds, and by the interpretation that the *Phaedo* gives way to becoming in its connections with the logical relations among Ideas. This text of Brochard's shows well on what adventurous bases this sovereignty of the dialectic has been constructed, even going so far as to include the sensible; a curious thing is that Brochard is led to say that participation has no effective location except in the sensible! At bottom, what is not Platonic is this, "that outside the Idea there is nothing real."[9] The existence of the soul, which is not an Idea, is itself sufficient to refute this.

It is better to acknowledge that philosophy remains within the between-two of the "numbered quantity"; we rediscover the problem of the "intermediary number" which is in question in the text (referred to several times) about the dialectic (the ὁπόσα = *hoposa* of *Philebus* 16d). The "eristic manner," to which Plato here opposes the "dialectic manner" (*Philebus* 17a), consists in stretching from the pole of the One to the pole of the many with-

---

[6] Victor Brochard, "Le Devenir dans la philosophie de Platon," in *Histoire de la philosophie* (avec L. Dauriac), Paris[: A. Colin], 1902, pp. 105–110 (AC).

[7] Brochard, *id.*, p. 109 (AC).

[8] *Id.*, p. 109 and p. 110 (AC).

[9] *Id.* (AC).

out reflection and without measure (which is the case when it is put in words).

It seems to me therefore that there remains something mysterious in the participation of the sensible in the Idea. To stop at "this" is to allow oneself to be fascinated by a presence which is not that of discourse; this is perhaps *to live*, in any case this is not "to philosophize." "In staying with the infinite multitude of individual things and with the infinite multiplicity that each of them contains is to prevent oneself, in each case, from taking a completed notion from this and from becoming a man who counts and numbers (*ellogimon . . . enarithmon*), seeing that on the basis of none of them were you able to attain any definite number" (*Philebus* 17e).[10]

For Plato, it makes no sense to speak of a "philosophy of the concrete." By the same token, the participation of the sensible in the intelligible is a relation that is *practiced* daily in the act of speaking, of naming, of defining, but which cannot be thought through as a relation intelligible in itself; everything happens as if, from brute existence to "meaning," there were a *leap* worked by the *legein*, by Speaking, and as if, inversely, from saying to perceiving, there were an inverse leap, a *chairein ean*, a "saying farewell" – which is silence. We shall see in the next chapter how the introduction of the demiurge partially resolves the difficulty.

b) A second aspect of the participation of the sensible in the intelligible was brought up in the *Parmenides* through the argument with respect to unknowable being. The "in itself" cannot be "for us." Here, the sensible is contingent and historical human knowledge, in other words, the soul. The argument therefore consists in

---

[10] The translation Ricoeur uses differs considerably from Chambry's (GF-Flammarion, 1969): "But the infinity of the individuals and the multitude which is in them cause you not to understand them and is why one cannot expect of you either an estimate or a count, because you never fix your vision on any number nor any thing." [R. Hackworth (*Collected* Dialogues): "the unlimited variety that belongs to and is inherent in the particulars leaves one, in each particular case, an unlimited ignoramus, a person of no account, a veritable back number because he hasn't ever addressed himself to finding number in anything"; Dorothea Frede (*Collected Works*): "The boundless multitude, however, in any and every kind of subject leaves you in boundless ignorance, and makes you count for nothing and amount to nothing, since you have never worked out the amount and number of anything at all." – Trans.]

saying that "the in itself" cannot communicate with the "for us." This is at bottom a different species of participation of the sensible in the intelligible, or at least of existence in essence, namely, the participation of the existing soul in the essence of the truth.

But was not this clarified indirectly by the dialectic of the *Sophist*? Yes, but only to a certain degree. The refutation of the Friends of the Forms is the indirect response to the thesis of the unknowable: at 248a, one admits that "through the body we have community with becoming by means of sensation, but with real existence (πρὸς τὴν ὄντως οὐσίαν = *pros ten ontos ousian*)" by means of reasoning, which requires that one assign to *ousia* the "power" of being known, therefore that minimal "passion" which authorizes placing being in the category of movement, if not as being that moves, at least as moved being (knowing being equals suffering, equals being moved, 248e). This is why it is necessary to forge the idea of the *pantelos on*, that is, of universal being or of total being, which envelops intellect, life, soul (249a). But there is no scandal in doing this thanks to the community of the great kinds: movement, rest, being (249b already says as much by anticipation: "it is necessary therefore to concede being to the Moved and to Movement").[11] "Known being" is therefore part of this dialectic of Movement and Rest, which includes the positing of every being. Plato does not give a soul to the ideas, but posits that very community of the soul with the Ideas that is knowledge itself.[12]

The dialectic of Being–Movement–Rest introduces in this way an intelligibility proper to itself into the obscure relation of the soul to being, which in the *Phaedo* remains obscure: the soul in this dialogue is only "akin" to the Idea (it is "what most resembles it") without being identical to it (which is why the soul's immortality is problematic, for it is the immortality of an existent and not

---

[11] Chambry's translation (*op. cit.*, p. 104): "It is therefore necessary to admit that that which is moved and movement are beings." [Cornford (*Collected Dialogues*): "In that case we must admit that what changes and change itself are real things"; Nicholas P. White (*Complete Works*): "Then both *that which changes* and also *change* have to be admitted as being." – Trans.]

[12] Ross is quite illuminating at this point: "His real meaning becomes clear in 249b, 5-10, where he says, in effect, that knowledge implies minds that are real and subject to change. He has not given up his belief in unchanging Ideas ... but he adds that minds subject to change must also be accepted as completely real ... that both unchanging Ideas and changing minds are perfectly real," cf. Ross, *op. cit.*, p. 110 (AC).

of an Idea). The Being–Movement–Rest dialectic of the *Sophist* structures this intentional relation of the soul to the Ideas; the Idea, as a power of being known, joins with the category of movement, all the while remaining at rest; and the soul that knows is at rest all the while it moves among all the relations. But this intelligibility that the *Sophist* introduces here remains partial. There remains in the soul a becoming irreducible to a dialectic of Idea which is indicated by such expressions as "to be in difficulty," "to seek," "to learn," "to forget"; this is why there has to be a myth – and myths – to recount this proximity and this distance of the soul with respect to the Ideas: absolute proximity in the "vision" which is also "consummation" ("to eat" symbolizing identification); absolute distance in the "fall"; but it is always in a myth that the soul is the Same or Other than the Idea.

So Platonism, to the degree to which it remains a philosophy of the intelligible, touches on this other limit: the obscurity of the becoming of the soul and of knowledge.

Chapter 9

The Genesis of the Sensible in the *Timaeus*

The *Sophist* resolves the problem of the participation of the sensible in the intelligible only partially: this participation retains something of the opaque, of the irrational; there is, therefore, an *unbridgeable gap* between the "vertical" participation (of sensible things in Ideas) and the "lateral" participation (of Ideas in Ideas).

Can the philosopher fill in this gap in another way than by dialectic? Yes, and this revival of the problem in the *Timaeus* will at the same time confirm our interpretation of the *Sophist*, like a recoil effect; this is because there is another explanation of the genesis of the sensible, in the *Timaeus*, as the *Sophist* is but a partial response to the problem posed at the beginning of the *Parmenides*. It is true that the answer of the *Timaeus* too is only a partial answer; at least it stops a little further on: it is not the sensible as a whole that is outside philosophic comprehension, but that "residue" of the sensible which Plato calls χώρα;[1] the irrational has been pushed further back; this is not nothing.

We are going therefore attempt to explain the problematic of the demiurge in the *Timaeus* as a continuation of the incomplete answer of the *Sophist* to the question about the possibility of participation that was raised at the beginning of the *Parmenides*.

The central idea of this chapter will be that Plato attempted to

---

[1] *chora.*

double the *formal causality* of the Idea through the *responsible action* of an agent, therefore to double the αἰτία by an αἴτιον.[2]

1 Saving the phenomena

The attempt in the *Timaeus* would make no sense if we were to lose sight of the fact that Platonism is not just the challenging of the sensible as *truth*, but its justification as *reality*. The *Phaedo* does not hesitate to call participated things "beings." What is therefore at issue is the universality of the being that is the being of the ideas *and* the being of things. The problem does not appear, so long as the image is only shadow and not yet a portrait. Even in his most "Orphic" and most "mystical" phase, Plato never was at the end of the movement that would tend to annul the ontological degree of this world; even the shadow is more than a simulacrum; it is a "semblance" which is already a "resemblance," since it can arouse the memory of the Idea, like "the lyre makes the lovers sing of love."

So, a mere *epistemological challenge* to the image-simulacrum cannot be the last word of the philosophy of the sensible; this challenge must be complemented by a *cosmological justification* of the image-portrait. Appearance, in accordance with the order of "scientific" purification, must become appearing, in accordance with the genesis of the "essences that have become" (to take up again the term from the *Philebus*).

We can follow this movement of the consolidation of the image from the *Phaedo* itself. The *Phaedo* calls the Ideas the true "causes" of becoming (*Phaedo* 100d); an illusion does not call for ideal "causes"; one can free oneself from an illusion practically, one does not justify doing so speculatively. Likewise in the *Phaedrus* the body is a reality prior to the "fall": the souls go about in winged chariots which are like their glorious body; the fall does not engender the corporeal but rather the "terrestrial," that is, the indication of illusion and fascination that afterwards attaches itself to corporeity and amounts to a prison and torture for the soul;[3] but the body is originally what the soul moves when it moves itself, the body is an organ before being obstacle. The

---

[2] *aitia* and *aition*.
[3] See below §4 (PR).

Philebus saves pleasure by giving it a place that, without being in first place, is not ignominious; it links this justification of pleasure, in second place, to a theory of the genesis of "mixtures," which is no longer a dialectical construction of the Ideas, but a genesis of sensible significations in the clarity–obscurity of the One–Many.

It is this line that triumphs in the *Timaeus*. But the great find of the *Timaeus* is that the genesis of the sensible is not possible except beginning from the *All*; a justification of "this" or of "that" – of the apple on the plate – is impracticable; it is *the world*, posed *en bloc*, that is the beautiful, good, and perfect image; "the God who always is and the God who must needs be born one day" (34a), the "visible God as the image of the invisible God" is the world . . . The mediation is therefore brought about through the idea of totality, which on the one side precedes its parts and thus clings to the ideal order by its formal character, and on the other side is immanent to its parts and thus inaugurates the sensible order, more exactly posits it as order and no longer as a chaos of fluctuating and variable images. And this intelligible–sensible mediation is brought about through the cosmic emotion of admiration for the *beauty* of the world ("the world is beautiful," 29a). This admiring synoptic vision is, it is true, linked to a cosmic schema that has been abandoned today, along with the sphere of fixed stars; we no longer know, or in any case we no longer *see*, the unity and indivisibility of the world; but even after Newton, Kant – the sober Kant – still acceded to the sublimity of the cosmic order ("the starry skies above our heads . . ."); Kant knew better than Plato that the All is an Idea and not an experience; but Plato had already known that the All is not a sum of experiences; in this sense the All is in the visible rather than in the sum of visible things; at least for Plato this totality adheres still to a visible figure, that of the sphere (33a) and of circular movement (34a). This is why vision itself is rehabilitated, as discovery of the cosmos (47a); to the eye, the individuality and unity of the world appear (31ab); in saving the phenomena, the form of the world also saves the eye of the body.[4]

So there is no direct justification of phenomena, but an indirect one, through the mediation of the All. This All will from now on be called κόσμος. The Pythagoreans had already given the name

---

[4] In the *Course*, the phrase is left without internal punctuation; one can put a semi-colon after the reference "(31ab)," as we have done, but then one ought to place one also after "the phenomena."

κόσμος to the Ionians' οὐρανός[5] (D.L. VIII 48)[6] in order to indicate that it is Law, visible order: Plato juxtaposes a last time the two titles οὐρανός – κόσμος (28b, with reference to the classic invocations: "if the name pleases him," as in *Agamemnon* 160). By the same token, Parmenides has been killed a second time: the world condemned as a fictive object on the path of opinion finds again the divinity that Heraclitus had conferred on it: "This world here, none among the gods or humans made it (ἐποίησεν),[7] but always it was, always it is and will be, eternally living fire . . .," Heraclitus 35.[8]

2 Cause (αἰτία) and agent (αἴτιον)

But if the world as a totality is the mediation between the Intelligible and the sensible, this totality calls for a new mediation; this latter bears a name: it is the Demiurge, as the link between the Paradigm and the Cosmos.

But here we have to consider an objection: someone will say: the demiurge no longer belongs to philosophical explanation, it is a myth.

Clearly it is necessary to set aside this objection; the demiurge does not belong to the mythic part of the *Timaeus*; it is after having spoken of the demiurge that Plato introduces the difference between the "plausible" and the "unwavering" (29b-d). The "plausible tale" (εἰκότα μῦθον)[9] that Plato then proposes corresponds to two questions: *why* the intelligible has not remained without effect and *how* it made a world; but not the question: *that* the world has a "worker" for its cause. It is the divine "gesture" that is mythic; but that the exemplary causality passes through the channel of a worker-like causality, that is necessary, and

---

[5] *cosmos* and *ouranos*, the earth and the heaven.
[6] The reference is to Diogenes Laertius. Chapter 8 of his *Lives of Eminent Philosophers* is actually devoted to the Pythagoreans.
[7] *epoiesen.*
[8] The *Course* has the reference as "35." In the edition established by Jean-Paul Dumont, *Les Écoles présocratiques* (Paris, Gallimard, "Folio-Essais," 1991), p. 73; this is fragment 30 [as it is in G. S. Kirk, J. E. Raven, and M. Schofield, eds, *The Presocratic Philosophers*, 2nd. edn (New York: Cambridge University Press, 1983). – Trans.]
[9] *eikota muthon* ("plausible myth").

true (πᾶσα ἀναγγκη τονδε τον κοσμον εικονα τινος ειναι, 29b).[10] It is
without recourse to myth that Plato poses (1) that "the world
is born, because it is sensible and tangible" and (2) that "all that
is born, is necessarily born through the action of a cause" (αἰτίον,
28a-b).

Plato is aware of the difficulty; he himself confesses: "In any case,
it is a great exploit to discover the author and the father (ποιητὴν
καὶ πατέρα)[11] of this Universe, and when one discovers him, it is
impossible to divulge him to everyone" (28c). Nonetheless, he
is no less sure of moving himself on a philosophical and not a
mythical terrain, for *here he integrates into his theory of causality the results of his theory of the soul, attained elsewhere in the
Phaedrus.*

The soul, according to the *Phaedrus*, is not solely that which
wants to escape, but that which moves itself by itself and, in so
doing, moves a body (the argument served to demonstrate immortality: "for that which moves itself" is an imperishable being; we
set this problem aside here in order to consider only the renewal
of the problem of the cause). By this power to move another
thing in moving itself, the soul acquires the dignity of a principle
(ἀρχή, 245d).[12] This ἀρχή is no longer just a reason for being, but
a responsibility for existence: "Every species of soul has charge
(ἐπιμελεῖται)[13] of the whole of that which is without soul" (246b).
It is a question, therefore, of a general qualification of the soul, one
might dare say, of a *structure of being* that finds itself as much in
human souls, the soul of the world, the demiurge (246b).

That the demiurge should emerge from this new dimension of
causality is confirmed by many texts from the end of Platonism:
the *Timaeus* again takes up the word ἀρχή (28b), attesting that the
demiurge is a first, not absolutely, but in the order of a worker-like
causality; for the question of the cause of the cause is extinguished
with the αἰτίον; there is a cause only of that which becomes, not of

---

[10] *pasa anangke tonde ton kosmon eikona tinos einai* ("The world must in
all necessity be the image of something." *Timee*, trans. Luc Brisson [Paris:
GF-Flammarion, 1992], p. 117). [Benjamin Jowett (*Collected Dialogues*):
"the world . . . must of necessity . . . be a copy of something"; Donald J. Zeyl
(*Complete Works*): "it follows by unquestionable necessity that this world is
an image of something." – Trans.]

[11] *poieten kai patera.*

[12] *arche.*

[13] *epimeleitai.*

that which moves itself in moving the *All*. The *Philebus* identifies the cause of mixture with the demiurge (27b).[14] The *Laws* (893 et seq.) confirms this splitting of causality, into the exemplary cause and what Plato characterizes as follows: "The movement that can put itself as well as all things in movement" (894b, and further on 895e); this causality is indeed spontaneous causality, the initiative of a soul; god finally is called "excellent soul" (ἀριστή ψυχή).[15]

3 The splitting of causality

This splitting of causality is pregnant with consequences.

First it attests that the genesis of the sensible could not be achieved on the basis of the dialectic exercises of the *Parmenides*; the dialectic of the intelligible does not allow itself to be extrapolated to the sensible; it is necessary that the laws of exclusion and inclusion that govern the ideal "mixtures" be handed over through the operation of a worker-like causality for which human artifice provides the symbol.

But this solution in turn opens a new cycle of difficulties. Up until now there have been two senses of ἀρχή; the reason for being and the initiation of existence; neither can supplant the other: *Timaeus* 27d–28 has posited conjointly the philosophy of the Model and that of the Artist; on the one side the break between the eternal order of the Ideas and of becoming which never really is; on the other the reference of what becomes to what is born and of what is born to what causes.

One could say that Platonism always calls for a mediation: the All of the κόσμος[16] was the mediation of the Intelligible and the Sensible, the demiurge that of the Intelligible and the All. Between the Intelligible and the demiurge Plato introduces an ultimate bridge: it is the demiurge's *Gaze* on the perfect Model. This Gaze, we know, is that of souls before the fall in the *Phaedrus*: "While the soul completes her tour, she has Justice in itself before her eyes, Wisdom before her eyes" (247c-d; 248b-e; 250b-d; 254b); it is the

---

[14] Chambry translates "the demiurge" by "the generation." [R. Hackworth (*Collected Dialogues*): "the fourth kind ... this cause"; Dorothea Frede (*Complete Works*): "the craftsman." – Trans.]

[15] *ariste psuche.*

[16] *cosmos.*

Gaze that is the sacred Meal[17] as well, the sacramental identification between the soul and being or the true. Such is also the Gaze that, in the *Timaeus*, joins worker-like causality to exemplary causality. But this gaze, how do we "know" it? To tell the truth, we do not "know" it; for it constitutes the goodness of the demiurge; we can say in a sense that this goodness of the demiurge is made manifest (σαφές, 29a)[18] since the beauty of the world[19] is the cipher; but the Sublime – is it Science? Is it not "right opinion"? Plato lets this be understood: it is not permitted (οὐ θέμις)[20] to suppose that the creator should be evil, that he should be "envious," for the "wise men" (φρονίμων)[21] (29c) have said so. Hence the sages and the pious alone know the ultimate mediation of philosophy, just as Diotima, in the *Symposium*, spoke in inspired terms of the sudden vision of Beauty of and just as the "sages of other times" announced the *Nous* that governs the All with wisdom and goodness in the *Philebus*. This is why, in the *Timaeus* as well, salvation (πρόνοια)[22] comes through plausible reasoning and not through science (30b-c) even though the demiurge would truly and necessarily be attained through thought.

That the supreme artisan Himself participates in the Good, this is the ultimate participation in which it is necessary to believe. This faith puts to flight the whole problematic of Greek tragedy and of the "evil god" who leads astray and strikes like lightning. This faith makes possible the passage from the dialectic of the Intelligible to the genesis of the sensible.

4 The residue

But this genesis is not a total one.

a) The action of the perfect Model, thanks to the agency of the "best soul," presupposes something opaquely given that represents

---

[17] "Model," "Artist," "Intelligible," "Sensible," "Regard," "Meal" are all capitalized in the *Course*.

[18] *saphes*.

[19] The word "world" is missing in the printed text, but this is certainly a typographical error, but *Timeus* 29a unequivocally indicates that it is a question of the world's beauty.

[20] *themis* ("it is not permitted," *ou themis* fits better here).

[21] *phronimon* (which is genitive in Greek).

[22] *pronoia*.

the gap between the real and the Good, between the image and the model. "Chaos," "errant cause," "place" (χώρα),[23] "wet nurse" or the womb of the real, "necessity," whatever name one calls it, this Other is not the *other* of the dialectic of the *Sophist*; for that Other was participated in by all the "kinds of being"; it is therefore on the side of the absolute Model, if we may put it that way; the χώρα of the *Timaeus* makes sense only in relation to the second species of causality, the one we have called worker-like causality; Non-Being is a "transcendental" of Speech; Place is the lower "limit" of the labor; this is what in the work is no longer worked; the artisan does his best, he cannot do everything: *Timaeus* 30a, 49a, 53c. So long as one has not introduced the second causality as a mediation between the ideal Model and the sensible Totality, one does not meet up with the χώρα. The χώρα belongs to the problematic of the demiurge or the great-soul, not to that of the kinds of being; non-being is still one kind of being; the χώρα is that for which there is no longer any genesis; as Plato says, Necessity does not allow itself entirely to be "persuaded" (*Timaeus* 48a). The χώρα is the gap between Necessity and Finality.

One will not say that Plato's God – at least if he is the demiurge[24] – is "powerless"; he is not powerless, for he is not at all a power. The demiurge does not will anything; he looks and through his looking he permits the Paradigm to be participated in; this is his manner of persuading. Also there is no scandal of evil for Plato, no lament as in Job; God is not a creator, but an orderer; Job laments that God has become his "enemy"; the Platonic thinker cannot complain, neither about the perfect models nor about the demiurge that looks at them; and Necessity is not a person, nor, properly speaking, "nothing," but rather the limit of the "persuasion" of the Good. This is how, no doubt, we have to understand the "God is innocent" of *Republic* X,[25] he is innocent, not at the end of an apology that exculpates him, but originarily, owing to the non-creation of matter. One might think that Hellenism thereby missed recognizing the enigma of unjust suffering and of deepening the problem of God under the prodding of this enigma. But, in return, it escaped the difficulties of theodicy.

"Corruption," in the world of things, therefore does not pose

---

[23] *chora.*
[24] See below, third part, chapter 2, §3 (PR).
[25] *Republic* X 617e.

any radical ontological problem, at least in the region of the transcendent; Platonism presupposes a sort of backward participation
that does not have a radical origin in the divine; everything which
is born is subject to corruption (*Republic* VIII 546a), owing not
to the powerlessness of God, but to the powerlessness of matter
to receive being. Goldschmidt has shown this point well in his
Religion de Platon;[26] he draws from this the conclusion that there
is no Platonic "tragedy."

But, in return, Platonism has the task of posing a principle of
unintelligibility – if one may still speak of a principle – at the
source of the real, an unintelligibility that the soul must in some
way repeat in itself in order to designate and name it with the aid
of some "bastard reasoning."

b) This is not all; one could say that there are, in Platonism, two
residues, two origins of evil: for human disorder seems to constitute a spontaneous and additional evil. It is true that the *Phaedo*
says: "Something bad is kneaded in with our soul" (66b); the body
seems, by its "lack of measure" (67a), to incarnate that Necessity
which does not allow it be persuaded; if one goes all the way to the
end of this movement of thought, matter would be evil and there
would be, according to Platonism, a calamity of existence. But
the same *Phaedo* reverses the movement; it is desire which nails the
soul to the body and not the body which nails the soul to desire:
"And the astonishing thing about this imprisonment, *philosophy
renders an account of it*, it is the work of desire and he who coop-
erates the most in wrapping the enchained in his chains is perhaps
himself" (82e). And even more strongly still: "The soul is then its
own executioner" (82e). This "psychic" initiative – if we may put
it so – of evil Plato named injustice, and no text allows us to reduce
to unity the Non-Being that dialecticizes being, the Necessity that
limits its expansion into the sensible, the Injustice that refuses the
light of the Good. All Plato's politics turns around an enigma of
an Evil that constitutes a "residue" supplementary to the genesis
of the sensible: Plato has marked out the different blossomings of
this enigma: it is the "whirlpool" into which the foolish Legislator
of vicious language is drowned (*Cratylus* 439c); it is the wicked-
ness of the "tyrant" according to the *Gorgias* and the *Theaetetus*;

---

26 Victor Goldschmidt, *La Religion de Platon* (Paris: Presses Universitaires de
France, 1949).

the perversion of language and that of power moreover always go together, since the "tyrant" reigns only with the help of the *false* arts of language, flattery, and persuasion (*Gorgias*). But, whatever may be the home for the proliferation of this human evil in speech and politics, the unjust soul in some way initiates the evil (cf. in the same sense: *Republic* II 379b-c; X 617e; *Timaeus* 41e–42d; *Statesman* 269e, 273b-c). Never does Plato refer the origin of evil back as far as the Principle of the Good; ethically unjustifiable, injustice is also ontologically irreducible.

Plato therefore is well aware of the *limits* of an ontology of essences; he explored these limits in both directions, toward the limit above and the limit below. Marked by the problem of language, from its Socratic origin, Platonism is a philosophy of intelligible determinations, therefore a philosophy of the *beings* and not of being. But Plato knows:

1) that the discrete multiplicity of the essential beings holds together only through the One-Good which is beyond essence, that is, beyond being as a dimension of discourse;
2) that the essential *beings* have *being* only through the non-being that makes them capable of mutual participation;
3) that the non-essential beings, which are also τὰ οντα[27] – the sensible things – imply an unintelligible beneath, which is the limit of any genesis of the sensible;
4) that that other, non-essential being, the existing soul, is beset by an injustice that is the limit of all philosophic education.

Plato thus leaves us an unfinished ontology, pregnant with many developments. It is Plotinus who will make it *a* system. Plato wanted to do nothing more than compose *dialogues*.

---

[27] *ta onta.*

Third Part

Being and the Divine

In chapters 3 to 6 of the first part, we have considered the *epis-temological* aspect of the discovery of being. It was also the epis-temological aspect of the Ideas of the One, being, non-being, and the other that we emphasized in the second part. Beginning from this function of the ontology of essences, considered as a "Science" – as SCIENCE – Plato works a "reprise" or, as Diès puts it, a "transposition" of religion. We would not have devoted a new section to this adventure of religion, transposed into reasonable religion, if this transposition had to do with religion alone. The Platonic transposition has to do with philosophy itself, which in a way *recharges* itself from the Sacred, thanks to this "reprise." It is this recoil of the philosophical transposition of religion on ontol-ogy that we are considering here. At the same time that religion becomes reasonable religion, reason and ontology are affected by a "religious" index that it is important to acknowledge.

What is more, this final turn of events seems to us essential for understanding the connection of ontology and theology in Aristotle. This connection is already operative in a way in Plato.

But one would take a wrong turn if one were prematurely to identify the religious problem of Platonism with the question of knowing whether there is a God in Platonism; not that this ques-tion would not make sense, but it is subordinated to a much broader question: what is the *divine* in Platonism?

We will ask ourselves in chapter 1 what this promotion of the "divine" to philosophic dignity means; it will then appear that in his philosophy Plato gives to the Ideas the prestige of the "divine" that the pre-Socratics before him had identified with the notion of Principle or of Origin (Ἀρχή = *Arche*).

In chapter 2, we shall consider the "divine" in its full breadth in Platonism. As Goldschmidt has shown, the religious function is assumed by the world of the Ideas as such. We shall ask:

1) what *recharging* of the Sacred this identification of the Forms with the "divine" signifies for the Forms themselves, whose origin we have retraced beginning from an ontology of lan-guage (first part, chapter 2);
2) what complexity the "divine" receives, in return, if one places

the ontology of the Ideas in the perspective of the Good from the *Republic* or of the One from the *Philebus* and the *Parmenides*. Is the "divine" not both *displayed* in the Ideas and *concentrated* in the Good or the One?;

3) how one passes, in Platonism, from the "divine" to God;

4) whether there is a passage from God to the gods which still matters to philosophy.

One sees in what sense Platonic ontology can emerge enriched from this investigation. It is not just a new attribute – θεῖον[1] – that being receives, but, perhaps, a certain tendency to personalize being. We shall see within what narrow limits this is true in Plato.

---

[1] *theion.*

Chapter 10

The Problem of the "Divine" and Pre-Socratic Philosophy

The problem of the "divine" takes priority over that of "God" in Platonism. It was through this integration of the "divine" with philosophy that it became possible for religion to be taken up within philosophy. We will show that this rational religion of the philosophers begins with philosophy itself.

This aspect of integration is one that Aristotle, preoccupied with his own investigation into the *division* of causality according to the schema of the four causes, masked in Books A and B of his *Metaphysics*. It is, however, the decisive point as regards the opposition between the Hellenic tradition, which reflects on the divine, and the Semitic tradition, which debates about whether there is one god or many.

1 Nature and the divine

The *primary root* of this philosophy of the "divine" has to be looked for as far back as the "Physicists," despite the purely "naturalist" interpretation of the school of Miletus. We will not tarry very long with Thales' saying – "everything is filled with gods" (though the aged Plato of *Laws* 899b did see in this saying the epitome of all philosophy) – which perhaps already presents a transposition of the gods of the myths into a *dimension of physis*. On the other hand, one can recognize the origin of this reprise of religion by philosophy in a meditation on the Principle (*Arche*) of nature. We will begin from the important text of Aristotle found in *Physics* III 4 203b1-15, which concludes with a reference to Anaximander:

> It is clear that the study of the indeterminate (or unlimited) is akin to that of Nature; and all (those who accept it) have good reason to hold that it is a *principle*; for, if it exists, it must affect things in some manner, and cannot do so except under the heading of a principle; for every thing must be as determined by some principle, unless it be a principle itself; but the indeterminate cannot be determined and so cannot depend on anything that would be its principle. Furthermore, being a principle, it can have neither beginning nor end; for everything that comes to be must have an end, and there must be an end point to every process of corruption. So the unlimited cannot be derived from any other principle, but is itself regarded as the principle of all things 'embracing and governing them all' . . . this unlimited would then be the divine: being immortal and indestructible, as say Anaximander and the greater number of the natural philosophers.[1]

But did Anaximander actually call the Infinite a "principle"? Simplicius affirms it in his commentary on Aristotle's *Physics*. This matters less than does the structure of argument that we find reconstituted here, and which offers us a striking summary of the key concepts of pre-Socratic theology: Infinite – absence of a beginning – principle – immortal and indestructible – divine: it is

---

[1] Pierre Pellegrin's translation of Aristotle's *Physique* (Paris: GF-Flammarion, 2002), pp. 175–6, has some fairly important differences. [The translation by R. P Hardie and R. K Gaye in *The Complete Works of Aristotle*, ed. Jonathan Barnes (Princeton, NJ: Princeton University Press, 1984) reads: "It is clear from these considerations that the inquiry concerns the student of nature. Nor is it without reason that they all make it a principle. We cannot say that the infinite exists in vain, and the only power which we can ascribe to it is that of a principle. For everything is either a principle or derived from a principle. But there cannot be a principle of the infinite, for that would be a limit to it. Further, as it is a principle, it is both uncreatable and indestructible. For there must be a point at which what has come to be reaches its end, and also a termination of all passing away. That is why, as we say, there is no principle of *this*, but it is this which is held to be the principle of other things, and to encompass all and to steer all. . . . Further they identify it with the Divine, for it is deathless and imperishable as Anaximander says, with the majority of the physicists." – Trans.

the manner in which these concepts are chained together that we must try to understand.

First comment

We have in this text a true deduction of the "divine." The Infinite implies the attributes Immortal and Indestructible, and these imply the Divine. "And this is the divine," says Aristotle. The starting point for this deduction is the positing of something that is a Principle. Here the *nature* of this Principle does not matter much; therefore it does not matter much that Aristotle (and Burnet)[2] are right to see here a material reservoir of becoming – although the very term *Physis*, just by its suffix, *-sis*, speaks of more than a simple given structure and contains the idea of an origin and of generation. The important thing is the *function* of this Principle; it provides a foundation *with no beginning* for everything that does begin. This function of an *Arche*[3] defines the "divine" and re-creates religion philosophically; the gods' immortality is transposed to the absence of a beginning in any principle: "and this is the divine."

Second comment

In this reprise, religion is both negated and retained. Negated, for the "myth" which sounds the depths of the "why?" gets lost in the endless creation of theogonies and cannot make the leap from indefinite genesis to the positing of a Principle, from something with no beginning to the beginning of things. Religion is also retained, for the Principle assumes the dignity that the poetic word

---

[2] A reference, without any further details, to "Burnet" (also repeated below). John Burnet is known for multiple works: *The Ethics of Aristotle* (London: Methuen, 1900); *The Socratic Doctrine of the Soul* (London [Oxford: Oxford University Press for The British Academy], 1916); *Aristotle on Education* (Cambridge: Cambridge University Press, 1913); and, above all, in France, for *L'Aurore de la philosophie grecque*, trans. Auguste Reymond (Paris: Payot, 1919), a translation of his *Early Greek Philosophy* (London: A. and C. Black, 1892).

[3] Did Anaximander himself call his Infinite a Principle? Even if the word is not there, Aristotle did not invent the idea. Cf. the text of Simplicius A 9, which confirms the attribution of *Arkhe* to Anaximander (Diels, *Die Fragmente der Vorsokratiker*) (PR). [Cf. Kirk, Raven, and Schofield, *The Presocratic Philosophers*, 106–7. – Trans.]

had conferred on the gods; "and it embraces them and directs all": W. Jaeger underlines the poetic and even more the *hymnic* style of these expressions, in a work which was precisely the first philosophy in prose.[4] In most of the pre-Socratics[5] – with Anaximenes, fr. 2, Empedocles, Anaxagoras, B 2 and 14, Heraclitus, fr. 14, Parmenides, fr. 12, 3, Diogenes, and even Democritus (B 30) – one finds these same expressions or other, similar ones for *celebrating* the divine principle of the Cosmos; the same accent of reverence is recognizable there, as a rational prayer of recognition. So the fundamental hymn communicates itself to philosophy through this reprise; at the same time that philosophy rationalizes the divine, it recharges itself using the primordial language of admiration and adoration. In this conjunction of reason and the hymn resides the Greek unity of philosophy and religion; but philosophy has the leading role; the divine predicate is retrieved only because it is speculatively disengaged from *Physis* and transferred from the traditional deity to the principle of being.

From this comes the ambiguous attitude with respect to popular religion. Xenophanes declares war on the ancient gods: "One sole god, the highest among the gods and mortals. By neither his form nor thoughts does he resemble mortals."[6] What does not "suit" the "divine" is refused to the gods; and first of all the "contour," the *morphe*; this is why all the Greek philosophers were at some time or another accused of atheism; the trial of Socrates is inscribed in the great trial of philosophy; Plato's attack on poetry and the myths in *Republic* II belongs to this line as well. However, the force of this atheism is religious and reaches back to the ancient hymn. And even when the Greek philosopher is not a-theist, his

---

[4] Compare this text on the Unlimited to the famous fgt [fragment] B1 (Diels), commented on by Nietzsche, E. Rohde, W. Jaeger, and Heidegger: "Whatever may be the things from which come those that are, it is in these things that destruction becomes according to necessity; for they mutually offer retribution and expiation for their injustice according to the ordinance of time" (PR). [In 1903, Hermann Diels published a monumental reference edition of the Presocratics – an edition that has been revised and expanded many times since.]

[5] Ross, *Aristotle's Physics, Commentary*, p. 546; this note by Ross moves in the same direction as that of W. Jaeger, *op. cit.* p. 31 (PR) [complete title: *Aristotle's Physics: A Revised Text with Introduction and Commentary* (Oxford: Clarendon Press, 1936)].

[6] Diels, B 23 (AC). [Kirk, Raven, and Schofield, *The Presocratic Philosophers*, p. 169.]

philosophy of the divine renders him indifferent to the opposition of monotheism and polytheism; Plato himself speaks of god and of gods; Parmenides, already, was not bothered by integrating polytheism to second place. The underlying reason is that philosophy bears more on the divine than on the gods.

Third comment

The positing of the *Arche* is not the fruit of a proof; any more than of a demonstration, it comes down to pointing to a foundation. This sovereign act, identical to "thinking" – *noein* or *phronein* – (like the Kantian *Denken* which posits the unconditional) is closer to the ontological argument than to any of the proofs arguing from effects. Philosophy is a return to the origin, a repetition of the *Arche*; this is the true meaning of Reminiscence. The *Physis* of the Ionians was the first positing of a first being by philosophy; the Parmedian One, the Platonic Idea, Aristotle's being as being are posited in this way;[7] or, rather, it is by being posited that the Principle, whatever it may be, posits the philosophic act, Thinking.

2 "The One" and the divine

Parmenides is the second root of Plato's rational religion. His indifference to God has been stressed (K. Reinhardt).[8] This is true, but it does not exhaust the question of the religious import of Parmenides' thought about being. It is even in him that we have the first full model of a rational religion. The religious tonality is given by the *Prelude*, which is not at all an *hors-d'oeuvre*; two moments need to be considered: the "voyage" and the "revelation" by the goddess. The voyage signifies a change of scene, the Odyssey of a thought that returns to the foundation; all the symbolism of "transport" (the chariot, the wheels, the greeting of the young women) announces a certain rapture of the mind by beneficial powers which cannot but already evoke Platonic Eros and, in a general way, Platonic "conversion"; the goddess's revelation signifies that the "Truth" is not so much a discourse articulated by man

---

7 A word or words seem to be missing.
8 [Karl Reinhardt, *Parmenides und die Geschichte der griechischen Philosophie* (Bonn: Friedrich Cohen, 1916).]

as the discourse of being, proffered by being. In this sense, one can speak of a "dis-covery" of being. Conversion and discovery have perhaps an Orphic model; but what matters is the philosophical style of the transposition: the destitution of which the initiate will be healed becomes "the wandering" of mortals; the "way" of salvation becomes speculation; the fervor of the initiate becomes absolute knowledge (B 1, 3: "the man who knows").[9]

Someone may object that the object of philosophic revelation by its absolutely non-religious character contradicts the movement of this revelation; but the tradition from Miletus seems already to have prepared the way for this idea, that the religious object for the Greek philosopher is not first a god or the gods, but the divine. The "it is" of Parmenides' *Poem* assumes the same function as does the Ionian *physis* and in particular as Anaximander's "infinite." What is new is that the Principle is no longer nature and can no longer be nature; the Principle excludes natural determinations; the ὄντα[10] of the *physiologos* are not true being; hence the negative style: the Principle is not many, nor in movement; it has neither beginning nor end.

We will also set aside the objection that the "it is" cannot be religious, even in a transposed sense, for it is merely thought. But the objection proceeds from a misinterpretation of "thinking and being are the same." It is not at all said there that being is reduced to being thought, but that being is the only thing there is to think, in the sense of being thinkable, that non-being is outside the field of νοεῖν.[11] It is precisely νοεῖν that is charged with religious feeling: for it is not an exaltation of *my* thought, but a subordination of Thinking to the Truth of Being. We rediscover the same subordination in the relation of the Platonic soul to the Truth of the Ideas: the idea requires being thought in this way and not otherwise; to philosophize is to submit to what the Idea demands (Goldschmidt). In this lies the religious function of reason: it is neither arbitrary nor empty, but very close to being and filled with it.

Someone may also say that the One of Parmenides has a form,

---

[9] Werner Jaeger: "The religious element resides more in the manner in which man is affected by his discovery and in his firm and resolute treatment of the truth-error alternative than in any classification of the object of research as divine" (Jaeger, *op. cit.*, p. 107) (PR).

[10] *onta.*

[11] *noein.*

that of a sphere, and that Parmenides is thus the father of materialism (Burnet): Empedocles' "elements," Anaxagoras' "homeomores," Epicurus' "atoms" are, someone else will say, rejections of the One-sphere. But what is certain is that this representation of the One with the resources of "physical" thought is essential to thinking Being; moreover, Plato was never held back by this aspect of Parmenides; but above all it is necessary to understand what sphere signifies; it signifies the height of determination; it is the "limit," πέρας,[12] that the Pythagoreans, in their tables of oppositions, placed in the same "series" as the Good.

So Parmenides adds to the theological universe of the pre-Socratics these two traits: the divine is the Truth opposed to opinion, the One opposed to the multiple. In so doing he has contributed to extending the speculation about the identity of Being with a god; the "mystery of being" he proclaims is a sort of self-revelation of the ontological dimension as such. Furthermore he orients ontology toward the side of limited, the finite. The breakthrough, brought about by Anaximander, on the side of a philosophy of the infinite tied to the idea of 'αρχή, of Principle, is closed. Plato will be embarrassed by the double qualification of the infinite as powerful, on the one hand, and imperfect, on the other.

It is Plotinus who will make the definitive choice for the Infinite and conjoin the Good, the One, and the Infinite: for the One, this is not that which thought thinks, the determined, the "finite," but that from which proceed both thinking and its indefinitely finite thoughts.

3 The other pre-Socratic roots of rational religion

We must add two more decisive influences to the two great Ionian and Parmenidean traditions, that of Heraclitus' λόγος, that of Anaxagoras' νοῦς.[13]

a) Heraclitus should have been put on the same footing as Parmenides; but Plato and Aristotle claimed to know nothing about him except as the philosopher of "flux," hence as the antithesis of Parmenides. Plato has even slandered him by creating an

---

[12] *peras.*
[13] *logos* and *nous.*

amalgam between him and Protagoras (and sophistic in general). It is the Stoics who, in seeking ancestors among the pre-Socratics, perceived the full breadth of this philosophy of the λόγος, for which "flux" is but a subordinate aspect; Plotinus will know how to integrate this doctrine of the arbitration of contraries into his own philosophy, in, it is true, a subordinate place (*Enneads* III, 1–3).

Yet Heraclitus' prophetic fervor is not less than that of Parmenides; it dissimulates itself by speaking using enigmas which gives an oracular turn to his revelation. This fervor does not apply to the "flux" but to the λόγος of the flux; thus this λόγος takes on for him the ontological dignity of Anaximander's "the infinite" and Parmenides' "it is"; it constitutes the eternal word that humans do not understand; not the words of Heraclitus, but the truth of the reality addressed to him (B 1); this word divides men into the "awake" and the "asleep," and makes its bearers solitaries amid a universal slumber.

This λόγος will alternate with νοῦς in Greek philosophy; it will designate the "immanent meaning" of the contraries, whereas the νοῦς will designate a separate, transcendent intelligence; this is why, after the Aristotelian νοῦς, the Stoics will return to the λόγος.

To what character of the λόγος, then, is Heraclitus' fervor attached? To the power of arbitrating and providing measure that it exercises at the very heart of contradictions; the admirable thing, for him, is that contradiction is not ruinous, but fecund: "War is the father of all and the king of all. Some it makes gods, others men, some slaves, others free men" (B 53). Father and King, this is the language of the ancient hymn (B 67 even says ὁ θεός).[14] What is astonishing, admirable, therefore, is the immanence of the Law, of Measure (B 94; B 114); we rediscover here Anaximander's δίκη,[15] which arbitrates among the elements and the forces in the great "trial" of nature; Heraclitus idealizes and glorifies it in a broad identification of the logic of the contraries, the cosmology of the forces, and the politics of men. This great identity is the κόσμος,[16] the immanent measure of all its conflicts (B 30). Whence

---

[14] *ho theos,* "the God."
[15] *dike.*
[16] *cosmos.*

the supreme oracle: "From all, one; and from One, all."[17] The equivalence of "totality-unity" (B 50).

One sees that Heraclitus no more provides a proof than do Anaximander or Parmenides; he unveils; he does not engage in induction, he exemplifies; on the basis of an example he grasps a universal meaning. Nothing, therefore, of a proof by means of effects; just the discovery of a foundation (B 54; B 123); just like the oracle at Delphi, not showing, not hiding, but "indicating" (B 93). Being then is not a problem, but an enigma. For Heraclitus, the enigma is that the One should be the Many, and Peace should be War.

b) We have to make a particular place for Anaximander, not only because of the theme of νοῦς,[18] but because of the "providentialist" ramifications of his thought which are important for understanding certain religious aspects of Socratism and in the end for what we have called the mediation of the Demiurge in the *Timaeus*.

It is true that Plato was disappointed by Anaxagoras' νοῦς, which orders everything, then reveals itself to be unusable for explaining the details (*Phaedo* 97b–99a). However, the *Philebus* rehabilitates him: all the sages, it says, are in agreement that νοῦς is "the king of heaven and earth" (28c), which has "governed" all things (28d), "ordered" all things. All these expressions lead back up through the pre-Socratics to the hymn to the divine.[19]

With νοῦς the accent is on the "unmixed" character of the principle, while the all is originally all mixed together: "The Infinite is sufficient unto itself; it is not mixed with anything; it is alone, itself

---

17 Heraclitus, fragment B10. Dumont translates more correctly: "And from all things the one / and from the one all things" (p. 68). [Kirk, Raven, and Schofield: "out of all things there comes a unity, and out of a unity all things" (p. 190). – Trans.] Did Ricoeur translate this fragment himself, or did he use an existing translation? In any case, the *Course* cites this formula in inverted order.

18 *nous.*

19 Karl Deichgräber, "Hymnische Elemente in der philosophischen Prosa der Presokratiker" ["Hymnic Elements in the Philosophical Prose of the Presocratics"], *Philologos* 88 (1933), p. 347. (Aristotle speaks of the "solemnity" of the theme of the "infinite" in Anaximander, *Physics* III 6, 207a18 – cited by W. Jaeger, *op. cit.*, p. 202 n. 42 (PR). [Pierre Pellegrin translates this as the "dignity" of the infinite; cf. Aristotle, *Physique* (Paris: GF-Flammarion, 2002), p. 193.] [Hardie and Gaye (*Collected Works of Aristotle*) agree with Pellegrin. – Trans.]

through itself." Because it is not mixed it "governs"; "It knows each thing and has the most extreme power." "Mind controls all things which have soul, from the greatest to the smallest."

These themes of the "sovereignty" of "government," of "embracing," "ruling," like that of "paternity" are thus the ultimate hymnic contribution from pre-Socratic philosophy; they are transposed from the gods to the divine, to the non-personalized principle of things: "Infinite," "Being," "Logos," "Spirit."

The new thing is that, beginning from Anaxagoras' νοῦς, a *semi-personalization* of the divine is outlined which comes to a close in Plato with the demiurge, through the identification with a moving and self-moving soul. This inflection is implicit in the very expression "putting in order" (διακοσμεῖν,[20] 28e). The question was to consider the principle not solely as a principle with a *final* character, but as a separated *efficient* cause. It is this move that Anaxagoras did not succeed in carrying through: whence Plato's disappointment and Aristotle's reservations (*Metaphysics* A 3, 984b15; 4, 985a17). Plato succeeded in splitting off the exemplary causality of the Paradigm only through the worker-like causality of the demiurge.

But this passage had been prepared by the providentialist and finalist theology issuing from Diogenes and attested to by Xenophon's Socrates (*Memorabilia* I 4 and IV 3),[21] which will blossom in the Stoic idea of Providence. It is there that one sees the split between the reign of the Goal [*Fin*] and that of "Necessity" as the counterpart to this personalization of the divine; the recoil effect was that Nature falls back to the rank of a blind and arbitrary mass; finality and mechanism are separated from and opposed to each other; this split, which was overlooked by the earlier pre-Socratics, can be taken as responsible for an important change in the realm of ontological thought, which becomes "metaphysical"; at the same time argumentation and the search for a proof are born, also overlooked by the pre-Socratics who posited the Foundation, which is to say both being and the thought of being (whether this be the "infinite," the "One," the "Logos"); an interpretation of the signs of finality, an indirect demonstration by

---

[20] *diakosmein.*

[21] The ordaining intelligence has a "design" (γνώμη); like a "worker" (δημιουργος), it "works" (δημιουργεῖν) (PR). [The Greek words are *gnome*, *demiourgos*, and *demiourgein*.]

works, by the arrangement of everything and the order of the parts gets substituted for this discovery; for, one argued, in order to give a reason for this order there must be something other than matter, than necessity; there must be an additional principle for which we have an example in human intentional activity. Historically, all the "proofs from the effects" will follow this line; but the ontological argument belongs to that breed of thought about being that includes Anaximander, Parmenides, and Heraclitus, where being allows itself to be thought in terms of the Idea that posits it.

This is the broad background of the philosophy of the "divine" and of "God" in Plato. In its admirable richness, two tendencies can be outlined: a major tendency, that of Parmenides (and of Heraclitus, little understood because obscure), a minor tendency represented by the series Anaxagoras, Diogenes, Xenophon. According to the former, the emotional charge borne by the myth and the hymns is transposed to a Principle for thought that wins the veneration of Reason; this principle is more "divine" than "god." In the other direction, the theme of the "Intelligence," which *thinks* order and *inaugurates* it, draws the "divine" again closer to "God." But this tendency will always remain subordinated to the preceding one at least up until Philo, that is, up to the encounter of Greek with Hebraic thought.

In any case, well before this encounter, Plato will try to bind together the two pre-Socratic traditions by unifying the philosophy of the Good with that of the Demiurge. And Aristotle, above all, will want to ground the fundamental identity of ontology and theology in reason, "of being as being" and the "first substance" (pure Act or Thought Thinking Itself).

Chapter 11

The "Divine" in Plato

In Platonism it is the Ideas, the Forms, that assume the religious function exercised by Anaximander's "infinite," Parmenides' "One," Heraclitus' "Logos," and Anaxagoras' "Intelligence." It is onto these that the solemn homage originating in the hymn and the fervor of the initiations is transferred. But this "transposition" (Diès) would not have been possible without the pre-Socratic tradition, which already involved such a "transposition" of worship.

1) Therefore, for our first task, we have to figure out in what sense the philosophy of the Ideas, which we have considered from an equally ontological and epistemological point of view, takes on a religious meaning.
2) We shall next ask ourselves what the new development of the ontological problem with the Idea of the Good and that of the One, and finally with the dialectic of the *Parmenides* and the *Sophist*, signifies for this rational religion. Plato's rational religion has to reflect all the tensions of Platonic epistemology, which we are going therefore to review again from a different point of view.
3) It will next be necessary to ask the religious significance of the theme of the Demiurge; in particular it will be necessary to situate this problem in relation to the double pre-Socratic tradition, the one that goes toward the "divine" and the one that goes toward "God."

4) Finally, the question arises whether there is anything philosophy can draw from the reference to the infernal gods of the
eschatological myths.[1]

1 The Idea and the divine

We have seen (in chapter 2 of the first part of these lectures) what
the ontological promotion of the Idea involves: first the validation
of language which had been put in question by the Sophists. It is
by means of a realism of significations that Plato replies to the
crisis of the word opened by the study of fallacies (*Cratylus* 386e,
389d). The Idea assumes the dignity of being, opposed both to
seeming and to becoming; this is the meaning of the refutation
of Protagoras in the *Theaetetus*; for example, the Idea is "true
be-ing," the τὸ ὄντως ὄν (*Phaedo* 66c).

This ontological promotion of significations takes place in the
same region as that of the pre-Socratics' "Principle." The Idea
comes to occupy a place and a dignity already circumscribed by
the earlier thinkers: the place and the dignity of that which is
One, of that which remains, of that which is through itself, of
that which is real and true. Plato recognized the pre-Socratic ἀρχή
in the Socratic definition. It is this recognition or identification
that immediately places the Idea in the sphere of the "divine";
because it is the foundation of naming, it is divine: "the Form is
divine, immortal, intelligible," *Phaedo* 80b (similarly: *Republic* VI
490b; V 476a; VII 532a;[2] *Phaedrus* 246d). The degree of divinity
being proportional to the degree of being, the most divine coincides with the being that is most being (Diès); one will notice the
emphatic doubled and tripled ontological formulas such as these:
τὸ ὂν ὄντως . . ., ὅ ἐστιν ὂν ὄντως, οὐσα ὄντως οὐσα[3] (*Phaedrus* 247e
et seq.). And, since the dignity of the Idea communicates itself to
Science (*Republic* V 476e, 477b; *Theaetetus* 146e), science too is

---

[1] On all of this: cf. Victor Goldschmidt, *La Religion de Platon* (Paris: PUF,
1949); Auguste Diès, *Autour de Platon*, vol. II: *les Dialogues – Esquisses
doctrinales* (Paris: Beauchesne, 1927); Paul Shorey, *On the Idea of Good in
Plato's Republic* (University of Chicago Classic Studies, 1895); René Mugnier,
Le Sens du mot θεῖος *chez Platon* (Paris: Vrin, 1930) (PR).

[2] These references to the *Republic* seem inexact.

[3] *to on ontos . . ., ho estin on ontos epistema ousa.*

divine. Plato thus joins up with Parmenides' ἀλήθεια,[4] which is not a character of our thoughts, but of being as being as discovered (*Republic* VI 508e).

So it is by means of the intervention of the pre-Socratic αρχή that the Platonic Idea assumes such a role.

This role is attested to by the transferring of fundamental religious emotions onto the Idea; the Idea taps into these emotions and in this way charges itself with a kind of rational sublime.

a) The theory of the Ideas takes up the theme of the "voyage," whose importance in Parmenides' *Poem* we have seen; knowledge is a migration toward the "intelligible place" (*Republic*), toward the "plane of truth" (*Phaedrus*); it is also a "flight," an "escape from below to above" (*Phaedo, Theaetetus*), an "anabasis" (*Republic*). This is why philosophical education is not a technique like others, which one can hasten; it requires maturity, leisure, and the hardships of the "voyage" of the initiate.

b) The starting point of this voyage is described in the language of Parmenides ("error") and of Heraclitus ("blinding"); this is an initial intellectual decline which is just as much "captivity" (*Phaedo* and *Republic*), a "whirlpool" (*Cratylus*), a "fall" (*Phaedrus*), "poverty" (*Symposium*). In this initial, closed, blinded situation, there is more than mere ignorance or a simple error, but rather an impoverishment that calls for purification.

c) The decisive crisis that gets things under way is a μετάνοια,[5] a "conversion," a resumption of the purification rites of the mystery religions. This purification, expressly named as such in the most "mystical" of Plato's texts (*Phaedo, Symposium, Republic* VI), is the implicit theme in the apparently purely epistemological preoccupations; hence this is what must be heard as underlying the "aporetic" method of a good number of dialogues. It is not just a question of getting to the true answer and laying the question itself bare, of somehow scouring and polishing the questioning; it is not even uniquely a question of joining an ethical function to this critical one, of undercutting the pretensions of the false know-it-alls through "irony"; it is a question of opening a void in the soul, a

---

[4] *aletheia*, "truth."
[5] *metanoia*.

night, an impotence, an absence that is the prelude to the revelation. For example, in the *Theaetetus*, Science is present-absent in everything it is not: opinion, right opinion, right opinion based on reasoning. That the aporia has the value of purification is attested to by the portrait of the philosopher inserted obliquely into the eristic of the *Theaetetus*, and serves as a counterpoise to the praise of Protagoras; philosophy is the defeat of life; it is necessary to lose the world to find one's soul and the truth.

d) Just as mystical initiation includes "degrees," the philosophic itinerary is marked out by stages; we have considered this problem from an epistemological point of view;[6] we were astonished that the opposition between two terms, being–appearance, could yield three or four "stages" or even more (if one compares the degrees of the *Theaetetus*, those of the *Republic*, and those of the Seventh Letter, without counting the aesthetic ladder of the *Symposium* and the *Phaedrus*); being will be "fifth," after the name, the definition, the image, science in the soul, according to *Letter* VII; in this way the logic of contraries, which knows only the extreme terms "ignorance–knowledge," is dramatized by the movement of a soul straining toward being as the limit of its approximation: "The soul is in labor on the subject of being,"[7] says the *Theaetetus* (187a). Spinoza's *Short Treatise* and *Ethics* will reproduce such a graduated ascesis.

e) Finally, the end of the initiation is indicated by intuition, by θεωρία.[8] We have discussed the epistemological problem of Intuition: is there intuition of an Idea? And, if there is no intuition of the Idea except via its connection to the totality of the Ideas and in its reference to the Good, does Intuition belong to the experience of this life, insofar as the whole system is not reached, if it can never be attained? But precisely because the theme of initiation is a theme "transposed" from religious experience, there is no need to inscribe it within philosophy in terms of some "given," of an

---

[6] First part, chapters 3–6 (PR).

[7] Chambry translates this as "The soul ... applies itself entirely to the study of beings" (p. 129). [Cornford (*Collected Dialogues*): "what goes on when the mind is occupied with things by itself"; Levett, rev. Burnyeat (*Collected Works*): "that activity of the soul when it is busy by itself about the things which are." – Trans.]

[8] *theoria*.

"actual presence"; it can remain in suspense, as the virtual term, as the symbol of the completion of philosophy. The bond between this eschatological fulfillment and pre-empirical existence on one side and Death on the other confirms once again the virtual, projective, symbolic character of the "transposition" of religious experience at this final stage of its unfolding.

So philosophy can enlist all the movements of the Orphic soul because the Idea is charged with the function of being the Principle, of the 'αρχή, which already with the pre-Socratics was identified with the "divine."

2 The Good and the divine

The divine, in Platonism, precedes God, because the Ideas are the very being of the divine; this is why they are that which "the thought of a god" contemplates (*Phaedrus* 247d); they are its nourishment and its vision (*ibid.*). Plato goes so far as to say that the thought of the philosopher alone is "winged," "for it always attaches itself as far as possible through remembering to *the essences thanks to which God is divine*" (*Phaedrus* 249c).[9]

But Platonism does not reduce to a philosophy of Ideas; the Ideas are transcended by the Good; the properly epistemological effort to integrate the vision of the Good with a total dialectic must necessarily have a significance for Plato's rational religion.

One can understand why: the Idea is indeed a principle of unity for homonymous things, but they are many; therefore there are *beings* (τα ὄντα, τα ὄντως ὄντα);[10] and we have lost the unitary function of the Parmenidean being; the "divine" gets reconstituted in a philosophy of being that is no longer a philosophy of the One; this distributive structure (εν ἕκαστον των ὄντων),[11] linked to the discontinuity of naming, implies a sort of distribution of the divine, a polytheism of forms (Goldschmidt). The religious function of a philosophy of the Good is to recover the problematic of the One in a philosophy that begins by parceling out Being; whence the ambiguity of the "divine" in Plato; it is both spread out in the

---

[9] Trans. of Mugnier, *op. cit.*, pp. 52–3 (AC).
[10] *ta onta, ta ontos onta* (the beings of being).
[11] *hen hekaston ton onton* (each one of the beings).

multiplicity of beings and *concentrated* within the unity of a final constitutive principle.

We are going to take up again the relation of the Ideas to the Good that we have considered from an epistemological point of view (first part, chapter 6) from the point of view of this double movement of the divine.

a) The philosophy of the "divine" tends on one side toward a philosophy of *transcendence* announced by the Plotinian One (*Republic* VI 508c–509b). An aim rather than a vision, the Good is "what every soul pursues"; it is the unitary foundation of the theoretical and the practical, of love and of knowledge. It is obscure (505e), one catches sight of it with difficulty (517b); so one will not say what it is, but only what it resembles (506e); in this way the unity of the apophatic method and the analogical method is posited. What we called, from an epistemological point of view, the principle of the final unification of Science – in opposition to the principle of distinct determination that presides over the constitution of the Idea – now appears to us as the foundation of the "divine." It is its function as "cause" that is underscored (508e); this has a double sense: the Good is the total "cause" of the being of the Ideas, since in the Forms everything is penetrable by the action of the intelligible cause, without its needing a helper or concurrent cause as is the case with nature (*Phaedo* 99b); furthermore, it is the "cause" of the power of knowing and of the power of being known for all the aspects and for all the Ideas.

So the Good assumes the function of *foundation*, of the 'αρχή, of the pre-Socratic tradition, like the Ideas but more radically than the Ideas; like the Ideas: this is why Plato also says ἰδέα τοῦ ἀγαθοῦ,[12] the Idea of the Good; but more radically than the Ideas: which is why it is said to reside "beyond essence." Plotinus will resolve this ambiguity by distinguishing between the One which is beyond the Ideas and the Intelligence which *is* all the beings, but already the *Philebus* seems to correct the ambiguity of the *Republic* by calling the supreme principle the One and no longer the Good.

b) The philosophy of the "divine" is, on the other hand, a philosophy of *immanence* which, we will see, restarts the philosophy of *transcendence*. We have looked at the epistemological side of the

---

[12] *idea tou agathou.*

dialectic, what Plato calls the "synoptic" activity of the dialectician, *Republic* VI 537c; the Principle here plays the role of goading knowing, by provoking regressive analyses leading toward a "sufficient" (*Phaedo*) and finally a "non-hypothetical" (*Republic*) starting point and to progressive syntheses aimed at the many.

The laborious, partial, and incomplete character of the dialectical exercises that Platonism proposes has an important religious significance: there is no total system, such that one could say that the vision of the One would entirely be recovered and reabsorbed into the dialectic; there are only dialectical fragments: for example, the construction of the five "kinds" in the *Sophist*; there is also a dialectical program; for example, the texts of *Phaedrus* 265d–266c, *Sophist* 253b–254b, and *Philebus* 16c–17a; *but nowhere does one find the complete system; if that were the case, the transcendence of the Good would be equaled by the system itself and Plato's philosophy would be Hegel's philosophy.* It seems clear that for Plato himself the Good finally escapes being put into relation; one might well say that it "illuminates all investigation but that it is not seen directly by anyone."[13] This is why each of Plato's dialogues, in its own way, is a complete work; each one uncovers a fragment of this system, without being able to profit from the systematic elements belonging to another dialogue; each one aims at the Good, but clings to a group of founding Ideas which are, for *this* dialogue, the "sufficient" but not non-hypothetical principle. Whence that mixture of conviction and interrogation that characterizes the apparently most "complete," least "aporetic" dialogues.

c) This rhythm of transcendence and immanence translates itself into several, explicitly ambiguous, Platonic notions that draw together the two intentions of Platonism.

For example, Plato often speaks of the "measure" both as the "power of the Good" and as the immanent regulation of the dialectical system of Ideas. We have studied the great texts on the "just measure" (*Laws* 283a–285a, *Philebus* 64e–65a, 66b), to which we could have added the text of *Timaeus* 30c on the Living Universal Thing. All these texts develop an indication from the *Republic*: the terminus of the spiritual Anabasis is the "cause" of what is good and beautiful. The discovery of the "just measure" – in politics, in ethics, in physics – therefore plays the role of a method of imma-

---

13 Goldschmidt, *op. cit.*, p. 39 (AC).

nence for the ascent to the foundation. One could say, in Kantian language, that the Unconditioned "schematizes" itself in the relations of finality and suitability that are the true "cause" of all the "mixtures"; it is from the perspective of this "schematization" that the *Laws* will call God "the measure of all things." I am quite ready to think that, if Plato substitutes the One of the *Philebus* for the Good of the *Republic*, it was because he had glimpsed that the Good was already such a "schematization" of the One through a final causality that outclasses the formal causality of each Idea, the dialectical relations of all the partial systems, and the structure of the total system which no philosopher can reconstruct.

This promotion of the Idea of Measure at the turning point of transcendence and immanence is not surprising; it is in line with Anaximander's well-known text on the Δίκη[14] that arbitrates among the infringements of phenomena on one another; it also recalls Heraclitus' aphorisms on the Measure, immanent within contradictions and identical to the Logos.

It is in the same immanent-transcendent style that Plato speaks another time of "total being" (παντελῶς ὄν,[15] *Sophist* 248e–249a); one might well think that what has just been said about the measure can clarify this difficult text. Let us recall in what circumstances Plato was led to invoke this notion. Seeking a definition of being acceptable to the upholders of change and the friends of the forms, he proposes calling being a power of acting and suffering; not only does he suddenly convert to a philosophy unthinkable to the ancients, to a dynamic or energetic notion (Being, is Force, is Energy!); the "passion," which is in question here, is the minimal passivity that has to be lent to being so that it can be known, it is the being-known of being. Between the soul and the idea there is, therefore, an exchange of power, a Making (ποῖειν)[16] on the side of knowing, a Suffering on the side of the ideas, even though it is the Idea that requires this and the soul that obeys. This is when Plato pronounces these enigmatic words (248e–249a): "And what, by Zeus! Shall we allow ourselves to be so easily convinced that movement, life, the soul, thought really have no place in

---

[14] *Dike.*

[15] *pantelos on*, total being or (at the end of the paragraph, in the quotation) "universal being."

[16] *poiein.*

the meaning of universal being, that it neither lives nor thinks, and that, solemn and sacred, empty of intellect, it remains there, planted without the ability to move? – Theaetetus. – It is a frightening doctrine that we would be accepting there, stranger."

This text becomes clearer, we believe, if one compares it to the declaration of the *Republic* 508e, according to which the Good is the common foundation of knowing and of the known, of Intelligence and the Intelligible, since it gives to the one to know and to the other to be known; in the same way that the light is the "milieu" between the fire of things and the fire of the eye, the Good is the mediation that makes possible the intentional relation of knowing; this mediation resolves the discontinuity the *Phaedo* had glimpsed between the soul and the Idea (Socrates declared there that the soul was what was "closest" to the Idea, what "most resembles it," without, however, being the idea). Therefore, the Good allows for a totalization of Intelligence and the Intelligible.

It seems to me that it is beginning from this point that it is necessary to understand the total or universal being of the *Sophist*; the Good, which was the *summum* of being in the *Republic*, here becomes the *sum* of being.[17] The accent is no longer on transcendence, but on the completeness within immanence. The "perfect" (τέλειος)[18] is "schematized" this time through the "all," the "total."[19] What follows in the text confirms this: the being that totalizes all the characters of the intellect, the soul, life, movement, and rest, this being is a totality and no longer an aim: "being *and* the all" (τὸ ὂν καὶ τὸ πᾶν,[20] says *Sophist* 249d) include movement and rest.

Plato therefore passes here from the transcendence of the Good to "the total being that embraces and contains at the same time all realities."[21] There is therefore no place here to see an intelligent soul of the world, as Diès did in the period when he wrote

[17] Diès, *Autour de Platon, op. cit.*, p. 556 (AC).

[18] *teleios*.

[19] Perhaps already in the *Republic* 511b, where the Good is said to be cause of all (πάντος [*pantos*]) (PR).

[20] *to on kai to pan.*

[21] Victor Brochard, "La théorie platonicienne de la Participation d'après le *Parménide* et le *Sophiste*," in *Études de philosophie ancienne et de philosophie moderne* (Paris: Vrin, 1926) (AC) [Brochard's article first appeared in *l'Année philosophique* in 1907].

his *Définition de l'être et la nature des Idées dans le Sophiste de Platon*;[22] for this divinity can appear only with the splitting of the transcendent causality into the exemplary and worker-like causality in *Timaeus* 92b, 34ab; what is more, one does not see what in such a soul would correspond to the synthesis of being, Intelligence, and life; finally, it would be necessary to admit that this is no longer the same totality that was in question in 249d; besides, Diès corrected his interpretation in the Preface to [his translation of] the *Sophist*.[23]

It therefore seems that the interpretation that most fits the over-all approach of Platonism consists in giving the total being of the *Sophist* a situation comparable to the measure or to beauty; the transcendence of the good is "schematized" as the totality that constitutes the essential determinations *plus* the thinking souls, in brief, in the In itself-For itself; this is because the Good gives the ability to be known to the Intelligible and the ability to know to the Intelligence, such that there is such a totality, an encompassing of Ideas and Souls; *Republic* 517c also says that the Good "dispenses and procures the truth and the Intelligence." When Plato speaks of dead being, he speaks of an in-itself, closed-in on itself, which would no longer be the known of knowing, the Intelligible for the Intelligences; and so Plato exclaims, "What a frightening doctrine we would accept there, Stranger!"

3 The divine and the demiurge

We have already studied the problem of the "demiurge" in Plato's *Timaeus* (second part, chapter 3); it was the epistemological aspect that interested us then, namely, the solution to the aporia of the *Parmenides* on the "participation" of the sensibles in the intelligibles; we arrived at this conclusion, that this "participation" is not justified by the participation of the intelligibles among themselves, but by the addition to the formal causality of the Ideas of the efficient, operative causality of a Worker.

This splitting of causality has to do directly with our investigation into the "divine" in Plato. In integrating into the investigation

---

[22] Paris: Alcan, 1909 (AC).

[23] Les Belles Lettres, "Guillaume Budé," 1925, p. 288, n. 1. "La somme de l'être," he says in the "Notice," p. 275 (PR).

of the "cause" of things his analysis of the soul in the *Phaedrus*, Plato integrated at the same time the second of the great pre-Socratic traditions concerning the Divine (chap. 1, §3), the tradition of Anaxagoras' νοῦς,[24] which, according to Plato himself, "governs" and "organizes" all things (*Philebus*). We have seen that, along this second line, a semi-personalization of the divine is initiated, up to the developments of a providentialist type that one observes with Diogenes, Xenophon, and Socrates himself. One may even ask oneself if this semi-personalization had not been a constant theme, however minor, in all the pre-Socratics: "govern," "organize," "rule," "embrace" are quasi-personal operations that the abstract and anonymous Idea of order cannot entirely exhaust. Whatever it may be, the worker-like causality of the demiurge consecrates this minor tendency of pre-Socratic philosophy; and this is not a concession to popular philosophy; the demiurge, we have seen, is solidly tied to the theory of the soul that reaches its maturity in the *Phaedrus*. *Republic* VI 507c and VII 530a, *Statesman* 270a, *Sophist* 265cd confirm it.

Having said this, the uneasiness we have felt in the theory of causality reverberates in the theory of the divine. The *personalized* causality is articulated through the *exemplary* causality by the demiurge's "looking" at the intelligible Living; this "looking," let us say, is the linchpin for this whole construction and finally for all the participations that go from the intelligible to the sensible; and this "looking" is an object of faith, since it signifies the goodness of the demiurge. The same enigma now takes the following form: what is the connection between the divine and God?

It does not seem doubtful that Platonism should be a philosophy that subordinates the personality of the demiurge to the exemplarity of the Ideas and, in this measure, a philosophy that subordinates God to the divine (reservation being made for a personalization, for all that improbable, of the Good itself or of the One). It is here that a passage from the *Phaedrus* finds its meaning: "The soul reminds itself through the forces of the things that make it that God is divine" (249c). God is divine because he contemplates the Ideas and the Good; his divinity is, in this ultimate sense of the word, participated in; no doubt for him the thesis of the *Republic* that the Good gives the Ideas to be known

---

[24] *nous.*

and the Intelligences to know is true; God is through the benefit of being, the divinity of being.

One can find confirmation of this in the fact that the whole charge of reverence and of devotion that philosophy borrowed from myths, liturgies, hymns, the sacred poetry, Plato transposes to the world of Ideas and not to the demiurge. It is the divine that is adorable in a plenary sense, then God, thanks to "the things which make it so that he is divine."

On the other hand, it is necessary to acknowledge that this philosophy of the Ideas does not exhaust all reason's power of veneration, since the Good from on high, the demiurge from below exceed its reality and intelligibility; if the divine is the intelligible, it is necessary to reckon with a supra-divine, if one dare put it that way, and an infra-divine which is god or at least the demiurge. In this sense, the Platonic philosophy of religion is not completed, any more than the "System" of the dialectic seemed to us to be.

One way of completing it would be to say that the Demiurge is the *place* of the Ideas, that the Ideas are *immanent* in this excellent soul; one can say so; but this interpretation, which Platonism does not exclude, goes beyond Platonism. For this to succeed an even more difficult synthesis would be necessary, that of the Good and of the Demiurge; certainly, the Idea of the Good is the "cause" of the intelligible and even of the visible according to *Republic* VII 517bc; it *gives* being and knowing; on this basis one might attempt a rapprochement between the Idea of the Good and the Demiurge;[25] but where is it said that the Good "looks" at the Perfect Model, as it is said of the demiurge? The texts on the Good and those on the Demiurge form two series which one does not need to try to unify. If Plato did not want to place the Ideas *in* the excellent Soul of the demiurge, it was perhaps finally in order not to "psychologize" them in the manner of the neo-Kantian interpreters of his works; instead he preferred to leave the unity of his religious philosophy hanging. To complete this unity is our work; no longer his.

---

[25] One can see a sketch of such a comparison in the text of *Philebus* 22c. Cf. Mugnier, *op. cit.*, p. 132 (PR).

4 The divine and the gods

Just how far down does this philosophy of the divine extend? It extends as far as souls and *par excellence* to the soul of the philosopher;[26] it also extends to the world. But Plato does not descend any lower than the *All* of the world; the visible Cosmos in the regularity of its circular movements. It is the "visible god," in the image of the invisible god, "the god who suffices to himself and who is most perfect, the world" (68e). The eternity of the world, bound to the eternity of the Ideas through the eternity of the demiurge, this is the ultimate terminus of this descending hierarchy of the divine. Someone will say that no one can ask for more! Certainly. For what is it that is not incorporated in the divine? Precisely the gods! Not that Plato ignores them, rather they belong to myth, not to philosophical discourse.

The religious tradition upon which the pre-Socratics and Plato drew includes a reference to gods that we have so far entirely neglected: namely, an appeal to their *eschatological role, in relation to man's destiny*. This tradition carries the themes of an absolute Judge, of a Tribunal of the dead, of a last Judgment, of eternal Expiation, of Punishment without any appeal. For the Greeks, this schema, which one may call the Judicial or Trial schema, was sometimes linked – at least in the tradition that Plato transposes – to that of the reincarnation which allows the Judges to inflict a degrading metamorphosis on evil-doers, and to the fabulous representation of "places" appropriate to this eschatology and more or less well suited to the overall topography of our visible universe.

What did Plato draw from the transposition of these myths? It is not necessary to seek an enlarging of the philosophy of the divine in the great eschatological myths (*Gorgias* 522e–527e; *Phaedo* 107d–115a; *Republic* X, 614a–621d; *Phaedrus* 246a–257b); it is not to his doctrine of being that they contribute but to the knowledge of the soul; they make up part of that "incantation" which the soul itself addresses to itself to exhort itself to become better, to "take care" of itself; they belong to a protreptic of the soul and not to an ontology of the Cosmos. This is the decisive reason that the gods, implied in the myths of Judgment and Retribution,

---

[26] We have left aside here the qualification of the soul as divine: the ontology of the soul would form another study (PR).

are not put in question as beings; they are incorporated into this appeal, this psychogogy, that the eschatology nourishes with its symbols and its narratives.

One can show this best with the *Gorgias*; the god-judge plays the role of revealer concerning the true situation of each soul at the end of its life; he reads on the soul alone the mark of its works; see, before him, the evil-doing soul, "entirely lacerated and ulcerated by the perjuries and injustices that each time its conduct has left imprinted on it . . ." (522a). In this sense no exterior *being* condemns us; "the sons of Zeus," remarks Goldschmidt, "do no more than render a verdict that we were first to pronounce on ourselves." If one transposes this absolute looking at the dead to the perspective of the living, the god who judges the naked soul is a figure of the philosophic gaze that pierces mundane appearances and discerns the ontological degree, if one may put it this way, of the just soul and of the unjust soul; the tribunal is a figure of the soul alone by itself in the face of its own fault.

This function of the revealer is perhaps more noteworthy still in the case of the degrading metamorphoses; the Bestiary, which Plato evokes long before Brueghel and Hieronymus Bosch, is composed in such a manner as to manifest the ways of souls through the symbolism of bodies.

Eschatology thus has a truth function within an ethical knowledge of the soul by the soul. The eschatological myths are in this way resituated by Plato in the *practical* perspective of a search for justice among the living: "For my part, Callicles, I give faith to these stories and apply myself to act in such a way as to present to the judge as healthy a soul as possible" (526d). It is even, more precisely, from the perspective of philosophers' political responsibility that the tyrant is denounced for his true nature – that is, the deceitfulness of his essence – thanks to the Judgment which brings it to daylight; and Socrates concludes: "When we together will have practiced this exercise sufficiently, we will then be able, if it seems good to us, to take up politics" (527d).

We meet the same practical, ethical accent in the other eschatological myths. "No loophole, no safeguard, except to render oneself the best and wisest possible" (*Phaedo* 107c–d); the infernal abodes, which the *Phaedo* describes with such care, are like the fantastic projection onto an appropriated countryside of the true condition of the good or evil soul, in a "sojourn suited to them"

(πρέπουσαν οἴκησιν,[27] 108c). But nothing indicates that the gods of
the Trial, implied in an oblique fashion in this philosophical fabrication, could have been attached, *as beings*, to the investigation
of the divine, whether as Idea, Good, Demiurge (and, it must be
added, Soul). For these "eschatological" gods one has attempted
no transposition, except at the level of "exhortation," that is, of a
species of right opinion. The *mythics* to which they belong constitutes this poetic incantation which sustains in its interior song the
prose exhortation through which philosophy gets itself under way.
It takes on its full meaning, but not a philosophical meaning, with
the final equation of Philosophy and Death that we have so often
rubbed up against.[28]

---

[27] *prepousan oikesin.*

[28] The reader would do well to finish this course by reading the *Laws*, the
Epinomis, and the documents on the final teachings of Plato, which unfortunately have not been dealt with here (PR).

II

Aristotle

Introduction

The connections between Plato and Aristotle, which we are study-
ing here from the point of view of the doctrine of being, are
singularly more complex than at first appears. Everything would
be simple if Platonism were the naïve realism that Plato himself
depicts through the characteristics of the "Friends of the Forms"
in the *Sophist* and if Aristotle were simply its contrary, that is,
a friend of the Earth. The opposition would reduce to that of a
philosophy of "essences" and a philosophy of "substances," given
the further assumption that the center of gravity of the Aristotelian
philosophy of substance is the theory of sensible and changeable
substance. But the Aristotelian substance is called *ousia* – a word
derived from the substantive participle τὸ ὄν, being: therefore it
is its ontological indication, if we may put it that way, that is
designated straight away; furthermore, what makes up the "beingness" [*étance*] of this "be-ing" [*etant*] (translating directly from
the Greek) is its form, its *eidos*; this same word, which we unfortunately translate as Idea in Plato and as Form in Aristotle, must
conceal both a continuity and a more subtle opposition between
Plato and Aristotle than first appears. This is still not the most
important point; neither Platonic ontology nor Aristotelian ontology comes down to a theory of Ideas or Forms; the keys to Platonic
"essentialism" and Aristotelian "substantivism" have to be looked
for beyond this.

We have seen that reflection on language – on the stable

significations that correct speech requires – led Plato to a first-degree ontology which we have characterized by the expression: Ideas as beings, as be-ings (ὄντα). But this first-degree ontology gets doubled with the question: What is the being of Ideas, if Ideas *are*? And we have seen how, in the proximity of its contrary, the Idea of the "Other," being becomes problematic in the *Parmenides* and dialectic in the *Sophist*. This puts us far from the naïve essentialism of the Friends of the Forms.

But Aristotle is no less radical; one could even dare say he is more so. Inasmuch as he does not start from a realism of significations, he does not pause at the intermediary stage of "true being" – of ὄντως ὄν – he goes directly to the question of being as being – τὸ ὄν ἧ ὄν.[1] In so doing, he finds himself as having posed the very question of ontology – Aristotle, the so-called philosopher of the concrete, the changing, the observer of animals and political constitutions.

There is, therefore, a level of ontology where Plato and Aristotle lend themselves to a *rapprochement* which remains unexpected, difficult, and where they will go so far as to exchange roles.

But where to begin? The question of the "order of reasons" is not easy to resolve with Aristotle. The *Metaphysics* is laid out in a scholastic order under which Aristotle's grand design lies hidden. We must therefore first deal with this question of order in the *Metaphysics*: we shall take as a guideline the interpretation of Werner Jaeger,[2] who proposes to substitute for this late, jumbled, and overloaded scholastic arrangement an order of *development*, a chronological order. We hope to show that this order of development, far from drawing us away from the systematic organization that we can disengage by paying attention to the scholastic one, will rather bring us back to it. Thanks to Werner Jaeger we better understand the nature of the difficulties Aristotle had to overcome to bring the old results of an ontology with a more theological

---

[1] *ontos on* and to *on hei on*.

[2] Werner Jaeger, *Aristoteles, Grundlegung einer Geschichte seiner Entwicklung*, Berlin[: Weidmann], 1923, translated into English in 1934 and 1948 (PR). [*Aristote. Fondements pour une histoire de son évolution*, trans. Olivier Sedeyn (Paris: éd. de l'Éclat, 1997); *Aristotle: Fundamentals of the History of His Development*, trans., with the author's corrections and additions, by Richard Robinson (Oxford: Clarendon Press, 1948). The Oxford edition of 1948 has been modified (thanks to Ruth Jaeger) from the Berlin edition that appeared in 1923; this is the one, it seems, that Ricoeur cites.]

character into the new project of a general ontology, centered on the notion of "being as being."

The first part will therefore be devoted to this enterprise: retrieving Aristotle's *"systematic" project* in the *Metaphysics*, by taking the detour of *"historical" interpretation*. The stages of development of the Aristotelian concept of First Philosophy will lead us in this way to the central theme of this Philosophy: the doctrine of Being as Being.

This first part will comprise four chapters. In the first one we will draw out the conclusions of the genetic method applied by Werner Jaeger to the *Corpus Aristotelicum*. In chapters 2 and 3 we will we look at how Aristotle readies his doctrine of being in a way that is alternately historical and problematic, in books A and B[3] of the *Metaphysics*. In chapter 4 we will attempt to interpret this doctrine, such as it is set out in books Γ and E. In this way we will have reached the highest level of Aristotle's meditation on the object of metaphysics. But, at this level, the *Metaphysics* still remains in a programmatic state, and we cannot yet see whether the realization lives up to the ambition; in particular we cannot yet see whether the project of a general ontology, centered on being as being, allows recapturing, recuperating, and integrating under the rubric of a realization and a fulfillment, the oldest results of a theology; it is this question that the historical method allows us better to pose, if it is true that this theology and this ontology represent two periods in Aristotle's thought; but it is no longer history that can decide whether the two programs exclude each other or whether the more recent, which is also the more far-reaching, the more radical, can encompass the older, which is also more precise and more determined.

The second part will be devoted to how the program of first philosophy is realized in a theory of the "separate," "unchanging," first substance. It is this realization of the program that alone can decide the coherence of Aristotle's system. The theory

---

3 Recall that the books of Aristotle's *Metaphysics* are arranged in alphabetical order, with the Greek letters in capitals: A (Alpha), B (Beta), Γ (Gamma), Δ (Delta), E (Epsilon), Z (Zeta), H (Eta), Θ (Theta), I (Iota), K (Kappa), Λ (Lambda), M (Mu), N (Nu). The books in turn are divided into chapters (designated by Arabic numerals). But in citing the *Metaphysics*, reference is made primarily to the Bekker edition (of the Berlin Academy, 1830–1836), with reference to its pages and columns.

of sensible substance will then appear to us as a "detour through
a lower level," a detour, we say, that prepares for the realization
of the program of ontology. We shall devote three chapters to this
detour so as to show sequentially that ultimately substance is not
constituted in its substantiality by matter – despite the reasons
that plead for this understanding (chap. 1) – but rather by its form
(chap. 2); at this point of our inquiry we shall better understand
how close Aristotle is to Plato despite his different philosophy of
reality; Aristotle's indifference to the singularity of individuals will
confirm that Aristotle is a philosopher of intelligibility and not
of existence. It is then that we will be well placed to broach the
continually delayed yet continually approached and prepared-for
question: is the special ontology of the "divine" or theology indeed
the realization of the general ontology of "being as being"?

We hope to show that Aristotle believed it was, and partly
verified it; but it will nonetheless be necessary to indicate at just
what point this partial success of the grandiose program of the
Metaphysics, as set up in Γ and E, is also a partial defeat.

Thus the question of the dismembering of the *Metaphysics* by
the historical method and the right to substitute a chronological
order for a systematic one (itself obscured by a scholastic one) will
remain in suspense right up to the last chapter of the course.[4]

---

[4] I must acknowledge my debt with respect to the works of Mansion
(*Introduction à la physique d'Aristote*), Le Blond (*Logique et méthode chez
Aristote*), Ross (his introduction to and commentary on his edition of the
Metaphysics), Robin (*Aristote*), Tricot (his introduction to and commentary
on his translation of the *Metaphysics*, 2 vol.), and above all Owens (*The
Doctrine of Being in the Metaphysics of Aristotle*, Toronto, 1953), to whom I
am indebted for the interpretation, developed here, of the systematic arrange-
ment of Aristotle's *Metaphysics* (PR). [The correct title of this work by Owens
in *The Doctrine of Being in the Aristotelian Metaphysics* (Toronto: Pontifical
Institute of Medieval Studies, 1951). – Trans.]

First Part

Being as Being

Chapter 12

The "Genetic" Interpretation of Aristotle's *Metaphysics*

What can one expect from the application of the "genetic" method to the works of Aristotle? A great deal, but not everything.

A great deal: namely, we can expect a better understanding of the *tensions* in this work, which at first presents itself as an atemporal block, made up of apparently contemporaneous parts. But not everything: namely, the replacement of a systematic interpretation by a historical one.

Let us look at this method in operation.

The genetic method, which had given such decisive results in elucidating the order of Plato's *Dialogues*, was not applied to the *Corpus Aristotelicum* until quite recently; it is Bonitz[1] and above all Werner Jaeger who have attempted to retrieve the *evolutionary scheme* of Aristotle's work, and thereby have profoundly renewed our understanding of it.

1 State of the Aristotelian corpus

Aristotle's *oeuvre* has come down to us through the Alexandrine editions, begun in the first century BC by Andronicus, a Peripatetic

---

[1] *Aristoteles' Metaphysik übersetz von Hermann Bonitz*, edited posthumously from his papers by Eduard Wellmann (Berlin: Georg Reimer, 1890). – Trans.

philosopher from Rhodes, in a state characterized by two decisive features.

a) First fact

It is a mutilated *oeuvre*, lacking the youthful writings of the Platonic period that would permit us to grasp the *passage* from Plato to Aristotle. This first fact tends to accredit the appearance of a monolithic Aristotle, forever cut off from Plato. Yet Aristotle spent twenty years with Plato, from the age of 17 in 365 up to Plato's death in 348/347; it is therefore a man of almost 40 who assumes his independence. It is a unique fact in the history of philosophy, Werner Jaeger notes, that a man so opposed to his master in philosophic disposition would remain so long a time in the shadow of a genius. It is Aristotle's experience of the Platonic world that allows him to take possession of his own, by a sort of liberating constraint. What is more, this Platonic period extended even beyond the death of Plato. Aristotle's departure from the Academy no doubt expresses a difference of opinion with Plato's successor (his son-in-law Speusippus)[2] far more than a break with the Academy as a whole. It was with a Platonic philosopher from Athens and others associated with the Academy from the provinces that he emigrated to Assos, until his departure in 343–342 for the court of Philip, where he became tutor of the young Alexander. So we have every reason to believe that Aristotle "had accepted Plato's doctrines with his whole soul, and that the effort to discover his own relation to them occupied all his life and is the clue to his development."[3]

We have, therefore, a *mutilated oeuvre*, one which does not allow us to see how Aristotle's thought got out from under from the Platonic "spell" (references: *Metaphysics* A3 984b8-11, and above all *Nicomachean Ethics* 1096a13-17).

The Platonism into which Aristotle was thrown is certainly not that of the *Symposium* and the *Phaedo*, but rather that of the bold self-critique of the *Parmenides*. We must represent to ourselves in

---

[2] The *Course* contains two small errors here: it has – certainly a typographical error – "Spensippus" in place of Speusippus; also, the latter is called Plato's "son-in-law," whereas he was Plato's nephew. In 348 Speusippus succeeded his uncle as head of the Academy.

[3] Werner Jaeger, *Aristotle, op. cit.*, p. 13 (AC).

a twofold way an Aristotle involved in the final stage of Platonism. On the one hand, he must have been associated with the abstract and methodological phase that would have started with the death of Theaetetus in 369. The self-critique of the *Parmenides* is a part in some way of this feature common to Plato and to Aristotle. In any case, it is at this level that Aristotle catches up with Plato. On the other hand, he must have been involved in the development of Platonism in the sense of an astral theology, which we can follow along the *Timaeus–Laws–Epinomis* axis (and about which we have not yet spoken in the earlier lectures).

It is essential to take into account these two characteristics: the self-critique of the metaphysics of the Ideas and the development of astral theology; for the "lost Aristotle" must have been the witness of the collapse both of the theory of Ideas and of the triumph of astral theology; these two phenomena are connected, for when the intelligible heaven vanishes, there remains the visible heaven of the celestial gods, and "dialectic" gives way to "theology." In the *Metaphysics* (Book Lambda) we still find the mark of this Platonism of Aristotle on his "theology."

But what remains from this Platonizing period? Bits and pieces. And yet, not only were Aristotle's dialogues known in antiquity, they were the only works known, the courses remaining unpublished or nearly so; some of those dialogues, like the *Protrepticus*, even enjoyed great success. For instance, the *Protrepticus* served as the model for Cicero's *Hortensius*, which will play a large a role in Augustine's conversion. The terminal point for this period would be the dialogue *On Philosophy*, from which we have the substantial extracts that Cicero cites so abundantly in the *De Natura Deorum* and which, up until the publication of the *Metaphysics* by Andronicus, were the only means of access to Aristotle's philosophy, in particular for the Stoics and Epicurus (which explains the ease with which these later thinkers slide into syncretism). This dialogue must have been the manifesto of the break with the Platonic theory of ideas following Plato's death and no doubt at the conclusion of a long debate both inside and outside the Academy (in particular concerning the Ideas of numbers). But this dialogue bears witness as well to two fundamental features of the transition period.

First, the effort to constitute a history of philosophy which plunges into the depths of the Orient of the Egyptians, the Chaldeans, and the Iranians (the "magi") and of the "theologians" of venerable Greek wisdom (the Orphics, Hesiod, the Seven

Sages, and Apollonian piety); the deeper meaning of this attempt at history was to show the unlimited number of the resurgence of the same truths. Every institution is a restitution (for example, Socrates with respect to the Apollonian religion).

The second feature is tied to the preceding one: the increasing importance of astral theology, which aligns Aristotle with the Plato of the *Epinomis*, is justified by this resurgence (like Schopenhauer rediscovering Zarathustra). With respect to the history of Hellenistic thought, this Aristotle is as weighty as the Aristotle of the treatises, for his astral theology makes him "the real founder of the cosmic religion of the Hellenistic philosophers, which, emancipated from popular beliefs, sought its objects of worship solely in the heavenly bodies."[4] He is thus the obligatory intermediary between the Academy's stellar religion and Stoic theology.[5]

Aristotle succeeds in sealing the pact between theology and astronomy (already the *Laws* identifies heterodoxy in astronomy with atheism), overturning the ancient pact between astronomy and the positivist spirit. But the religious promotion of the heavens parallels exactly the decline of the Ideas.[6]

b) Second fact

Not only is the Aristotelian corpus presented as a mutilated *oeuvre*, but also as one whose initial editions covered over its internal evolution. It presents itself as a collection of courses and treatises meant to be taught (whence the name "acroamatic" writings: *acroasis* = act of listening) which, unlike the lost dialogues, had not been published (let us take note of the curious situation: his successors, in particular the Stoics, knew a Platonizing Aristotle whom we have lost and were unaware of the Aristotle of the treatises, our Aristotle).

---

[4] Werner Jaeger, p. 138 (AC).

[5] For the preceding, cf. Joseph Moreau, *L'Âme du monde de Platon aux Stoïciens* (Paris: Les Belles Lettres, 1939) (AC).

[6] Cf. the discussion of the chronology of the περὶ φιλοσοφίας [*peri philosophias*] by F. Nuyens, *L'Évolution de la psychologie d'Aristote* (Louvain: éd. de l'Institut supérieure de philosophie, 1948), pp. 100–106, and Moreau, *id.*, pp. 114–129 (PR). [The *Course* has "Nuyens, *Le Problème noétique dans la psychologie d'Aristote*, pp. 100–106," but to our knowledge no such book exists.]

These treatises were not secret, rather they had a scholarly purpose. Their internal order is systematic and in no way historical (that is, with respect to their contents, not according to the times when they were edited): Logic, Physics, First Philosophy, Ethics, Politics, Rhetoric, Poetics.

It is as though Aristotle had done no thinking between his departure from the Academy in 348–347 and the foundation of the Lyceum in 335, and as though this work had sprung up as a single block during the thirteen years when Aristotle directed the Lyceum: thirteen "full" years after twelve "empty" ones! (The anti-Macedonian faction flamed up again following Alexander's death in 323 and posed a threat to Aristotle accused of impiety like Socrates, and, before him, like Protagoras and Anaxagoras. Aristotle fled to Chalcis, to die there shortly thereafter.)

Whence a problem: How to reintroduce time and history into a mass of treatises that the editors have deliberately arranged in a systematic order based on their contents?

The problem is not made any easier, it is even aggravated, by the role of the commentators and the use that the tradition has made of Aristotle (those commentators whose work has come down to us can be listed in tiers from the second to the sixth century (above all the sixth) and are particularly the neo-Platonists concerned to associate Plato with Aristotle; then come the Arabs; then Albert the Great; then St Thomas). History is absolutely foreign to their concern. Whereas Aristotle situated himself historically, and even "invented the notion of development in time" (W. Jaeger), tradition has embalmed him in the system. It is not only his adversaries who have furnished him with theses and theories torn from any law of development. Aristotle, Werner Jaeger can say, is "the only great figure of ancient philosophy and literature who has never had a Renascence."[7]

2 The general sense of the development of Aristotle's *Metaphysics* (according to Werner Jaeger)

It is Werner Jaeger – following (it must be said) Bonitz – who has systematically attempted an interpretation of Aristotle in terms of "development" (itself strongly influenced by Goethe: form built

---

[7] Jaeger, *id.*, p. 5 (AC).

up through a development). The general sense of the enterprise is this:

1) the existence of an initial and abiding Platonism in Aristotle;
2) the progressive disengagement of Aristotelianism from its Platonic straitjacket.

Comment. These two themes are connected: initial Platonism and organic development. For an Aristotle without history is also an anti-Platonic Aristotle.

W. Jaeger's effort focuses on two principal points:

• reconstituting "the lost Aristotle" so as to give the starting point (we have given an account of this in the first section);
• rediscovering within the systematic edifice the traces of the successive stratifications allowing us to build a bridge between Aristotle's "Platonism" and "Aristotelianism."

This effort results principally in extricating an *Urmetaphysik.*

a) The evolution of the problem of being

Without going into the details of W. Jaeger's demonstration, we can state right away what does not make up part of the original *Metaphysics* and matters for our inquiry into the meaning of being in Aristotle. Essentially the group of books Z–H–Θ (Zeta, Eta, Theta). This group of books is devoted to the theory of sensible *substance*, that is, of forms immerged in matter.

The second part of these lectures devoted to Aristotle will show that this is the starting point for the properly Aristotelian ontology: whereas Plato begins from the *significations of language,* Aristotle will start from reality in its physical *individuality* if not its singularity.

It was only little by little that Aristotle became aware that the theory of material and perceptible substances could preface a new theory of being and belong to philosophic inquiry.

The *problem of being,* prior to the reworking brought about by the insertion of the theory of substance (Z, H, Θ), is to know whether there is a *supra-sensible reality*: the question is Platonic in its very formulation; it remains Platonic in its answer, if one considers that theology (astral or not) takes the place of the theory of Ideas; hence metaphysics is a "theology" (and more precisely an "astral theology"). To look for being is to look for *a* being (or beings). The introduction of the theory of substance is going to re-equilibrate the meaning of being by incorporating sensible beings into genuine philosophy. By the same token, the notion of being will need to be pushed beyond the bifurcation of the sensible and the supra-sensible, and metaphysics will be an ontology. The end point, from the historical point of view, is therefore what we would consider the starting point from the systematic point of view, i.e., the well-known theory of "multiple meanings of being" (E 2–4), dominated by the notion of "being as being," totally dissociated from that of a supreme, supra-sensible being. It is there that we must seek the ultimate and fragile synthesis of Aristotelianism: in a kind of "ontological phenomenology," in W. Jaeger's language; this elucidation of the multiple significations through which being is spoken of will allow integrating the theory of substance with first philosophy. We understand why E 2–4, this *tenon* of the entire *Metaphysics*, should be in this place, *after* the great introduction of A through E 1 and *before* the *piece de résistance* about substance (Z, H, Θ).

In this way, this sovereign ontology is capable of reigning over both the entelechies of change (according to the theory of substance) and the pure Act of divine thought, "within which the old Platonic doctrine of transcendent and immaterial Form still remains as conclusion, but no longer holds the center of interest."[8] One sees the fecundity of the genetic method: it dramatizes the investigation and gives the key to the skillfully concealed *tensions* between an ontology (a theory of being as being) and a theology (a theory of the supreme being).

b) What belongs to this Urmetaphysik

Book A – A brief history of philosophy including the critique of Platonic Ideas (A 9). Aristotle still says *nous* as if he were still a Platonic philosopher; on the contrary, the second critique of Ideas (M 4–5) testifies to an already established break; the tone there is more curt and scornful. However, A seems already to draw up an inventory of already consolidated arguments.

The parallelism with the *peri philosophias* is striking owing

---

[8] Jaeger, *id.*, p. 204 (AC).

to the use of the genetic method in order to found a theory of "causes."

Book B – It develops the program of first philosophy, called "the science that we are seeking," and does not announce the theory of sensible substance of Z, H, Θ; the group Z, H, Θ is not the execution of the plan of B. It is, rather, in Book N that one must find the answer to the question posed by B. What is this question? It is a Platonic question: What realities truly exist outside the sensible realm? Are they the Platonic Ideas? And if they are not, what are they? B proceeds by positing *aporias* and develops four of them concerning the nature of the sought for science and eleven concerning its content. This method of *aporias* is, however, quite different from Plato's, because it does not betray any real perplexity, but rather serves as a dramatization subsequent to the discovery of the solution. These are therefore purely pedagogical aporias.

Books Gamma, Epsilon 1 – E (less E 2–4),[9] reply to the four first aporias concerning the science that we are seeking.
    (*Comment*. Book Delta does not belong to this series, it is a lexicon of already established Aristotelian terms.)

Book K 1–8 – This forms a small whole by itself: it is a summary of B Γ E, attesting to an initial stage of elaboration. It is important for a genetic analysis: W. Jaeger calls it "crystal-pure":[10] the theory of "meanings of being" (E 2–4), which would have allowed for the insertion of the theory of sensible substance into a philosophy which at first only looked for supra-sensible substances, is not yet elaborated. K8 (1064–1065) plays this role of a "bridge" between the Introduction (A–E 1) and the theory of supra-sensible being.
    Metaphysics, in this period, is therefore still the science of immaterial things.

Comment: W. Jaeger sees even K 1–8 as prior to B Γ E1 and contemporary with M 9–10: in effect, one asks whether the sought-for science does *or does not* include sensible substances (= alternative);

---

[9] As the following will show, this somewhat complicated reference signifies the break in book Epsilon between chapter 1 and the following chapters 2–4, which occupy a separate place in the development.

[10] Jaeger, *id.*, p. 208 (AC).

B asks whether, *beyond* the sensible, there is a supra-sensible being. So, one goes from "either . . . or" to "not only . . . but also." And yet K already holds in balance two senses of metaphysics:

- being as being;
- being as unmoved, eternal, transcendent.

Book Lambda (except for chapter 8: very late) is also an independent work which contains an overview of all of Aristotle's thought, one which remains quite rare.[11]

Book M 9 (1086a21 and following) –10: a short preface, full of allusions to A, B, and Book N.

Book N: it forms a single body with M. It is this ensemble, M 9–10 + N, which would have been replaced by the better preface M 1 and by M 1–9, more thorough than N.

Conclusion

1) The principal fruit of the genetic method is to set the tension between two conceptions of metaphysics into an evolutionary perspective:

   - According to the one, the object of metaphysics is distinguished from that of physics and mathematics in that it is unchanging and independent (1026a13); hence, metaphysics is a science above the others but comparable to them; it is the science of the "noblest kind," of the highest being – in short, metaphysics is theology.
   - According to the second, metaphysics is the science of being as being and all the sciences carve out their objects according to a certain perspective (as in some matter, or as measurable). The break is no longer between the sensible and the supra-sensible, but between being as such and being from a special point of view. Metaphysics is ontology, that is, a general theory of being and its species. One can say then that

---

[11] See Mansion's critique, *op. cit.*, in Nuyens, *op. cit.*, p. 26 (AC). [Augustin Mansion, *Introduction à la physique aristotélicienne* (Louvain: l'Institut supérieure de philosophie, 1913); an expanded edition was published in 1987).]

first philosophy shifts from the (more Platonic) theological
pole toward the (more Aristotelian) ontological pole.

2) Werner Jaeger's method has not been seriously criticized, either
   in principle or in its grand lines.[12] What has been challenged
   is the chronology, not the general idea of development: that
   suffices for our investigation. It has been questioned whether
   the speculative philosophy in its essentials belongs to the
   intermediary period and whether the mature period, that of
   his supervision of the Lyceum, was more experimental and
   education-oriented. If so, it is necessary, in reaction to Werner
   Jaeger, to push the completion of the *Metaphysics* more in the
   direction of the mature period, and conversely to see as earlier
   the works on logic, physics, natural history, and the history of
   culture. The vision of an Aristotle moving from a metaphysical
   phase to an empirical phase is the most contested point.

That said, at bottom the real question remains whether the tensions that the genetic method reveals and spreads out over time
amounts to a ruinous contradiction for Aristotle's "System." This
question cannot be resolved by the historical method, but by internal comprehension of the work and the confrontation of the project and its realization.

Let us consider, therefore, this project, insofar as (1st) it seeks
itself, by means of history (Book A); (2nd) it dramatizes itself, by
means of the "diaporematic" method (Book B); (3rd) it posits
itself, in the form of a program (books Γ and E 1).

---

[12] See Nuyens, *id.*, pp. 17–25, for a summary of evaluations of Werner Jaeger's
work (AC).

Chapter 13

Philosophy: Its Intention and its Memory

Aristotle's editors have placed at the head of the *Metaphysics* Book A, which constitutes an introduction to philosophy by means of its history. We do well ourselves to begin at this beginning, first of all because it must be contemporary with the περὶ Φιλοσοφίας[1] and attests to an early state of the *Metaphysics*, next because it culminates in a critical examination of Platonism, finally, and above all, because it allows us to catch sight of the very meaning of philosophy. It is through this very meaning that Aristotle holds on to Plato, in spite of the critique of Platonism. One can say that the critique of the Platonic theses is carried out from within a "philosophic intention" that remains fundamentally Platonic.

Aristotle's plan in Book A is significant. Aristotle does not take up the history of philosophy without first having justified its destination. His history of philosophy is not that of a pure historian: the history of philosophy is inseparable from his own project. This is a project that is initially posited as mature and only afterwards recaptures its own childhood. (This shows, we note in passing, that the whole meaning of a history of philosophy cannot be anything other than a work *of philosophy*.)

---

[1] *peri philosophias.*

1 The philosophical intention

There is a unity of philosophic design in Plato and Aristotle. It is
the science of first principles and first causes; it is not necessary to
separate chapter 1 and chapter 2 of Book A of the *Metaphysics*,
which, in a single breath, defines science as the knowledge of
causes and the "science that we are seeking" as the knowledge of
that which is first in the order of principles and causes. "The goal
of our present discussion is to show that, by the term wisdom,
everyone commonly understands what treats of first causes and
first principles" (A 1 981b27).

a) The break between the practical and the theoretic

"The praise of philosophy" that constitutes the opening of Book A
stands on the essentially Platonic terrain of disinterest: knowledge
for the sake of knowledge. The first statement of the *Metaphysics* is:
"All men naturally desire to know"; Aristotle finds this instinct even
in *seeing* and its curiosity. If Aristotle proceeds by a kind of genesis
of science beginning from the sensible (a procedure which at first
sight seems anti-Platonic, one which has been seen as an "indirect
critique of Platonism, for which science and its object stem from
the transcendent world"),[2] this genesis is an emergence: the animals
are limited to images and to memories: "They participate, but only
feebly, in empirical knowing, whereas the human kind of knowing
raises itself up as high as art and rational thought." This division
into levels (*empeira*, τέχνη,[3] *logismos*) is by no means a "genealogy
of logic," but the marking out of a, no doubt, progressive upsurge,
but surely irreducible in its dynamism: memory consolidates itself
in experience (limited to ὅτι),[4] then experience surpasses itself into
"technique" through judgment, already universal, but the prisoner
of practice; finally science surpasses *techne*, through knowledge of
the cause, the "why", *dioti*; sensation remains mute about the why;
hence science – contemporary with teaching – appears to Aristotle
as a fruit of leisure and of wonder. It is important to understand

---

[2] Tricot, *Métaphysique*, p. 4, note. [This is a translation with commentary of the
    Metaphysics by Jules Tricot (Paris: Vrin, 1933, 1953) and is the one that the
    Course generally cites, albeit at times rather loosely.]
[3] *techne*.
[4] *hoti* ("that," i.e., the experience and the affirmation of existence, in contrast
    with *dioti*, the "why").

this double discontinuity. Leisure is the sociological occasion, if one may put it so. "Egypt was the cradle of the mathematical arts, because there the greatest leisure was available to the priestly caste" (A 1 981b24); the priest appears as the man of leisure.

Wonder, as detachment from making and know-how, as taking a step back, is essentially linked to the question *why?* Nothing is more Platonic, since wonder comes from *Theaetetus* 155d.[5] It is as a Platonic thinker that Aristotle repeats: "It is in fact wonder that pushed the first thinkers to philosophical speculations, as it does today" (A 2 982b12, and the following material on the role of the *aporia* that will occupy all of Book B). This may well be why Aristotle is more sensitive to science's line of descent from myth rather than from techniques (against Herodotus and the moderns, such as Bergson): the *philomythos*, owing to both his leisure and his response to the ignorance deepened by wonder, is parent to the *philosophos* (A 2 982b17-20). This break brought about by leisure and wonder is the same break as that between the *practical* and the *theoretic*.

b) The break between the free man and the slave

This first break is equivalent to that between the free man and the slave, which is a political break (cf. A 2 982b25-27). We find here the conviction that true superiority among men is due to *education* and not to power or entitlement. The one who arouses "admiration," who becomes "superior" to others, who is considered "most wise," is the one who wonders and who knows the cause. Aristotle simply invokes the universal consensus with respect the dignity of wisdom so understood; he dispenses with any other proof.

c) The "divine" and the "too human"

This is why the "theoretical," the "free" (the "dignified," the "superior") is finally the "divine." "The most divine science is

---

[5] A somewhat misleading statement. Chambry's translation of this passage of the *Theaetetus* says that "philosophy has no other origin than the feeling of astonishment" (GF-Flammarion, 1967), p. 80. [Levett, rev. Burnyeat (*Complete Works*): "For this is an experience which is characteristic of a philosopher, this wondering: this is where philosophy begins and nowhere else." Cornford (*Collected Dialogues*): "This sense of wonder is the mark of the philosopher. Philosophy indeed has no other origin." – Trans.]

also the highest in dignity, and only the science we are speaking of must be considered most divine, and considered so under a double heading; because a divine science is both that which God would possess, and that which would deal with divine matters" (A 2 983a5 7). One will note the identification of the object of philosophy with God, that is, with the first being ("in current opinion, God is a cause of all things and a first Being") and not with being as being; this again attests to the connection with Plato.

One could not be closer to Plato: the harmonics of the "divine" are, as with Plato, the atemporality and the perfect rest of the soul that knows (cf. also *De anima* I 3 407a32 and following).[6] We will see, in the doctrine of the intellect, that the act of thought is withdrawn from movement and becoming. "The intellect more resembles a rest and a halt than a movement, and the same with the syllogism. And what is more, nothing is sovereignly happy that is difficult and forced; if movement by the soul is contrary to its essence, it is contrary to the soul's nature that it will be moved." Even more strongly *Physics* VII 4 247b13: "Reason knows and thinks by rest and a halt." We are very much in line with *Meno*, which compares science to a knowing that is "chained down," unlike unstable *doxa* which are like the statues of Daedalus.

2 Philosophy and its past

The history of philosophy, as Aristotle understands it, has a double precondition. First because it is preceded by a *positing of meaning or a philosophical intention*: philosophy is the science of first principles and first causes; next because it presupposes the properly Aristotelian theory of the four causes: the *Metaphysics*, here, connects up with the *Physics* and presupposes it. This is an important remark, for, if the theory of substance – if not in its definitive form, at least in its initial elaboration – is not originally at the interior of the *Metaphysics*, metaphysics at least presupposes the fundamental principles of physical knowledge. What is the impact of this preoccupation on the historical reconstruction that follows?

Book A of the *Metaphysics* does not constitute an attempt to evaluate other philosophies in terms of their own problematic, but

---

[6] "On the Soul": Ricoeur, no doubt from habit, cites this book of Aristotle's by its Latin title.

rather Aristotle's (both Metaphysical and Physical): more exactly, for Aristotle the possibility is excluded that other philosophies should have posed a problem other than his own: for his is, if we may put it this way, the *problem in itself*. So, previous philosophies cannot be anything other than aberrations or rough drafts of Aristotle's philosophy: transposed into Aristotle's language, they must appear as omitting one of the causes and the exclusive consideration of another, in brief as an inadequate statement of the system of causes in its entirety and its architectonic. Let us consider four different examples of this treatment of the thinkers of the past:

a) In Aristotelian language, Ionian philosophy appears as a reduction of all the causes to the "material cause," as a hypostatization of matter elevated to the rank of the in itself, when in reality, which is to say in Aristotle's philosophy, it is only a mere correlative of the intelligible form. The variety of philosophies within Ionian philosophy reduces to a permutation among this or that material principle: water, air, etc., and to a discussion of the number of material principles: one? *four* (Empedocles)? *an infinite number* (Anaxagoras)? A true Procrustean bed, from which the complex Ionian philosophy emerges diminished and amputated.

b) Philosophy's progress, by way of contrast, will come from "the constraint of the truth itself" (the same thing a little further up: "But at this point in their course, reality itself traces out the way for them and requires of them a more profound investigation,"[7] namely, the investigation of the "why of change" that matter cannot explain. Anaxagoras and his *nous*, already referred to by Plato in the *Phaedo*, is the witness to this constraint. So the truth of itself cuts a path through history, and history is less contingent *event* than the *advent* of the true: this is why the historian of philosophy can both narrate and criticize. Anaxagoras – with his *nous* that "puts all things in order" – alone appears as having good sense in comparison to the ramblings of his predecessors (A 3 984b18). History and orthodoxy coincide in this judgment.

This advent itself comes about through an obscure presentiment; the first philosophers touched on the truth, "as in battles poorly trained soldiers carry on, rushing about on all sides and

---

7 A 3 984a18.

often striking lucky blows, but without science playing any part" (A 4 985a14-17). What history makes come forth is therefore an *ex*-plication of the causes (in the sense of a de-simplification); this *ex-plication* begins by means of the *dis-tinction* of the material cause and the formal cause: from that comes the exceptional significance of Empedocles and Anaxagoras in Aristotle's eyes. This appears clearly in the conclusion of Book A, which, on top of the critique of Plato, takes up again the book's overall movement (cf. the 12 first lines of A 10).

c) But this aligning of all these philosophies in terms of a unique problematic, that is, an "etiology," seems particularly arbitrary in the case of the Pythagoreans, something which is all the more important in that Aristotle connects Plato to Pythagoreanism, whether by actual descent or mere resemblance (A 6). Aristotle explicitly states that the examination of Pythagorism will be conducted from the narrow perspective of the investigation of principles: "we have treated all these points elsewhere with more precision; if we return to them here, it is to grasp what these philosophers posit as principles and how their principles fall under the causes that we have enumerated" (A 5 986a12-15). The Pythagoreans will therefore be assimilated to the natural philosophers because "they also" (986b16-17) know only the material cause: number will be a sort of material cause, all the rest being *pathe kai hexeis* (modifications and states) of this matter. (A discussion among the commentators seeks to establish whether the efficient cause goes under this heading of *pathe kai hexeis*, or, according to Ross, a vague premonition of the formal cause. In any case, there is a problem in reconciling this interpretation, which casts Pythagorism off to the side of natural philosophers, with the interpretation that makes numbers *models*.)

Aristotle is clearly bothered by the feeling that it is difficult to bring the Pythagorean distinctions into his own problematic of the four causes: limit and unlimited, even and odd, one and many, left and right, etc., which is to say the primordial contraries, for which one term is a principle of order, perfection, limitation, and the other of disorder, lack of limit, imperfection (cf. the admission of difficulty at A 5 986b5-7: "But as for the way in which it is possible to bring these under the causes about which we have spoken, this is what is not clearly articulated by these philosophers, they seem though to arrange their elements under the idea of matter, since it is beginning from these elements, taken as immanent parts of all things, that according to them substance is constituted and shaped."

d) The case of *Parmenides* is even more embarrassing for Aristotle: the negation of movement and of the many does away with the problem of the "principle" and the "cause": so one must say that "the discussion of their doctrines cannot in any way enter into the framework of our present examination of causes" (A 5 986b13). It is solely because of an inconsistency that Parmenides re-enters the Aristotelian scheme of history, namely, through his proposing the famous "path of opinion" that reintroduces the sensible plurality: a sign in Aristotle's eyes of that constraint of the facts (*id.*, 986b31) already referred to with regard to Anaxagoras' *nous*.

3 The critique of Platonism

a) Preliminary question

What is it that Aristotle understood about Platonism? His whole critique is governed by his reading of Plato. Two aspects need to be considered.

First of all, it is a dogmatic and naïve Platonism that is depicted by Aristotle: almost the philosophy of the "world behind this one" that Nietzsche mocks; a sort of *thing-ism* of the Ideas. The way in which he represents the *motivation* of Platonism is already characteristic (books A, B): Plato's starting point is Heraclitean (by way of his teacher Cratylus): "Sensible objects are in perpetual flux and cannot be objects of science." Further along Aristotle adds: "Plato will remain faithful to this doctrine."[8] Plato is the philosopher who has despaired of the truth of the sensible, and, according to the phrase from the *Phaedo*, "took refuge" in the Ideas, in brief who sought true reality *elsewhere*. The encounter with Socrates is the second motif; Socrates taught him to "define" and to "seek the universal." But "his first formation" (that is to say, the Heraclitean one) led Plato to think that "this universal must exist among the realities of another order than that of the sensible things" (A 6 987b1 5 et seq.).[9]

---

[8] The same phrase appears in A 6 987a33-34.
[9] Tricot, whose translation Ricoeur apparently is citing, has put "beings" in

It is striking that the divorce between Aristotle and Plato is already sketched out in this interpretation of the motives of Platonism. Plato despaired of sensible reality; Aristotle has made the opposite wager or oath; a science of physical things is possible; that is indeed why, from the first book of the *Metaphysics*, it is the *Physics* that lends the *Metaphysics* its categories of explanation: the "four causes." This different wager is the motive for Aristotle's incomprehension. The model of existence, if we can put it so, is originally situated in different dimensions; for Aristotle, it is near to us, it is here; for Plato, it is out there; so Plato could only appear as the philosopher who granted intelligible things *the existence which can belong only to things*, who has emptied sensibility of its reality, led, one might say, by Heraclitean intimidation to transpose reality "out-there."

It is in short in the most naïve terms that Platonism is depicted, almost in those Plato himself attributed to the Friends of the Forms in the *Sophist*, or to the young Socrates in the *Parmenides*: the Ideas are "separate" from the sensible and the "homonymous" sensible things participate in them through an "imitation" similar to that of Pythagorism ("the name alone has changed," notes Aristotle). It is astonishing that Aristotle can say: "In any case, this participation in or imitation of the Ideas, whatever may be its nature; this is an investigation that they have left undecided" (A 6 987b12-13). Astonishing when one recalls the critique of the various representations of participation, in terms of imagery, in the *Parmenides*. In sum, Plato believed that these grosser interpretations of participation were mere caricatures from which he could free himself; Aristotle sees in this caricature the true face of Plato.

Second aspect: not only is Platonism taken in its least critical and most dogmatic articulation, it is projected onto the very plane of the Aristotelian problematic of the *explanation of the sensible real*: Plato "seeks to apprehend the causes of the beings that surround us . . ." (A 8 990b1). We must not lose sight of the fact that this critique is introduced indirectly in that part of Book A dominated since chapter 3 by the enumeration of the "four causes"; it is again recalled in chapter 7 (between the "exposition" and the "critique")

<hr>

place of "things." *Metaphysics* vol. 1 (Paris: Vrin, 1991), p. 30 – this comes from the *editio minor* in comparison to the one that appeared for the first time in 1933. Remember that these citations Ricoeur makes to Tricot's translation are generally not very literal.

that "none of those who have treated the problem of the cause has said anything that could not be included among the causes which we have ourselves determined in physics . . .",[10] and that Platonism is what got closest to the "quiddity" and the "formal substance"; finally chapter 10, after the critique of Plato, concludes: "That the causes that we have enumerated in the *Physics* should be the very same ones that all the philosophers have, it seems, sought, and that outside these causes we cannot name any others, as the preceding considerations obviously show . . ."[11]

So, Plato's "philosophical act" is unrecognized; if it is true that the Platonic problematic is the possibility of meaning and finally of language, this problem is reduced to Aristotle's, which is that of *sensible reality* considered in its *dioti*, in its "why," and not in its brute presence, in its ὅτι. This is important for understanding the critique of Plato: it can only consist in this: to make apparent the defeat of a *naïve* Platonism confronted with the *Aristotelian problematic*.

b) We can now move quickly through the critique of Plato. It is doubtful that we can expect what Robin expects in his *Théorie platonicienne des Idées et des Nombres d'après Aristote* (1908), namely, separating out Aristotle's genuine testimony about Plato from "what seems added out of a dogmatic and polemic interest." In fact, it is not just the critique that stands on Aristotelian ground, but already the interpretation of Platonism and its own philosophical intention.

Robin (laying aside the discussion of the *meta-mathematics* which would have been the object of Plato's oral teaching) lays out Aristotle's critique of the Platonic ideas in three moments:

1) the hypothesis of the universals;
2) the absurdity of participation;
3) the incoherent delimitation of the field of the Ideas.

There is no question of taking up again this scholastic examination of Aristotle's own quite scholastic argumentation, presenting Aristotle's riposte to a quite scholastic Platonic argument; it is much more interesting to try to catch sight of the properly

---

[10] A 7 988a20-22.
[11] A 10 993a10-12.

Aristotelian motivations for the critique. So:

1) The critique of the *reification* of universals supposes, on the one hand, that the reality Plato confers on the Ideas is the same as that which Aristotle recognizes in individual substances; the Ideas are then treated as *individual substances*; to realize essences is to substantialize them; on the other hand, what Plato speaks of as an Idea is what Aristotle speaks of either as "universals" or as "quiddities." This second point calls for an explanation: under the name of universals, Aristotle means the arrangement into genera and species for a classifying thought, an arrangement running from the highest genus to the last species; Aristotle agrees with Plato in saying there is a demonstration or science only with respect to these universals (Book B 4 999a24-32). But universality is extrinsic and accidental with respect to the essence of the thing; in other words: that an attribute repeats itself in multiple subjects is not inscribed in the essence, which in principle could be the essence of a single thing. Universality is thus an accident of the thing and not a thing. But the argument is not comprehensible unless one knows that for Aristotle what is real is the subject of attribution and not the attribute; substance is precisely that which cannot be attributed to another thing, that which is never attribute but always subject. The mark of reality is thus placed on the *thing* to which this or that happens. Platonism appears then as a sort of monster: where the universals are treated as separate individuals, as primordial individuals, whereas they are only classes of attribution. The incompatibility of universal and substance underlies the entire critique (cf. B 6 1003a7-13; K 2 1060b21; M 9 1086b21; M 9 1086b32-35).

What remains is that Ideas are not universal "kinds," but the actual *quiddity* of things. In Aristotle's language, the quiddity is the τὸ τὶ ἦν εἶναι = *to ti en einai* – word for word: the "what was (given) to be" (we shall explain this expression later on,[12] here

---

[12] If we want to grasp the expression more closely, we must translate with St Thomas (*De Ente et Essentia*): *quod quid erat esse*, "that which has been given to something to be," says Tricot (*La Métaphysique d'Aristote*, traduction, introduction et commentaire, 2 vol., p. 23, n. 3) or "that which the thing cannot not be" (Ravaisson), its total definition, without reference to some extrinsic or accidental fact whose meaning belongs to something else. (Comment: Why the use of the imperfect in the *ti en einai*? Is it a philosophical imperfect presupposing a "let us say"? An imperfect of duration? Or rather

we are going straight to the intention); the quiddity is the unified whole of the elements of the definition, that which properly
belongs to the defined, that which the entire Western tradition will
call the "essence" or the "nature" of the thing, whose explanation
is found in *Metaphysics* Z 5 1031a12.[13] What Plato substantial-
izes, in "separating" the definition, is therefore, in Aristotelian
language, the *ti en einai* that represents the essence of the defined
and its quiddity (Robin). We are right at the point where Plato
and Aristotle both create a philosophy of the Form or the Idea, but
where the meaning that each gives to the form excludes the other's
absolutely; the Idea or Platonic Form is a unit of signification, a
grain of meaning; the Aristotelian form is a principle of existence
or, if one can put it this way, a unit or grain of existence; from the
very first definition of the four "causes" at A 3 on, form is the first
named of the four causes, under the two synonymous names of
ousia eidike (formal substance) or *to ti en einai* ("quiddity").

If, therefore, the Platonic idea is transposed into Aristotle's language, Platonism's vice consists in "separating" the *quiddity of a
thing from the thing itself*, as a result in detaching the form from
the matter, which makes no sense, since reality is the concrete
composition of the form and the matter, *the individual which
is there in the indivisibility of its meaning and its presence*. In a
philosophy of concrete individuality, which has as its model the
organism, the living individual, the form can only *be* immanent
to the matter; to realize it separately is to treat as substance that
which is the very "nature" of the substance. The quiddity and
the thing make one, in a philosophy of the concrete individual,
whereas the Idea and the thing make two in a philosophy of signs,
of speaking, of thinking by means of signifying words.

Hence, the Platonic Idea could no longer appear except as a use-
less and absurd doublet of true reality. This is the point at which

---

an anteriority of the form to the composite? It is a literary reminiscence of
Antisthenes, who defined the logos as *ho to ti en esti, delon* = ὁ τὸ τὶ ἦν ἐστὶ
δῆλον) (PR) [*delos* means "clear, evident, manifest." But with this accepted
meaning the saying becomes even more untranslatable. Approximately, translating exactly on the basis of Tricot: "That which was given to it [to the
logos to be] was, insofar as it is, manifest" – In the *editio minor* of Aristotle,
Métaphysique, trans. J. Tricot, vol. I, books A–Z (Paris: Vrin, 2000), the note
found on page 12].

[13] Aristotle's explanation of quiddity is developed above all in Z 6; it is simply
announced in Z 5 1031a12.

Books Z, H, Θ, the central books about substance, will end up: the full and genuine existence of things *suffices* (cf. Z 6 1031a15-28; 1031b3-18 and 1031b31–1032a2; Z 10 1035b27-31). "If the beings which are not affirmed of another being, but which are of themselves and which first exist, *they suffice*, even if the Ideas were not to exist . . .. It follows from these arguments that each being is one with its quiddity, and that this identity has not come about by chance" (1031b13-14 and 19).

Projected in this way onto the "physical" plane of Aristotelianism, the Idea is a universal kind taken as a substance, a quiddity detached from the thing.

2) The absurdity of participation is no longer a comprehensible objection in the absolute sense; it can only be understood starting from a philosophy that excludes the immanent participation of forms in their matter.[14]

3) As for the extent of the world of Ideas – its "population," as Ross puts it in his book on the *Theory of the Ideas in Plato* – Aristotle insists on two difficulties of direct interest to our ontological investigation.

On the one side, the hypostatizing of universals as substances led Plato to exclude unduly certain Ideas about which there is nonetheless knowledge, such as the ideas of individual things, of artificial things, the ideas of negation and privation, the ideas of relations; an unjustified exclusion, for there is knowledge, under the form of attribution, of negative terms such as not-human, of relative terms such as the Equal, and even of the perishable individual "about which there remains an image in thought."

This critique is surprising: has not Platonism, from the *Phaedo* to the *Sophist*, explored relations under the heading of the "communication of kinds" and has it not given them as a foundation an Idea, the Idea of the "Other"? The same can be said with regard to negations; Robin admits: "Aristotle seems, if one refers to his own assertions, to have an inexact interpretation of Plato's doctrine about negations. It is doubtful that Plato would have made the False a real non-being and an ideal principle. But it is possible that, in a completely different sense, he would have made a place for

---

[14] This argumentation will be found in Léon Robin, *Aristote* (Paris, PUF, 1944), pp. 81–120, which we draw upon here (PR).

non-being in the world of Ideas, and that in non-being he would have seen a positive principle of existence of a world of Ideas. For another thing, it is possible he also would have said that non-being is not nothing and that, being the very negation of the reality of the Idea, it does not have its place among the Ideas. But surely it would be necessary not to take his assertions in an isolated fashion or to interpret them literally."[15] Similarly: "There is little likelihood, given the argument of the πρὸς ἕν,[16] that Plato would have denied there could be Ideas of the Relative."[17]

In truth, Aristotle does not do justice to what we have called Platonism's second degree ontology; yet it was Plato that was the first who, in order to give an account of ideal "be-ings," introduced the dialectic of the Idea of being, which rests precisely on the ideas of relation and the other. Is it not rather on account of the very privilege given to "substance," in the theory of the multiple accepted meanings of being according to Aristotle, that relation is pushed to the other extreme in the series of the categories? Is it not this downplaying of relation in a philosophy of substance that Aristotle projects onto the philosophy of Plato, reduced ahead of time to a substantialism of Ideas?

On the other hand, Aristotle reproaches Plato for having treated as Ideas, that is, according to Aristotle, as "Universals," as "Kinds," the Good, the One, and Being. The argument against the Idea of the Good should to be connected to the critique of it given in Book I of the *Nicomachean Ethics* (1096a17-23; 1096b8-25);[18] the Good cannot exist "by itself" because it is not a genus that envelops the goods corresponding to the various kinds of life: pleasures, honor, prudence, and contemplation. In this way the ever so subtle connection that Plato established between vision and what is envisaged in books VI and VIII of the *Republic* is lost. The sense of Aristotle's critique appears clearly in the case of the One and that of Being: these are principles for the Platonic philosophers because they are supremely attributable; but the most universal attributes are precisely those farthest from reality, from substance, hence the most difficult ones to hypostatize. Furthermore, it is

---

15 Robin, *Aristote, id.*, p. 187 (AC).

16 *pros hen.*

17 *Id.*, p. 189 (AC).

18 *Éthique Nicomachéenne*: this form of the title comes, to all appearances, from Paul Festugière's *Le Plaisir* (Paris: Vrin, 1936), a translation of Aristotle, *Nicomachean Ethics* VII 11–14 and X 1–5.

even more doubtful that they would be "kinds" (hence Universals, hence Ideas). Being, to start with it, "is said in multiple accepted meanings"; these are the accepted meanings, elaborated in the theory of the categories, which possess the rigor of the "kinds": substance (being is a thing that is), quality (it is, because it qualifies the thing which is), etc.; thus the pseudo-Idea of being gets distributed among the categories. As for the One, it is diversified in a manner parallel to that of Being; the One is *a* being, in the sense of one substance, one quality; right away each of the categories is being or a being, without having to participate further in the alleged "kinds" Being and One.

So Platonism is decapitated both of its *aiming* at the Good, which the *Philebus* radicalizes in the Idea of the One, and of its second-degree ontological *dialectic*. One may well be dismayed at the absence of understanding and sympathy for works like the *Sophist* and the *Philebus* on the part of a philosopher who has lived for twenty years with the master. Moreover, does not the dialectic of the kinds of being in the *Sophist* lie in the same vein as the theory of being as being, and as the theory of categories, which are interconnected by an analogical connection that oscillates between homonymy and synonymy? Aristotle, as regards all this, is obsessed by his conviction that reality is on the side of subjects of attribution and that Platonism is summed up entirely in a vast hypostatization of the attributes of affirmation; thus Platonism as a whole must pass through this narrow gate: there will be nothing to it other than attributes, kinds, Universals, set up as substances. The entire second-degree ontology is "reduced" in advance by this decree of condemnation.

Chapter 14

Philosophy and its "Aporias"

Older commentators saw in Book B the true beginning of the *Metaphysics* and in Book A a merely historical preface. In fact the two books form a single unit: it is the "wonder" of Book A that gets developed into an "aporia."[1] Plato had already linked ἀπορεύω[2] and aporia, to be perplexed and to seek; Aristotle for his part compares the state of aporia to that of a man who is chained down; Plato called it being numbed. Moreover, the development from wonder to perplexity is prepared for by the sequence of trial and error presented in Book A, which functions as an education about truth through history.

Why does not the *Metaphysics* proceed according to the rigorous method of *sylloptique*,[3] but rather through an exposition of difficulties, through a development of aporias (whence the expression diaporematic, meaning "to seek one's way through difficulties")? Moreover, this method is the least rigorous one, one that stems from the less noble method than demonstration which Aristotle calls dialectic, giving this word the pejorative sense of a confrontation of opposed theses.

---

[1] Owens, *op. cit.*, p. 116 (AC).

[2] *aporeuo.*

[3] This unknown word is doubtless a mistake. We may conjecture that what is at issue is "syllogistic," the science of logical laws with respect to statements, which Aristotle founded and which leads us to consider him as standing at the origin of formal logic.

If the *Metaphysics* had to proceed dialectically, it is because there was nothing more prior that one could analyze and from which one could deduce the first propositions of Philosophy. There is thus an affinity between the First and the Dialectical, however inferior dialectic may be in the order of demonstration; this is why extricating the theme of First Philosophy by means of *history*, on the one hand, and *aporia*, on the other, remains the only road to take. In effect, it is the principles concerning the four causes posited in Book A that *create the problem*, which will then to some degree be resolved by tracing the antinomy that lies at the heart of common opinions. (Werner Jaeger underlines the Platonic atmosphere in all this: these are "questions within the sphere of the supra-sensible" and situated on the terrain of Platonism's crisis concerning the nature of the suprasensible. We shall see at the conclusion of this section what this is about.) Book B does not "untie the knots," but locating them already provides an indication of the way in which they will be untied.

Book B develops fourteen aporias: the method is scholastic and fastidious. There is no question of reviewing them all here; we shall content ourselves with drawing attention to the first four, not simply as examples, but rather because they provide the controlling theme of Book Γ and of E 1, which concern us in this chapter: and above all we shall try to understand the function of these aporias.

1 The four first aporias

They have as their center the difficulty that one must think of the causes as being four in number. We shall see that the answer will be given by the "as being" (*e on*), taken as the basis of a unique science.

First aporia

If there are four causes, four dimensions of research, how will there be *one* science? Is it not necessary that they arrange themselves under a unique genus as contraries? (In virtue of the adage that for contraries there is a single science.) But the causes are not contraries.

Aristotle adds that if *certain* beings, such as motionless beings,[4] fail to fall under *all* the causes (in fact, they have neither an efficient nor a final cause), a *unique science* is not possible. He means by this that, if a being eludes one of the four ways of questioning, it does not belong to the question of being as being; the science of being must be the science of *all* beings. This aporia can only be resolved if the science of being as being also encompasses sensible things, disengaging itself from the Platonic framework of motionless being, for the aporia would not let us anticipate what we might find out with respect to efficient and final causality among the motionless beings.

Shall we say, then, that there are four sciences? But each has a dignity that permits it to claim sovereignty: it is equally dignified and sovereign to know the final, the formal, or the efficient cause. Aristotle emphasizes that "formal substance" is "the knowable *par excellence*" (B 2 996b13-16),[5] seeming to insinuate that this is to reduce the other "causes" to this one which first philosophy will employ; we may instead perceive here the primacy that substance will have in the series of the accepted meanings or categories of being; already here knowledge through the *einai*[6] (line 16) presupposes the theory of the categories; here the first category (*ousia*, substance) coincides with the formal cause. So the reduction of every type of being to *ousia* is already prefigured here.

Conclusion: the perplexity proceeds from the conviction acquired in Book A that wisdom has to do with the four causes; the result is friction between a still Platonic conception of wisdom as the science of unmoving being (excluding efficient and final causes) and some more properly Aristotelian notions (one science for different things = a science of the contraries: three of the four causes have an equal right to establish a science of wisdom). There

---

[4] Note the Platonic example of the motionless beings and of the Good in itself; the claim is not even that they lack matter – because for the Platonists the large-small = the material – but rather efficient and final causes. This quite Platonizing antithesis between sensible and supra-sensible things is constantly present in this text. In this sense the science that is sought for is equivalent to the science of motionless being; it this science which does not make use of all the causes. Thus the aporia oscillates between the two conceptions: the Platonic conception of true being (*ontos on*), the Aristotelian conception of being as being. (PR)

[5] In the *Course*, an imprecise reference to 993b13.

[6] *einai*: the infinitive of the verb "to be."

is a hint here that points in the direction of a reduction of "cause" and "being" to *ousia in the sense of form*.

Second aporia

The opposition is going to arise no longer from within (among the four causes), but from without, from the conflict between the science of the causes taken all together and the science of the "principles of demonstration," that is, of the axioms or indemonstrables.

The interesting thing is that the assertion of this aporia sums up the four causes in terms of *ousia* (cf. 996b31); the science of the four causes is called the science of *ousia*. Whence the aporia. Shall we say that there are multiple sciences of the axioms themselves, as many as the sciences?[7] The origin of this aporia lies in what we do not yet see at this stage: the indemonstrables or *substance*.

Conclusion: it is, therefore, from a properly Aristotelian logic that the difficulty is born: the common axioms constitute a supreme universe. The solution insinuated at 997a14 will be that there is no science of the axioms as such: *the reduction to* ousia *will at the same time provide the root of all universality*: the science of the axioms can be neither definitional (*horistike*), since they are immediate, nor demonstrative (*apodeiktike*), under pain of reducing them to a single genus and, along with them, all their consequences.

Third aporia

Are there different kinds of *ousiai*?[8] How can it be, then, that there is only *one* science?

It is therefore understood that the "science sought for" is the "science" of *ousia*.

Comment: the aporia results from the fact that *ousia* is treated like a genus. The solution will be to restore all the substances to a primary type of *ousia*; but to do so in a non-generic way, following a different line of affiliation than that of the subordination of species to genus.

This aporia is resolved at Γ 2 and E 1. Not only are universal,

---

[7] *Sic.* Meaning perhaps: "as many sciences as axioms," or "as many axioms as sciences"?

[8] *ousiai*: Greek plural of *ousia*, therefore "substances."

form, cause, and being reduced to *ousia* according to Book A, but *ousia* itself is reduced, within its own sphere, to a primary example, that of a substance *par excellence*.

Fourth aporia

The science of the *ousiai* – is it also the science of accidents? The argumentation supposes that essence (*ti esti*) and substance are identical. The aporia proceeds from the conception of demonstrative science as a science of the accidents *per se* of substance, but still not a science of substance itself, which cannot receive attribution unless one considers it in its *ti esti*.

In the background we find the difficulties of "participation" according to the *Parmenides* and the *Sophist*. It remains to connect the accidents to substance by means of the doctrine of the categories or the multiple ways by which being is spoken of, and to create a science of substance that envelops the demonstration of the accidents and therefore of the "forms" in the Platonic sense.

Conclusion concerning the four first aporias

Can one reduce these aporias to the question of knowing [whether] the "science that we are seeking" will be *one* and independent (Natorp, Jaeger)? What is also in play is what is at stake in this science, "being as being," the key and solution to the metaphysical problem. But this stake does not appear clearly, because Aristotle does not start from nothing, but from presuppositions of diverse origins.

In these first aporias, Aristotle is put in an awkward position in part by Platonism, in part by his own logic or physics. Therefore it is both the scope and the object of this "science" which are in question, without our being able to distinguish the two.

2 The function of the aporias

1) Reference to a type of auditors

Have the aporias fulfilled their goal, which was to locate the "knots" where the intellect stumbles? Yes, if one considers that the reflection takes its start from matters that are familiar to a certain

type of "auditor," the "auditors" of the Lyceum, who were familiar *with Platonic thought and the presuppositions of Aristotelian
logic and physics, and with the whole background of contemporary doctrines in physics.* Book B allows us to draw up a list of
these "preliminaries" to Aristotelian ontology. They are referred
to here from the point of view of being obstacles to understanding the four causes; in determining these obstacles, Book B makes
manifest the "knots" and sketches their "unknottings"; it is true
that conceptions quite foreign to one another are reinterpreted in
the language of Aristotelian physics and logic, and that an entire
current of thought, from Heraclitus (in the physical order) to
Protagoras and Antisthenes (in the logical order), plays no role
(it is only after the solution of the aporias concerning the axioms
that he will justify the principle of non-contradiction, whereas this
ought to be obstacle number one). But then, the "auditors" were
not recruited from that side.

2) Reference to the four causes

It is not necessary, therefore, to see in all this a discussion of the
principal problems of First Philosophy, but only of those which
concern the four causes for a certain type of auditor; the objections are not constructed in a systematic manner, but from a
well-defined historical context. It is a question of the obstacles
to the empirical establishing of the causes. On the other hand,
we need not reduce the doctrinal background, as W. Jaeger does,
to the "crisis of Platonic doctrine"; the Platonic point of view
is *one* of the obstacles. At least if we do not call Platonic all the
problems that are indeed common to Plato and the entire earlier
tradition. Instead these are above all obstacles that are proper to
Aristotelianism in its physics and its logic: the causes are already
the causes of sensible things (cf. the examples: the bed, the house,
the four elements, Socrates; the Ideas are considered in them only
as "sensible natures" to which gets added the characteristic of eternity. Mathematical properties cannot be separated from bodies).

3) No reference to a solution

We may not even assume that the questions spoken of in Book
Lambda are essentially *metaphysical*, and still less that their solutions are. These do not go beyond the project of locating the

obstacles to understanding the four causes established empirically as the problems investigated by wisdom. In this sense, this is an amplification of the *initial wonder*. In fact, there is no possible demonstration of what is first; so one must proceed through the "dialectical" confrontation of opinions; the opinions of others serving to raise *wonder* to the rank of an *aporia*.

4) The central place of substance

It is the formal cause that lies at the end of the road. It retains the meaning it has in Book A, where the formal cause is already the ultimate subject of predication and of accidental change. What is more, the quiddity seems to coincide with the formal cause, but not with the universal in the sense of genus–species; for the quiddity is *such* a thing; but Book B does not press any further.

Chapter 15

The Object of
"First Philosophy"

1 The abrupt positing of being as being (Γ 1)

Book Γ of the *Metaphysics* opens with an abrupt declaration:
"There is a science that studies being as being and the attributes
that belong to it essentially." One cannot prove that there exists
such a science. It is a fact. What will be demonstrated is the irre-
ducibility of this science to any other: "It is not to be confused
with any of what are called particular sciences, for none of these
sciences consider being as being, but rather, carving out a certain
part of being, it is solely the attribute of that part that they consider: such is the case with the mathematical sciences." (Note: Do
not become attached to the word "part," which has the appearance of suggesting a regional division within a common domain;
we shall see that this "extensive" reading is not a good one.)

The argument therefore supposes that being as being has been
granted; it establishes only that being as being must be the object
of some science under penalty of remaining overlooked. The one,
and rather obscure, indication that this brief and enigmatic chapter 1 contains is the one that connects this declaration about being
as being to the history of philosophy found in Book A: "Since we
are trying to discover the first principles and the highest causes
..." The allusion is supported by an example from Book A:[1] the

---

[1] 986b15.

natural philosophers sought for the elements of things on the side of matter; at least they saw aright the need to look for "first principles"; what is necessary therefore is to do with respect to being as being what they had done in the limited direction of the "elements." There is, therefore, no demonstration of the object of metaphysics; we shall see why later. One takes a stand on the basis of conclusions established empirically in Book A, namely that, *in fact*, the science of being as being was at work in the earlier think-ers and all that Aristotle will do is extricate it (cf. the "we also"). The possibility of this science will be investigated starting from its factual existence.

What, therefore, does being as being *mean?*

If we adhere to the mere appearance of the expression, we are first struck by the substitution of the expression *e on* for the Platonic *ontos on*; *as*, and no longer *truly*: metaphysics no longer bears on what is *truly being* but on being *as being*. It is true that, in addition to this first expression, two others are given in the text cited above:

- being as being "and what belongs to it essentially" (*per se*);
- none of the particular sciences considers being as being "in general" (universally) (on the connection of these three terms, cf. *Anal. Post.* I 4 73b26 and 74a3).[2]

Necessity and universality still have, no doubt, a Platonic reso-nance, but the guiding theme is the "as." The expression is com-prehensible if we consider that Aristotle's starting point is no longer in the *logoi*, in the significations in themselves, but rather in the individual things. It is the being of these things as being that is going to be studied, no longer the *true* beings, the *logoi*, in opposition to *apparent* beings; and, if one still speaks of the universality and necessity of the being of *these* things *here*, one already catches sight of the link with the *ti en einai* of Book A, which indeed designates the essence of that which exists and not the essence as existing; one also catches sight of the link with οὐσία, which we translate so badly as substance, and which properly

---

[2] *Analytica Posteriora* = [in French] *Analytiques Seconds* [in English *Posterior Analytics*]. It should be remembered that for a long time Aristotle's books were cited by their Latin titles and in Latin translation.

is "the be-ingness" of things. Book A had prepared this series
of equivalences: be-ingness, form (Aristotle says: οὐσία εἰδητική,
eidetic be-ing), being. This chapter is going to be taken up with
grasping the principle of how the series ties together.

Let us say for the moment that "wisdom" is identified with the
question: what does it mean to exist, to be, precisely for that which
exists and initially for individuals? It is the universality of the being
of be-ings that is at issue, abstracting from any differences in their
natures; we are going to think about all that exists *simply as existing*. In doing so, we have not abandoned the definition of wisdom
as investigating first causes and first principles. We have simply
recognized in the question of being the question of principle, as
indicated by the last words of the end of chapter 1 of Book A.

2 Being as being and *ousia*

Aristotelian ontology is marked out by four propositions which
together form the skeletal structure for the set of books A–E 1 of
the *Metaphysics*.

- "Wisdom is the investigation of causes and first principles of
  things." Philosophy is *etiology* (Book A).
- "There is a science that establishes being as being and the attributes that belong to it essentially." Philosophy is *ontology* (Book
  Γ 1).
- "It is with regard to substances that philosophy ought to
  apprehend principles and causes." Philosophy is the *theory of
  substance* (Book Γ 2), or *ousiology*.
- "If there exists an unmoving substance, the science of this substance must be prior and must be first philosophy" (Book Γ 1).
  Philosophy is *theology*.

The last lecture led us from the first to the second proposition;
the causes that we seek are the causes of "be-ingness," of the fact
of being for what is. It is necessary that we understand *how* this
vast proposition, of such formidable universality, is determined by
Aristotle in a twofold way: by the reduction of being to substance
(the third proposition) and of substance to separate and unmoving
substance (the fourth proposition). We shall attempt to understand the properly Aristotelian reasons for this double reduction,

where the problem of being may get lost insofar it is rendered determinate.

Let us first consider the first determination of the ontological problem.

Facing the immensity of the problem of being as being, Aristotle seeks a principle of determination; but, the first aporia has closed one way; the way of generality. Being cannot be a universal that caps all the species, on pain of absorbing all the sciences into one single science. He thus offers a principle of determination that consists in ordering a series of significations in such a way that the first signification serves as a reference for all the others through a special system of references, but without all these meanings being subordinated as species to a common genus. An example, Aristotle's own at Γ 2, will illustrate this non-generic but "analogical" universal: the word *healthy*, which is said about what preserves health, gives it, expresses it, and receives it. The right to speak of health in all these cases rests on a principle of common naming which lies midway between synonymy (the same meaning is attached to different words) and homonymy (the same word but different meanings), because there is a *first meaning*: what is healthy *par excellence* is the organism itself; it is in relation to this primary case that health extends to the cause, the effect, the sign, and the helper of the health of the body. Aristotle calls [this] universality *pros hen* = πρὸς εν (relative to a single term). This universality determined by a basic example is not a superior genus, or a species coordinated with other species, but the first in an *ordered series of homonyms*. In the same way, the series of the significations of being constitutes the categories of being, which do not allow themselves to be reduced to common identical principles. Πολλαχῶς λέγεται τὸ ὄν – ποσαχῶς τὸ ὄν σημαίνει οἷς ὥρισται τὸ ὄν (= *pollachos legetai to on – posachos to on semainei hois horistai to on*).[3] Being means, in succession: substance, quality, quantity, relation, etc. – what the scholastics called the *transcendental termini* – which realize the same community by analogy through a relation to a first meaning that serves as the type for the signification.

What is the first of the analogues? *Ousia*. But what is meant by

---

[3] What is in question is the sentence that opens Γ 2: "Being is said in multiple accepted meanings" – and, further on, the sentence: "Being is related in many ways to that which limits it."

ousia? We translate it by substance, which has the serious defect of not retaining the root "to be." This translation is instead an *apt commentary*: in effect, substance is always implicitly posited, in the books preceding the group Z H Θ (which are the books on substance), as that which subsists through change (cf. A 3 983b10: "[. . .] Whereas substance subsists under the diversity of its[4] determinations . . ., the substrate remains, namely Socrates himself"). The substance of change is its very possibility in *Physics* I-2, I 8, II 1. The substance–accident opposition is therefore the primary cleavage in Aristotelian ontology: what "happens," the event, is not as such being: that an event *be* cannot be said except by referring to that to which the event happens; the grass is green; green *is* not the first heading, but the grass *is*; if I say that the green *is*, I mean the grass is green. Such is the tie between being and substance, looser than synonymy, tighter than homonymy.

Comment

The list of categories in Aristotelianism always remains quite empirical (as Kant remarks in the *Critique*, in seeking *Leitfaden*, a complete and organized enumeration of categories). The category is taken from language and, if we may put it this way, from the ways of *speaking of being* in the common culture; thus, in Γ 2, this list is elaborated, in gross terms: affection of . . . leading toward . . . (generation and corruption), quality, cause, effect, generation, negation of substance or of one of its derivatives. Thus, remarks Aristotle, by means of this system of intermediate references from one signification to another, substance makes its being beam forth as far as into non-being: an elegant solution to the problem broached by Parmenides and resolved in different ways by Plato (the "other") and Democritus (the "void"). For Aristotle, to say non-being is, means [that] there is an absence or privation of a form which is, by rights, first (the same at 1004a10-16 and 1032b3-6). So, finding the "accepted meanings" of being in experience, he refers them to and organizes them around a first meaning, without making recourse to the unity of a genus: "This, therefore, is the substance[5] whose principles and causes the phi-

---

[4] The French of the *Course* has *ces* instead of *ses*, "these" instead of "its," which is obviously an error.

[5] Tricot's translation has "the substances" (*op. cit.*, p. 112). [W. D. Ross: "If

losopher must apprehend" (1003b18). Aristotle wanted to push this primacy of substance to the extreme and strictly to subordinate the principles of logic or axioms to it by subordinating every axiom to the principle of identity and by interpreting this principle ontologically. Aristotle asks himself: in what sense can the axiom be said to be universal? Because it is said of the first in the order of *being*, namely *ousia*, *a being* is what it is: here is the ontological foundation of the principle of identity. The principle of identity is thus the logical expression of the principle of substance and not of thought's pact with itself. There is therefore no autonomy to logic, which is a propaedeutic to theoretical science. The instrumental function of logic is laid out in the situation of the principle of identity. There is a conflict among the attributes belonging to a single subject. The logic of contradiction situates this between the thus ... and the thus ... of attribution. Book Γ is going to be a trial between Heraclitus and Protagoras, as was Plato's *Theaetetus*. There is no indefinite thought, otherwise there will be no thought at all.

To negate the principle of contradiction is to negate that a being should be what it is, to take back from it its quiddity (its thinkability as substance, that is, its determination). It is reality that, by its equality to itself, founds the possibility of maintaining the stable reference to the subject itself throughout the duration of my affirmation. The definition of substance as permanence of being and as support of change is thus the root of the principle of identity.

Critical conclusion

This dominance of the problem of substance is of capital importance for the history of philosophy. It governs not only scholastic philosophy, but Cartesian, Spinozan, and Leibnizian philosophy. To say *is* is to say *subsists*. The problem: what is it that subsists? is thus equivalent to the question of being. But at what price?

1) Is this not to shrink the ontological problem, as Plato had said in the *Sophist* in positing being as the *triton ti* between permanence and change? Is this not to plunge ontology back into the alternative of constant change or immutability?

---

then, this is substance, it is of substances that the philosopher must grasp the principles and the causes." – Trans.]

2) Did not Aristotle shrink the ontological problem in a second way? In substituting the problem of substance for the problem of being, he introduced the enumeration of *substances*. He thus travels in reverse the path that Plato had traced from beings as Idea to the being of the Ideas. Aristotle will go from being as substance to beings that are substances: we see this in Aristotle's conclusion at 1003b17-18; from here we catch sight of the second vicissitude opened by book E 1: to seek the substance that is first among the substances and that determines a "first philosophy":[6] 1004a3-10 (which is perhaps interpolated, and in any case there is a parenthesis in the development concerning the forms of being).

3 That ontology is a theology

Book E, chapter 1, furnishes the final determination of "wisdom" (or philosophy) in defining a first philosophy, or "theology." It takes as already acquired the identification of etiology with ontology and of this with the investigation of "substance" (the first twenty-five lines of E 1 assure this suture).[7]

How will we take this new step? Through a rapid classification of the sciences according to the degree of being of their objects. This classification is therefore a classification in relation to substance. Whereas the first books of the *Metaphysics* oppose the universality of wisdom and the *particularity* of the sciences, E 1 offers a hierarchy of three sciences which form a "series"; in the same way that a while ago substance in general was the first term in a "series" of analogues, corresponding to the multiple ways in which being is spoken of, in the same way the series physics–mathematics–theology can be considered as a sequence marked

---

[6] Cf. already in Γ 2 the text 1004a3-10 inserted into the development of the forms of being: perhaps it is simply an interpolation reflecting the final state of the *Metaphysics*; it announces E 1 (PR). [This note is in part a repetition of the phrase which follows in the text.]

[7] E 1 nonetheless introduces a difficulty that is not easy to interpret: it is said that science *demonstrates* substance in its *ti esti* ["what it is"] and in its *ei esti* ["whether it is"], what we translate as its essence and its existence – and even that it is the same act of intellect that grasps the "what it is?" and the "whether it is?" What does this "is it?" about which there is no longer any question in the *Metaphysics* and which is omitted in the resumé of K signify? (PR)

out by the diverse meanings of the word substance; there are "secondary" substances relating to a "first" substance, just as there is a "second" meaning of the word being (accident, quantity, quality, etc.) and a first meaning: *ousia*, substance.

In what sense can one speak then of a "first" substance? What is this leading-meaning to which the other substances refer? We must acknowledge that E 1 is not very explicit; first of all the opposition among three terms is reduced in reality to two, for mathematical beings figure here only as something to remember; their definitive status will be fixed only in books M–N; the principal accent therefore bears on the opposition of physics and theology. Physics is called the science of "not-separate" and "not-unmoving" substances (1026a14).[8] These two words call for comment: "not-separate" has to do here with "formal substance" in the sense of Book A, which is inseparable from its matter; Aristotle therefore does not contradict himself when he calls sensible substance "separate": it is a question then of substance as "composed" of form and matter; it is separate in this sense that it can exist as an individual distinct from all others. As for the opposition between unmoving and moving, that takes us back to an essentially Platonic preoccupation.

What then will "first" philosophy and its object, "first" substance, be? First philosophy is the science "of beings at once separate and unmoving" (1026a16).[9] Aristotle does not state here what they are and how they are; the text obviously reserves the possibility that there could be many of them; the unicity of God according to Λ 7 and 9 as well as the multiplicity of unmoving movers according to *De caelo, Physics* VIII, and *Metaphysics* Λ 8 inscribes them in the framework traced to theology, which is thus the science of the divine more than of God; nor must we lose sight of the fact that the doctrine of the *Nous* of (*De anima*)[10] Book III is an aspect of this philosophy of substances (the reference in the *Metaphysics* is at 1026a6).

---

[8] In the *Course*, there is an erroneous reference to 1035b27. There is a difficulty in this passage, for, according to Tricot's translation, "Physics, in effect, studies separate beings, but not unchanging ones." Ricoeur does not entirely clarify this problem in the commentary that follows. [W. D. Ross: "natural science deals with things which are inseparable from matter but not immovable." – Trans.]

[9] *Id.*: an erroneous reference to 1036a.

[10] (*De anima*): between parentheses in the *Course*.

In defining "first philosophy" – a science of first, separate, unmoving substances – by theology,[11] one does not say anything about the precise nature of its object; we would be mistaken in prematurely identifying it with the god of Book Λ 7 and 9.

Conclusion to chapters 1 to 4

Having arrived at the end of this first part, we are ready once again to take up the problem posed by W. Jaeger concerning the coherence of Aristotelian ontology. Is there an incompatibility between *two* systems of thought, one that ends in "being as being" and one that ends in the god of Λ 7 (and in the unmoving movers of Λ 8 and *Physics* VIII)? Must one renounce having a universal ontology and a first (and, in consequence, particular) ontology fit together? Or, put more strongly, an ontology properly speaking and a theology? W. Jaeger does not believe so; according to him the different parts of the *Metaphysics* "did not arise out of the same act of reflection."[12] It is this doubt that is implicit throughout W. Jaeger's entire interpretation and which condemns him to presenting a purely *historical* interpretation, exclusive of a *systematic* interpretation of the *Metaphysics* such as the one that offers itself in its current order; we are faced with "periods" and no longer with logical "moments" of a system. What are we to think of such an interpretation?

We have seen the interest of a historical interpretation of the *Metaphysics* in chapter 1. But does this "evolutionary" reading exclude a "systematic" reading of the *Metaphysics*? This comes down to asking whether the elaboration of the current, not chronological, order of the *Metaphysics* is devoid of all sense, or whether the chronological order is the sole *meaningful* order of the *Metaphysics*. But, in order for the current order be meaningful, there would have had to be a reasonable passage from the one conception of ontology to the other, from the general ontology to theology, from the science of being as being to the science of separate substance.

But Aristotle has not overlooked this aporia: he elaborates it

---

11 1026a18.
12 Robinson's English translation, p. 218 (AC).

himself at E 1 1026a23:[13] "One might ask oneself whether first philosophy is universal." Answer: "If there exists an unmoving substance, the science of this substance must be prior and must be first philosophy, and it is universal in this way because first" (E 1 1026a28-32). This answer by Aristotle is the key to his *Metaphysics*. Hamelin, Owens, and Tricot[14] have opted in favor of Aristotle's coherence for the reasons that are condensed in this sentence of his. Let us try, then, to understand this decisive answer.

How can that which is "first" be "universal"?

We can understand this answer from Aristotle with the aid of the solution that he brought to a similar difficulty: the difficulty in passing from being as being to the *series* of the accepted meanings of being: substance, quality, quantity, place, time, etc.; Aristotle, on that occasion, clears a way between two untenable positions, one of which would consist in making being a genus which "caps" the categories as species, the other which leaves the accepted meanings of being in a dispersed state; the principle of the solution lies in an "analogical" and not a "generic" unity: the first accepted meaning of the word being – *ousia* – is the first of a series in which all the other terms refer to this primary meaning. If now we apply the same kind of reasoning to *ousia*, we will say there is a substance or a group of substances that realize to an eminent degree the nature of substance and that are the reference term for the whole series of substances which come after it. It is the same type of unity (πρὸς ἕν)[15] – analogical – that allows one to pass from τὸ ὂν ᾗ ὂν to ᾗ ουσια and from ᾗ ουσια to θεος.[16] It is in a similar sense that Tricot writes:[17] "The first being is nothing other than

---

[13] The same error in reference in the *Course*, which has 1036a.

[14] Octave Hamelin, *Le Système d'Aristote* (Alcan, 1907; Paris: Vrin, 1931), p. 405; Owens, *op. cit.*, pp. 176–177; Tricot, *Métaphysics, op. cit.*, pp. 172–173 and 333–334 (AC).

[15] *pros hen.*

[16] From *to on hei on* to *hei ousia* and from *hei ousia* to *hei on theos* (from "being as being" to "as substance" and from "as substance" to "as being god").

[17] Tricot invokes the unity of consecutive order in 1005a11 (see his note on p. 190) that Aristotle distinguishes from unity πρὸς ἕν. It would be necessary to make precise the connection between the two principles of serial order: the πρὸς ἕν and the τὰ τῷ ἐφεξῆς. Owens (p. 176) holds himself to πρὸς ἕν from Γ 1: unmoving substance is the first example of substance, as substance is the first example of being (PR).

being as being, because it is first in being, bare of all potentiality, pure form, which is realized as true substantiality whose study constitutes the *Metaphysics*."[18] What is *supremely* being is the first example of what *being in general* is; what will remain to be determined: 1) why the act that is pure and without potentiality is substance *par excellence*, 2) why substances mixed with potentialities are "hung" on substance without matter and "dependent" on it.

These are the two difficulties which will occupy us in what remains. The first one will not be resolved until we have established, through actual examination of the least noble substance, that it is form that makes for the substantiality of substance. The second will be similarly resolved if one establishes that the line of descent of all substances from the supreme substance rests on *finality* – on the attraction of Desire, as one will later put it – lacking a line of descent by means of causality, of creation. The connection through finality will assure the reference of all beings to the first being. "If the scale of beings is presented as a series hierarchized from least to most perfect," says Tricot, "the science that has as its object infinitely perfect being extends its hold over all the lesser beings considered as beings."[19] In other words, to know God would be to know the being of every being. But Aristotle has not yet established the double series of proofs that justify the passage from general ontology to theology: the reduction of substance to form is worked out in the group Z H Θ and the nature of supreme substance established in Book Λ, and thereby the connection to finality of all the other substances to the "unmoving" substance (if one may in any case speak of demonstration with respect to mere allusions). This is why, in Book E, Aristotle again gives a hypothetical turn to his answer: "If there exists an unmoving substance, the science of this substance must be prior and must be first philosophy and it is universal in this way because it is first." It is this answer, still hypothetical and in a way held in suspense, that assures the coherence of the *Metaphysics* in its current order and justifies the very revisions whose history W. Jaeger has attempted to trace.[20]

---

[18] Tricot, *id.*, p. 172 (AC).

[19] *Id.*, p. 173 (AC).

[20] Cf. Gilson on the chronological and the pedagogical orders in the *Metaphysics*, in Owens, *op. cit.*, Préface, p. vii–viii (PR).

Second Part

Being and Substance

Introduction

Let us first recall the results Aristotle attains by the end of the introductory books of the *Metaphysics*, A–E 1:

1) Wisdom is the science of first causes and first principles.
2) The science of first causes is the science of being as being, but is not being as being an empty term if one intends to treat it as a supreme genus and its signification as distributed according to the categories? Does the object of metaphysics vanish for all that? NO, if in the series of accepted meanings of being there is one that dominates and to which all the rest refer in a relationship of homonymy by analogy (*kath' en* = καθ' ἕν).
3) This first term is substance; everything about which one says "is" refers to that which is *par excellence*: *ousia*. Z 1 puts it this way: "And in truth the eternal object of all present and past investigation, the problem always in question: What is being? comes down to asking: What is substance?" (1028b2-3).[1]
4) Finally, philosophy is the science of the substance that comes at

---

[1] This movement of thought is strikingly summarized in the first pages of Rodier's article "Remarques sur la conception de la substance" (*Année philosophique*, 1909): pp. 1–11, reprinted in *Études de philosophie grecque*, pp. 165ff. "In other words, complete being is substance and all the other things about which one affirms being are not within *ousia*'s extension as its species, but within its grasp as its parts" (p. 169) (PR).

the head of a hierarchy of substances; it is the science of what is most divine. It is *theology*.

Having arrived at this point, one would expect a determination of this substance *par excellence*, the elaboration of a theology: in fact, this theology presents itself as an empty framework, since we do not know whether there is a divine substance or what it is. (Owens notes that this way of proceeding is adapted to a certain type of auditor who already admits there is something like a theology; Aristotle does not proceed radically in some sort of intellectual void, but on the historical basis of a knowledge that is physical, logical and physical.)

But this is not what the *Metaphysics* offers us. Apart from a quite important group of chapters which conclude Book E and to which we shall return (E 2–4, which considerably enlarges the notion of being so as to create an entry to other directions of research and which Jaeger sees as the chapters that suture the *Metaphysics* together), the *Metaphysics* moves on to the fundamental books Z H, devoted to *sensible substance*.

The treatment of the first substance that ought to bring a first philosophy or theology to its conclusion is thus put off until the group Λ M N. What does this procedure indicate?

If one follows Werner Jaeger, one will content oneself with a "historical" answer and see in the insertion of books Z H Θ a testimony to Aristotle's evolution: leaving behind the alternative of the sensible and the intelligible, of the moving and unmoving, Aristotle no longer identifies the object of philosophy with the unmoving; by inserting the theory of *sensible* substance he entirely surpasses this wholly Platonic alternative and makes possible a philosophy of being as being that envelopes both species of substances.

But if, as we have shown, the current arrangement is, even if late, a meaningful one, if one can pass from being as being to being as first of beings, the theory of sensible substance must have a function in relation to this final program that justifies the current arrangement of the *Metaphysics*.

Aristotle's intention in integrating the conclusions of his *Physics* (and his *Logic*) with the *Metaphysics* must have been to use the knowledge of sensible substance as a "long detour" in order to get past sensible substance. The expression "long detour" is Platonic, it is true; but it is in a specifically anti-Platonic sense that Aristotle takes this detour, since it is a detour "from below" and not "from above." To fill the empty framework of the "theology" it is necessary to pass through the world, in order to find there the indication of what true substance, first substance, might be, namely, as we shall see, substance without matter or potentiality. Thus Aristotle "wonders" like Plato; but he does not "convert" like Plato; the long detour of Z H functions as a worldly stage in his philosophy.

We take up therefore the group Z H, which constitutes something like a reprise of the physics (and the logic) of sensible substance in the *Metaphysics*.

We will treat first (chaps 1 and 2) sensible substance for itself.

We will ask ourselves up to what point Aristotle creates a philosophy of "the individual," radically opposed to the philosophy of "signification" by which Plato gets under way, and if Aristotle is not still 'platonizing' in his philosophy of forms – even sensible ones (chap. 3).

Only then (chap. 4) shall we be able to relate this doctrine to the great theological "design" of the *Metaphysics* and ask ourselves whether Aristotle has fulfilled his program and attained his goal.

Chapter 16

Sensible Substance: Substance as Substrate

If substance is being *par excellence*, substance in turn is determined according to many accepted meanings. (Note the way in which Aristotle's thought proceeds, which, never ceasing to come up with new meanings, picks out the most important one and moves in this way from one determination to the next.) The whole analysis is going to be oriented toward the identification of substance with its form or more exactly its "quiddity" (τὸ τί ἦν εἶναι);[1] but this identification is singularly laborious and makes Z in particular one of the most complex books of the *Metaphysics*, where multiple preoccupations and above all multiple presuppositions are interwoven.

One difficulty immediately blocks the way: *ousia* means four things (beginning of Z 3), only one of which, in fact, the fourth one, is truly perplexing: *ousia* means quiddity, universal, genus, and subject. "Universal" and "genus" cause us no difficulty, because it will be easy to show (Z 13 and 14) that the universal and the genus are "in another thing," therefore do not exist "in itself" (with reference to itself, *kath'auto*). On the contrary, Aristotle hesitates about arranging the two remaining meanings in relation to each other; substance, on the one hand, is what it belongs to something to be, therefore its *ground of knowability*. Substance, on the other hand, is what "lies under" the substrate or subject (ὑποκείμενον).[2]

---

[1] *to ti en einai.*

[2] *hupokeimenon.*

1 The double meaning of "substrate"

What is it that pleads in favor of the identification of substance as substrate? What is it that makes it difficult to make that identification? It is the double meaning of the word substrate, which pleads both for and against the identification. The subject, *from the logical point of view*, is the subject of attribution, as all the rest affirms; *from the physical point of view*, the subject is that to which determinations happen: it is matter. So everything invites us to identify substance with the subject of attribution, while making us loath to identify it with matter. Let us look therefore at the two sides of the question.

a) The logical subject

It is this primary sense that is the first one affirmed at Γ 3: "The subject is that which all the rest affirm and which is not itself affirmed of anything"; and, further on, "substance is that which is not predicated of a subject, but . . . on the contrary, it is about what all the rest are affirmed." This identification of substance fits well with an initial trimming down of the idea of substance, one that makes it a *kath'auto pephukos* = καθ' αὐτὸ πεφυκός (Z 1. Tricot translates: "that which has its own existence").[3] In this sense substance is "the real and determined subject": this subject is "the substance and the individual";[4] it is *that about which* one says all the rest. For Rodier, "substance properly speaking, is what is always subject and never attribute, in the same way that the categories are what is always attribute and never subject."[5]

This first trimming down therefore takes place on the level of language. Le Blond has shown the weight in Aristotle's work of what he calls "schemes of language," and which, according to him, interact concurrently with "schemes of industry" (more exactly of artificial production) and "biological schemes" (more exactly of generation and spontaneous movement).[6] Many of the difficulties of the Aristotelian theory of substance, according to Le Blond, have

---

[3] Z 1 1028a23.
[4] Tricot, *op. cit.*, p. 348 (AC) [Z 1 1028a26].
[5] Rodier, *op. cit.*, p. 170 (AC).
[6] Jean-Marie Le Blond, *Logique et méthode chez Aristote* [Paris: Vrin, 1939] (AC).

to do with the conjunction of these grammatical, manufacturing, and vitalist schemes. Consequently, we first approach substance starting from the language schemes. ("Without a doubt, the most important analysis of this whole book [the *Physics*] which ends with the notion of substance and that of matter is guided by the form of the propositions in which every change is expressed.")[7] The grammatical analysis presupposed here is brought to light in *Physics* I 5; it can be stated something like this: all change moves from one pole to the other of a pair of contraries, and this displacement from one pole to the other is done on the basis of a "subsisting" principle (190a15-24). For example, we say, "a man subsists when he becomes educated and he is still the same man" (190a6-12), whereas "being unlearned and illiterate do not subsist, neither as simple nor as united to their subject."

The opposition between a – permanent – subject and its changing attributes is further accentuated in that the pair of contraries (into which change is logically analyzed) conceals the opposition between the negative and the affirmative (uneducated, educated) so that the substrate is discerned through its being opposed to privation. (Le Blond cites the noteworthy commentary of Simplicius: "He begins by showing the difference between privation and the substrate starting from language before showing it in the nature of the things.")[8] The subject is not the starting point of the change (from uneducated to educated), but *that which is changed*. An assimilation is therefore brought about between the attribute (κατηγορούμενον, *Physics* I 6) and the accident (συμβεβηκός),[9] and one can even say that "the distinction, so important in his philosophy, between substance and accident, appears here as the transposition of the grammatical subject–attribute pair."[10] To be sure, this does not explain all the determinations of substance, above all not those of unmoving substance, the last object of philosophy as theology, but it does explain at least two things: first of all, the very first coincidence of the two meanings of substance, the subject of attribution and the substrate of change (Δ 7 1017b10), a coincidence assured by the grammatical analysis of change itself (it is

---

7   *Id., op. cit.*, p. 310 (AC).

8   *Id.*, p. 312, n. 1 (AC).

9   Reading for attribute and accident: *kategoroumenon* and *sumbebekos*. The reference in the *Course* is erroneous: Aristotle speaks of the attribute and the accident in *Physics* IV 186a9ff.

10 Le Blond, *op. cit.*, p. 312 (AC).

precisely from there that, in a little while, the difficulty will arise, since the substrate of change will not be form but matter); next it explains that the true substance – the first substance, as Aristotle puts it – is the individual. This thesis is fundamental in *Categories* 5, 3, and *Physics* I 7: for if one can say "the just is white," "just" is certainly the subject in this proposition, but one cannot say about it that it is "never an attribute"; finally, there are only individuals which are never attributes, which are the final (Δ 8 1017b23) or first (Z 3 1029a1) subjects; Z 16 1041a4 will say the same more energetically: "Nothing general or common is substance," and this too will create difficulties, this time no longer through the possible confusion of substance and matter, but through its clashing with the theory of science; in effect, if it is true that there is science only of the general, how will there be a science of substance? We do not say that the aporia is insoluble, and in fact Aristotle does resolve it: we say only that the schema of language which identifies substance and subject, subject of attribution and subject of change, leads to a philosophy of individuality with all its difficulties.

What are we to think of this influence of language schemes on the theory of substance? We know the severity against Aristotle with which Brunschvicg concludes his *Les Âges de l'intelligence*.[11] But we must say two things in defense of Aristotle.

First that these language schemes do not determine everything in his philosophy, precisely since they interact with the other schemes drawn from human art and the natural productions of life.

But above all that he has not simply projected an already completed grammatical analysis onto the theory of substance; one can even say that the exorbitant privilege of the attributive proposition was consolidated through the fecundity of the physical analysis of reality into substance and accident that it allowed; it is necessary to know how to retrieve the effort directed at the *intelligibility of the sensible* that the analysis of reality into substance and accident represents, in leaving behind a Platonism that remains Heraclitean when faced with the sensible. The Greek language oscillates between two propositional analyses: the subject–verb analysis, as one sees in the *Theaetetus* and *Sophist*, and the subject–copula–attribute analysis; does one speak about the subject's *actions* or

---

[11] Léon Brunschvicg, *Les Âges de l'intelligence* (Paris: Alcan, 1924).

to *qualify* the subject? *to do* or *to be*?[12] Privileging the attributive proposition (Socrates is educated) over the verbal proposition
(Socrates speaks) allows ordering the qualities in terms of pairs
of contraries; it is this analysis into *contraries* that enhances the
standing of the adjectives at the expense of the verbs; the attributive proposition also confirms the privileging of the verb *to be*
imposed by Parmenides, by the Eleatic Sophists and their aporias
of attribution: whence the recoil of the theory of substance on its
own verbal instrument.

b) The material substrate

If substance is defined as the first subject, is it not necessary to say
that the true subject, the *hupokeimenon*, is matter? Z 3 undertakes
to dissipate this difficulty, directly issuing from the previous analysis, and which creates an obstacle on the path that will lead to
identifying substance with form, and first substance, the ultimate
object of investigation, with form without matter.

Let us see how Aristotle himself presents the difficulty in Z
3 (beginning from 1029a10): if one removes everything that is
attributed to a subject, what remains? Undetermined matter, it
seems, since one will have removed all the quantitative determinations (length, width, and depth); what remains is that which all
these determinations determine, that is, the purely undetermined,
the matter: "I call matter," Aristotle clarifies, "that which is of
itself neither determinate existence, nor of a certain quality, nor
of any other of the categories by which being is determined"
(1029a19-20). One arrives at the paradox that matter will be substance to such a point that the substance will be its predicate: X
is a man. In other words, matter does not have the determination
of the first category, which Aristotle expresses as follows: "All the
categories other than substance are predicable of substance, and
substance itself is predicated of matter" (1029a23). And Aristotle
concludes: "To consider the question under this aspect, it results
therefore logically that matter is substance" (1029a27).

One will note that this analysis, conducted like the analysis of
a piece of wax in the *Second Meditation*, leads to a diametrically
opposed result. Descartes says: what remains when everything
changes is a determinable space of diverse materials, because it

---

[12] "To do" and "to be" are in English in the *Course*. – Trans.

is what is *intelligible*; Aristotle's grammatical analysis prevents him from stopping at a *quantitative* determination of substance, because every magnitude falls under the category of quantity which is spoken of not under the heading of being, but under that of attribution; measurement is on the side of the attribute, not on that of the subject. Hence it is necessary to go all the way to undetermined root.

How will Aristotle get out of this difficulty? By returning to the meaning of substance: it is not enough to say that substance is subject. It is necessary to add: *determined* subject. Substance must be *ti*, something. Z 1 had prepared this riposte: "a real and determined subject ... the individual" (1028a27). Only the One, the individual, has its own existence (*kath'auto*). This precision is in reality a turnabout in relation to the analysis of language, because the individual is no longer an "X" *without* its determinations, but "such a One" *with* its determinations; so, the other categories are not external to substance, but rather the explanation of the determinations that make a substance a determined something. Tricot puts it well: "It would be ... to denature (Aristotle's thought) to understand that substance can exist without the other categories, for a substance with no determination whatsoever is an impossibility as obviously as is a quality without substance. In reality, Aristotle means that, unlike the other categories, substance alone can exist in a separate state. Substance is nothing other than the individual thing, *complete by itself*, with all its qualities and its relations; and as such, it can exist separately."[13]

One thus comes to say that the priority of substance over the categories (quality, quantity, etc.) is the priority of the concrete over the abstract, of the individual over its properties, therefore of the implicit totality of determinations over their explicit analysis in terms of the categories. The primacy of the *determined* comes therefore to *limit* the apparent consequence of the subject–predicate analysis.

But is this answer tenable? In what sense do the accidents happen to substance if substance contains its determination? Is it not necessary that substance be absolutely not determinable in order to be absolutely determined? Owens notes that only the divine substance will ultimately be not determinable, precisely because it

---

[13] *Metaphysics*, trad. pp. 348–349 (AC) [Ricoeur cites Tricot's translation as published by Vrin in a single volume in 1933].

is without matter and that this answer is compatible only with difficulty with the status of sensible substance, which is said to *receive* its determinations. If it receives them, what does it have that it has not received? And, if it has received everything, what is it if not radically undetermined matter? We have to ask ourselves therefore about the status of matter in Aristotelian substance, in order to understand in what sense it is and is not substance, and to make apparent the identity between substance and form, toward which all this analysis tends.

2 The status of matter in Aristotelian substance

This is a question that Z 3 does not resolve. Z 3 goes straight to the identification of substance with quiddity, which is the principal plan of books Z H. The problem can be resolved only by putting the form–matter pair together with a new one, *potency–act*, which one can say is Aristotle's true discovery.

a) The Aristotelian style of explanation

A few words first about the significance of those thought frameworks that present themselves in pairs. Their situation in the Aristotelian edifice is difficult to make precise, for they are called principles (*archai*: the first books of the *Physics* are called *peri archon* by Aristotle himself, when he refers to them), without their being established *a priori* or proceeding from experience. They are rather functional or structural analogies, both *suggested* by common experience and its regularities and *imposed* on experience as an interpretive grid. According to Le Blond, they stem from an "organization of the given" that compensates for the fragmentation of science based on its disparate objects through a unity of style or way of proceeding; their uncertain situation between the empirical and the *a priori* is due to their function in investigation which entirely escapes the logic of the Organon, which has more to do with putting an already constituted knowledge into shape; according to *Physics* I 1 184a12–184b15,[14] they permit analyzing indistinct ensembles; therefore these "principles"

---

[14] Text commented on by Le Blond, *op. cit.*, pp. 284–291; he cites Werner Jaeger: "Analysis is the soul of Aristotelian thought" (PR).

are the instruments for an analysis of the real different from the division into homogeneous parts in the manner of Democritus: for to divide into causes is not to divide into things. In this way, Aristotle takes up anew the old problem of the one and the many. At the same time it appears that the real genius of Aristotle lies not in the classifying thought of genera and differentiating species, but in explanation. To classify is always to situate in a context that allows discovery and recognition. To explain is to analyze the object itself by making it known through its elements. As a result:

1) The notion of matter stems from an *explanatory* analysis rather than a classifying one.
2) This functional analysis takes place through correlative terms; so it is vain to seek a matter in itself, an absolute one, one aspect of the real plays the role of matter in relation to another aspect that plays the role of form.
3) Finally, this explanatory scheme of a correlative type amounts to a rational organization of experience that is neither *a priori* nor properly experimental. Le Blond sees in this the conjunction of the schemes of language, industry, biology.

We shall take the pair matter–form as far as possible without making recourse to the pair potency–act (by remaining with the viewpoint of matter), then we shall see how the potency–act pair completes the meaning.

b) *The correlative function of matter*

In his *Introduction à la Physique d'Aristote*, Mansion emphasizes that the matter–form pair is a static pair.[15] He refers to the way a being is structured such as it is, such that it finds itself realized (a bed, a person, an animal). The pair potency–act is a dynamic pair: it introduces becoming. But the distinction, as we are going to see, is quite unstable, because matter plays many roles. Matter could be defined without reference to potency if it were always considered as fundamentally *passive* (that which receives determinations) and therefore as in itself undetermined and finally absolutely unknowable. Inert, unlimited, unknowable, so it is in Z 3, which for that reason eliminates it from the definition of substance

---

[15] Mansion, *op. cit.* (cf. p. 159), pp. 134–5 (AC).

that is determined as individual. But matter is never treated by Aristotle as the purely undetermined; it is a correlative: the wood is matter for the bed, the tissues for the organs, the human for science. Le Blond shows that this oscillation comes from the fact that undetermined matter is suggested by the language schemes (it is what remains when one eliminates the attributive determinations); determined matter is the material of the industrial schemes; it is what one draws the thing produced from. The three expositions (*Physics* II 1–3, *Metaphysics* Z 7, and *Parts of Animals* I 1) confirm that the analysis is no longer static but always refers to stages followed in a process of production. Matter is then an analogical function common to all productions and presupposes the fundamental analogy between human art and nature; on the one side, art imitates nature (example: digestion as cooking, respiration as bellows, etc.); on the other, the procedures of art clearly show the proceedings of nature. For example, in *Physics* II 3, the oldest exposition, the examples are almost all examples of fabrication. [*Metaphysics*] Δ 1, for that matter, goes directly from handy work to rule-governed art and wisdom. *Metaphysics* Z 7–9, further perfected, sets aside accidental production and subordinates production by nature to production by industry for understanding things (cf. the syllogism of "invention: for such a goal, such means, for such means, such material which governs the syllogism of realization"). We are faced therefore with a distinction of an analogical character, transported from the experience of things being made in nature. Whence a first retouching of the idea of matter: it is no longer identified with an internal, undetermined, unknowable substrate; instead it represents the least determined in relation to the most determined in a process of fabrication.

Yet Le Blond corrects this first interpretation through a second one: "If the distinction of causes is based on making things, the deeper study of each of the causes is carried out from a biological point of view."[16] That is going to introduce an important change in matter, which not only acquires a relative determination but loses its inertia and calls for reference to potency. It is the biological scheme that governs the great distinction of movements into natural ones and violent ones: the locomotion of the living and the throwing of a projectile. In this perspective, what does matter signify? It has the same signification as the organ does with respect

---

16 Le Blond, *op. cit.*, p. 356 (AC).

to function, that the eye has for vision (*On the Soul* II 1, 412b18), that the differentiated tissues (hand–face) have in connection to the organs.

Suddenly a new meaning of matter appears, based on the model of the connection of desire to the desirable. *Physics* I 9: "It is, therefore, the matter that desires the form, as the female desires the male" (192a23, 200a42, 200b5).[17] We are close to the Platonic Eros, the son of poverty; matter is then the system of means and obstacles by which a form makes its way into existence.

But then the – once plain – borders become blurred among the four causes: the form tends to be confused with the end in the biological scheme, while it is distinguished from it in the productive scheme (*Metaphysics* H 2 1043a14, and more plainly still *Physics* II 8 200a3), whereas matter becomes the necessity that allows and prevents, sometimes collaborating, sometimes a principle of defeat, of chance, of monstrosity.

c) Matter and potency

The potency–act distinction is the peak of the metaphysical analysis of the real, but also the highest difficulty, for the idea of potency introduces considerable difficulties in turn. Let us look first at how Aristotle introduces this notion. Next we will examine, in d), the aporias of potency.

In truth, the *Metaphysics* does not really succeed in slowing down the recourse to this distinction. From the point of view of the structure of the *Metaphysics*, this ontological distinction is introduced only in Book Θ, but it is foreseen in the system thanks to the distinction of the meanings of Being presented at E 2:[18] to be by accident (E 3–4) – to be in the categories – to be as true. But in reality this notion is introduced much earlier. H 1, which epitomizes Z, says: "I call matter that which not being a determined being in act is in potency solely a determined being";[19] and H 2 begins: "Since there is unanimous agreement about the subject considered as substrate and as matter, and it is this which exists in potency, it remains for us to speak about what is the substance of

---

[17] Uncertain references, except for 192a23 (AC).
[18] In fact "beginning from" E 2. Tricot titles E 3 "The Nature of the Accident" and E 4 "Being in the Sense of True" (AC).
[19] H 1 1042a25.

sensible things considered as act" (cf. the series H 2 1042b9-10; 1043a32-b2; H 6 1045a23-24; 29-30; 1045b18-19).

Let us look now at how the notion of potency is introduced in *Physics* III 1–3 (cf. equally *Metaphysics* Δ 12 and Θ).

The notion of matter is conquered with difficulty in Book I of the *Physics*, against the Eleatic and Platonic tradition of non-being which renders a physics impossible; every effort to distinguish matter from non-being in the proper sense tends at the same time to draw it to the side of substance. It is through the introduction of the considerations on "nature" at the beginning of Book II that the apparent privilege of matter is dethroned. Let us here also take a look at the two faces of the question in Book I and then in Book II.

Book I, chapters 7–9, arrives at the idea of matter through an analysis of generation; for there to be generation, it is necessary that there be a passage from a contrary to a contrary and a permanence of something; but, the initial term (*ek tinos*) is designated negatively in relation to the final term (*eis ti*); it is therefore a *privation* (not-white, not-musician). But, in that the subject is distinguished from the contraries as a third principle, the subject that remains is thereby distinguished from the initial privation. It is this analysis that governs the distinction between matter and non-being. For privation is the true non-being, non-being for itself. Therefore the matter is the subject that remains: to say that the man is not-musician by accident is to say that the matter is non-being by accident.

Aristotle thinks to escape here the Eleatic aporias about the impossibility of generation: for from non-being nothing is born, nor from being becoming. If one distinguishes the subject and the starting point of generation, one has at the same time the permanence of being (as subject) and generation starting from non-being (as privation); but it is evident that this is so in both cases by accident (for it is neither necessary that the man become educated, nor that the uneducated start to become educated). What is more, Aristotle ([*Physics*] I 9) thinks he has caught Plato's mistake; Plato too has confused matter and non-being in confusing the subject that remains and the privation that gets abolished in the positive contrary wherein the form realizes itself; in particular, Plato has grouped together and confused in the Dyad of the Large and Small the double function of privation and substrate.[20] This concern

---

[20]   192a10-11.

to render physics possible, by distinguishing the matter–substrate and the initial privation in the play of contraries, tends to put matter in first place: "it is almost and in some manner substance" (I 9 192a6),[21] whereas privation is not substance in any way. Everything that distinguishes matter from privation, and therefore from nothing, puts matter on the side of being, of *ousia*. This is why Book I ends with two aspects that glorify matter, if one may put it this way:

- "The subject of desire is matter, in the same way that a female desires a male and the ugly the beautiful; except that it is not ugly in itself, but by accident" (192a22-24). This means that what there is negative in desire is not the desire as such, but the privation of something, therefore the non-being by accident.
- It [matter] is non-generable and imperishable: it is true in a precise sense (cf. 193a10-13); this text should be compared with the passage of *Physics* I 7 cited above.[22]

Nothing therefore lets us foresee the primacy of form. Yet Book I concludes with this warning: "Now let us continue our discourse by taking a new starting point." This new starting point is going to be the introduction of the idea of *nature* which has not yet appeared, since one has solely sought for "the existence of principles, their nature, and their number" (*Physics* I, end).

The introduction of the idea of nature is going to give the advantage to form, as the consideration of the determined and the individual in *Metaphysics* Z 3 has done. The *rapprochement* imposes itself even more in that *Physics* II 1 says straight away that to have a nature is to be a substance (192b33). But to have a nature, to be by nature or according to nature, is to have in itself, immanently (not externally as in art) and essentially (not by accident), the principle of its movement and its rest (this definition of nature is given in 192b21-22). Will someone say that matter constitutes nature? "In a sense," yes (193a28): in a sense, one calls nature the matter that serves as the subject immanent to each of the things

---

[21] In the translation by Annick Stevens (Paris: Vrin, 1999 and 2008): "The one, matter is at hand [*proche*], and in a certain manner a be-ingness [*une étance*]" (p. 96). [Hardie and Gaye (*Complete Works*): "the matter is nearly, in a sense *is*, substance." – Trans.]

[22] Rather I 8.

that have in them a principle of movement and of change. But, in a more decisive sense, the permanence of the substrate no longer suffices to define a being as existing "by nature." What is going to disqualify matter is that it is on the side of potency, whereas form will be on the side of act: "For each thing is said to be what it is more when it is in act than when it is in potency"; and the neighboring argument: becoming moves *toward* the form; "therefore it is the form that is nature" (193b18). The recourse to the potency–act pair (that is, potentiality–fulfillment) introduces a criterion for substance, parallel to that of *determination* on the level of the thinkable, of the identifiable invoked at *Metaphysics* Z 3; this time it is a question of a criterion of *fulfillment*, of *perfection* attained in the finite.

So, *Physics* II identifies *ousia* and nature; but nature is the principle of movement: it is the structure of movement that is now going to impose the difficult notion of potency; potency is what makes movement possible and movement is what makes physics possible. By taking potency up within the framework of a study of movement, one acquires only one of the senses of potency, but the most fundamental one as [*Metaphysics*] Θ 1 1046a1 recalls (Θ 1–5 will remain within this framework of the potency of motion which is potency *par excellence*, κυρίως),[23] which is based on [*Metaphysics*] Δ 12 1019a15. The first two meanings that Δ 12 gives to potency refer to movement: "One calls potency the principle of movement or of change which is in an *other* being or in the same being as other"[24] (example: the potency to build which is in an other than the house, the potency to heal which can be found in the sick person, but not as actually getting better). In the first sense, potency is the potency to do something, the capacity of an agent to produce a movement "in an other." In the second sense, potency is the potency to undergo, to receive a change or a movement from an other (or from oneself as other).

From where does Aristotle draw this notion? From an inspection of reality? Not at all: the way in which it is introduced in *Physics* III shows very well that what is at issue is a sort of preparatory ontological axiom with which one approaches the real. *Physics* III 1 begins brusquely: "First it is necessary to distinguish that which is fully in act and that which is partly in act, partly

---

[23] *kurios.*
[24] Δ 12 1019a15.

in potency, and what in the determined individual τὸ δὲ τι, or in quantity, or in quality, and similarly for all the categories of being" (200b26-27). Aristotle, armed with this distinction of act and potency, comes then to change, which is *manifest* (as nature itself is "*manifest* among the manifest things," 193a5). This distinction being posited allows constructing a definition of change, which too is posited: "Being given the distinction in each genus of that which is in entelechy and that which is in potency, the entelechy of that which is in potency as such, this is movement" (201a10). One gives examples of this, applications that allow elucidating the meaning of each of the "schemes of industry" (Le Blond), once one will have stated which aporias the definition of movement in terms of potency is meant to resolve. The example of construction is clear. It is an example of movement as growth (therefore of quantity): construction is more than the constructible (pure potency); the house builds itself (is built) actually; this actuality in the potentiality is translated by the substantives ending in –*sis* (οἴκησις, δόμησις, μάθησις, ἰάτρευσις, κύλισις)[25] (or, in French [and English], in –*tion*: construction, rotation). But if we do have examples, in no way do we have proofs. Why? Because this notion does not spring from nothing, even if it precedes experience and in some way is encountered in it; it is the solution to the aporias transmitted by the Ancients: [*Physics*] III 2 begins thus: "The proof that this explanation is good is taken from those which the Ancients[26] have given us with respect to movement and from the difficulty of defining it otherwise."

What difficulties does Aristotle have to face? The defeat of thought regarding "passing" as such, passing from nothing to something or from something to nothing (generation and corruption). (The passage of something from nothing makes for a difficulty; Δ 12 makes precise that potency is oriented toward being-more and that in the other direction it would be better to speak of impotence), passage from one place to another, from one quality to the other, from one size to the other. This defeat can be overcome only if one escapes from the at first glance invincible dichotomy between the determined and the undetermined (or the

---

[25] *oikesis, domesis, mathesis, hiatreusis, kulisis* (*oikesis*: "action of dwelling"; *domesis*: "action of building"; *mathesis*: "action of learning"; *iatreusis*: "action of healing"; *kulisis*: "action of rolling"; cf. *Physics* III 1 201a9).
[26] Tricot's translation: "the others." [W. D. Ross agrees. – Trans.]

indefinite, 'αόριστον,[27] cf. III 1 201b25). The idea of potency allows opening a middle way that would be a new way: potency stands *between the possible and the real*. For this, it was *necessary* to distinguish potency and act and to elaborate the difficult notion of an *act of what is in potency*, in brief, the idea of an "imperfect act." "Movement is indeed a certain act, but an incomplete one; and that because the thing in potency, of which the movement is the act, is incomplete. This is why it is certainly difficult to grasp its nature: in effect, it would be necessary to place it in privation, or in potency, or in pure act; but none of these seems admissible. What remains therefore is our way of conceiving it as a certain act; but an act as we have defined it is not easy to understand, nonetheless it is admissible" (201b30–202a2).

d) The difficulties of potency

Potency is therefore implicated in movement as "passage," but what is it in itself, since movement, about which one says that it is *manifest*, is not exactly potency, but the act of that which is in potency insofar as it is in potency? Bare potency is therefore not manifest, but thought as a "principle" (one had spoken in this way of the substrate in *Physics* I). But is it thinkable? If potency is called a "principle," it is, it seems, thinkable. Is that the case?

We must admit that the word *potency* introduces not only a new ontological dimension – namely, unfulfilled being, the passage to being – but also new hesitations; for this notion, destined to seal in some way the ontological signification of matter, is handed over to the same oscillations among multiple interpretive schemes: 1) it is, on the one hand, the possible demanded by language, in particular by every judgment about the future and more generally by every judgment that does not bear on the eternal; in brief, it is the possible as a modality of judgment, in other words it is the contingency in an affirmation; but the possible so understood has only negative determinations; according to [*Metaphysics*] Δ 12 1019b27, this is "something whose contrary is not necessarily false"; in particular in relation to future contingents, it is the possibility of escaping the principle of non-contradiction (of two opposed propositions, one is necessarily true, the other false), which is valid only for the past or for the present; 2) but potency is, on the other hand, a tendency

---

27 *aoriston.*

– whether it be as a capacity to do, or as an aptitude to undergo; it is therefore something like an inclination (*nisus*), a thrust; this is the true Aristotelian sense, the one that dominates the relationship of matter to form and allows one to say: "Matter reaches toward the[28] form" (Θ 8 1050a15); it is this second meaning that subordinates the industrial schemes to the biological ones; for, as Le Blond says, the marble does not want to be "God, table, or basin." It is only in the biological scheme of potency that the definitions of potency take their full meaning as faculty rather than bare possibility. Even passive potency, that is, "the faculty of being changed or moved by another [being] or by itself insofar as other" (*Metaphysics* Δ 12 1019a19), even though it should be only a potency to submit, is already a potency for something. One never attains pure matter which is an abstract limit because one never encounters the possibility of anything whatsoever, but the determined aptitude; as Tricot says in his commentary on Δ 12: "The patient is in a state of undergoing, of responding by a sort of connivance to the incitations and motions of the agent":[29] this is the *ordinatio ad finem* of the scholastics. The change therefore refers back, through its "imperfect act," not to "pure indeterminacy," but to the "capable of"; one only ever grasps the determinate in its potentiality. Pure possibility indifferent to contraries is incapable of rendering an account of the fact of change: change implies determinate powers pinpointed through their relation to the occurrence of "forms," not the bare contingency of the possible. (We leave aside the difficulties introduced by Book Θ, beginning in chapter 5, which puts in question the still simple analysis which preceded it.)

What is the result as regards matter? That matter is not "I know not what thing in itself, opaque and inert, impenetrable to thought, and that one could conceive of only by divesting a thing of all its qualities; it is exclusively the indeterminate in relation to something more determined."[30] "We should really say again that what is matter relative to a more determined thing is form relative to a simpler thing: and also that everything that is form in relation to its simple elements is matter for a more complex thing. In brief, as substance, matter and form are relative terms."[31]

---

[28] Tricot's translation has: "toward *its* form." [W. D. Ross agrees. – Trans.]
[29] Tricot, *op. cit.*, p. 284 (AC).
[30] Rodier, *op. cit.*, p. 171 (AC).
[31] *Id.* (AC).

"Potency" has therefore attested to the relativity of matter to some form; even though it is always the form that one names and that one thinks.

Chapter 17

Sensible Substance (continued): Substance as Form

Introduction

a) The situation of this doctrine in the Metaphysics

The entire Aristotelian analysis of substance is oriented in one direction; since one only knows matter if it is already form (the wood in relation to its proper matter) or form in potency (the future statue), everything that there is of intelligibility and of being in sensible substances is concentrated in the form that metaphysical analysis distinguishes from the matter. In turn, this extraordinarily laborious analysis (one of the longest in the *Metaphysics*: it occupies nearly all of the interminable Book Z, principally Z 4–12, plus a good part of Book H; it is what is taken up anew in Book Θ with the distinction of act and potency). This complicated analysis is meant to set up the investigation of the being or the beings that are pure forms, pure acts. As a result, this identification of substance and form is the goal of the group Z H Θ and, in its turn, the way to the "theology" of group Λ M N.

b) Structure of the argumentation

The reduction of substance to form answers to two converging orders of consideration: logical and physical. The form is everything knowable about things; the form is the whole reality of what produces and what is produced. This double demonstration is carried out following a quite subtle order: first logical in Z 4–6, then physical (Z 7–9), then logical again (Z 10–12), the physical demonstration serving in a way as an intermediate stage in furthering the logical one.

Let us try to follow the movement in its main lines, reserving to the end the difficulties Aristotle accumulates; but we must understand that all this effort pushes toward saving the Platonic spirit of rationality while doing without the Platonic ideal models, the paradigms; it is not by chance that the word *eidos* is common to the two philosophers; but against Plato there is the question of showing the physical and logical identity of the *eidos* with the thing itself; it is not a model of a thing, it is the thing itself in its intelligibility and its immanent reality.

1 The logical identity of the form and the thing

Taken from the logical side, that is, as the possibility of definition and demonstration, the form is identified with *to ti en einai* = το τί ἦ εἶναι, which the Latins translated by *quidditas* (quiddity); this is something more precise than the *ti estin* = τί ἐστιν. Bergson would say that the essence is the ready-made suit that fits many; the quiddity is what the thing is *kath' auto* = καθ' αὐτο, *per se*, by itself. Δ 18 elaborates this notion of the *kath' auto*, "Callias by himself, is Callias and the quiddity of Callias"; the example of the proper name, as adhering to the individual man, is very illuminating; Z 4 repeats: you are not the musician, for you are not as yourself a musician;[1] so the quiddity is what cannot be lost without the thing ceasing to be itself.

Z 6 will attempt to establish rigorously the identity of the quiddity and the thing: that is, that a thing and its quiddity are not other but the same: "Each being does not differ, it seems, from its own substance, and the quiddity is called the substance of each thing"; so begins Z 6. But this demonstration cannot be pushed very far, because it is not at all evident that for things produced by others, as is the case with sensible things, there should be an unchangeable intelligibility; it will be necessary to make recourse to a properly physical demonstration, that is, to a study of production, to estab-

---

[1] Z 4 1029b15.

lish 1) that what one understands in the cause is again the form; 2) that, in production, the form is not engendered but communicated by the cause. Hence it will be true that the Platonic ideas do not have the exclusive privilege of being through themselves.

At least, this first analysis has made apparent what the stakes are: the quiddity is the principle of knowability of things: "We have scientific knowledge of each being when we know the quiddity of this being" (Z 6 1031b6, similarly at 1035a7-9);[2] not just the stakes, but the Aristotelian style: the quiddity is daughter to the Platonic Idea, but identical to the real. When I know the quiddity I know the very reality and not its model; and, when I know the reality, I grasp the intelligible and not its shadow. The whole effort is therefore to uncouple the quiddity from the Platonic universal and to couple it to the existing individual. We shall see how far Aristotle went down this path of identifying the form and the individual (chapter 3).

2 The physical identity of the form and the thing

How does the physical analysis restart the logical analysis? At first glance, physics[3] moves us away from the goal, since it is a composition of form and matter that is produced. But, on a closer look, "having a nature" is to be defined by the form; if this is true, the requirement of the definition and the reality of the nature exactly overlap.

How to attain this goal? By showing:

- that production is a transmission of form;
- that, in production, the form is not engendered, but pre-existing.

---

[2] The second reference does not seem to correspond to the passage cited.

[3] Z 7 recalls the most important frameworks for physical analysis: the distinctions among natural, artistic, and fortuitous production; the distinctions among: production according to substance (birth and destruction), quantity (increase and diminution), quality (alteration), and place (transporting). Note that Aristotle terms "movement" (μεταβολή [= *metabole*]) any change in size, quality, and place; but he sets apart production according to substance, which is a movement from nothing to something and no longer between two contrary "somethings," the word "change" (μεταβολή), which here covers all four sorts of "passings," of movements, becomes synonymous with the word "movement" (PR).

a) It is a reflection on *efficient* causality that governs the first point of the demonstration (Z 7); in the case of natural production, for example sexual generation, the transmission of the form is obvious; "the man engenders the man,"[4] the cause and the effect have the same form in different matter (we already note that the logical analysis and the physical analysis are not oriented in the same direction to solution of the problem of individualization: if the quiddity is the meaning of the individual, the principle that makes it knowable, the formal identity of cause and effect prevents the form from being perfectly individuated since the cause and the effect are numerically distinct; we shall return to this in the next lecture).

In the case of artificial production, the situation is more delicate: isn't there an architect who makes the house? Certainly, but it is the quiddity of the house in the mind of the craftsman that produces the house; this is so much the case that Aristotle can write, not without some paradox: health comes from health, the house from the house. "So the efficient cause, the principle mover of doing well, is the form that is in the mind if health is the fruit of an art" (1032b22). In this way gets sketched Aristotle's reduction of cause to reason and of the relation of causality to an identity in meaning in Meyerson's sense:[5] Hamelin also has strongly emphasized this.[6]

b) This reduction of the cause to the reason is pushed further along by the radical affirmation that, in the production of something, what is engendered is the individual as composed of matter and form. But neither the matter "from which" one makes the thing nor the form "that" the thing has become are engendered; if the artisan produces a bronze sphere, he produces neither the bronze nor the sphere. Aristotle is arguing here from absurdity (Z 8); if the sphere as such were engendered, it would have been from "something" which would be form–matter and the production of something would demand an infinite chain of intermediaries. Whence the conclusion (1033b17-19).

At first glance Aristotle seems to have struggled against Plato only for a superior Platonizing in the sensible, if one may so put it,

---

[4] 1032a24.
[5] Émile Meyerson, *Identité et réalité* (Paris: F. Alcan, 1908; Vrin 1951).
[6] Hamelin, *Le Système d'Aristote, op. cit.*, pp. 271–273 (AC).

in place of a Platonizing in the intelligible, in the "supra-celestial place"; but we must be careful to note that:

1) The unengendered cannot in any way be said to be eternal. Only the non-sensible forms (God, the guiding principles of the spheres, and reason) are eternal; as for the sensible forms, either they pre-existed in another individual of the same species that has transmitted them or they have sprung up "without time passing" (ἀχρόνως)[7] "in an indivisible instant" (ἐνατομῷ νῦν);[8] as one commentator notes, such is the case with quiddities of quantity or quality.

2) These unengendered forms are in no way paradigms; Aristotle even declares firmly at least twice (Z 6 1031b15-18 and Z 8 1033b20-21) that, if the Universals were in themselves, a singular individual never would be born (similarly at Z 13 1039a3). This affirmation renders even more urgent the problem of individuality of the form which appears to be part of the logic of the anti-Platonism. In this text, however, Aristotle is quite cautious; he always reserves the expression *tode ti* (one such, the this) for the composition: this bronze sphere. The sphere in its roundness is not the materially existing individual but rather its quiddity, and Aristotle here calls it a τοιόνδε,[9] a *quale quid*. Tricot translates: "a thing of such a quality." We shall ask to what point the quiddity so termed is individual.

What interests us here is that the consideration of the causes does not take us away from the consideration about the forms but on the contrary leads us back to it. Aristotle even pushes the reduction of the cause to the reason so far that he will go as far as saying: "As with syllogisms, the principle of all production is the formal substance: for syllogisms begin from the essence and productions begin from here as well (1034a30, which concludes Z 7-9). Tricot emphasizes how Aristotle has an analytic conception of causality, here compared to the connection of premises and conclusion (causality, he notes, tends to be confused with "logical development of an essence," with the "deductive movement of

---

[7] *achronos.*
[8] *enatomo nun.*
[9] *toionde.*

explicative thought");[10] seeking the middle term of the syllogism
or the cause is the same thing. In this regard, Descartes, and
above all Spinoza (*Ethics* II, 46), will only reinforce this analytic
side; it will remain so up to the revolution of Hume and Kant,
who begin from a temporal and no longer a rational analysis of
causality, from a succession of events and not from a transmission of an identical form or a transformation of some quantity of
movement. The Aristotelian analysis of causality thus works to
the glory of the form: what is knowable in the cause is the form.
Owens emphasizes how Aristotle is indifferent to the "existential
problem,"[11] that is, to the fact that a new existent arrives. What
interests him is that the new event, the building of the house,
makes manifest a meaning, the form of the house being identical to
the house thought of by the architect; it is the identical thinkable
in the effect and in the cause that interests him, not the new event.
The advent of the form and not the event of the existing thing.
This is really a Platonic heritage, albeit one turned against Plato,
against his universals-paradigms.

3 Logical consequences of the physical analysis

Strengthened by this reduction of the cause to the form, we can
return to our problem of the identity of the thing and its form.
This identity is henceforth true of produced things. We can now
say more strongly: the form is the ground of the *definition*. We
catch sight in this way of the fact that the theory of the form has
as its goal to insert the whole logic of definition into the reality
of things. Substances through their forms are realized definitions;
conversely, one can say they are definable realities. This bringing
together of the *definition* and the *form* occupies Z 10–12; it is carried out through the intermediary notion of *logos*.[12] In this way,
in Aristotelianism the definition receives an ontological status that
clarifies the ultimate meaning.

   Still, how is a definition presented? With its "parts," which are

---

[10] Tricot, *Métaphysique, op. cit.*, p. 397 (AC).
[11] Owens, *op. cit.*, pp. 221–222 (AC).
[12] Cf. Tricot's note on *logos*, I, 400; he notes in it an oscillating meaning: notion,
      definition, form, explanatory discourse. Thus in the first line of Z 10: "The
      definition being a statement . . ." Ross translates this as *formula* (PR). [Cf. the
      lexicon in Tricot's translation of the *Metaphysics*, vol. 2, p. 304.]

genus, species, etc. It is a question of understanding that the parts are the "parts" of the form itself, an articulation of the meaning, let us say, not of the parts of matter; to put it another way, they proceed from an analysis of the form, not from a division of the thing taken as a material composition. "If one does not perceive clearly which parts are taken in the sense of material parts and which are not, neither will one see what the definition of the thing must be" (1036a28-30). The distinction is easy for the hoop which, [made] sometimes of wood, sometimes of bronze, remains the same in different matter; but the face, for example, which is always made of flesh and bone, lends itself less easily to the distinction of the parts of the definition and the parts of the matter. And nonetheless this is necessary if the form is not to be *posterior* to its material parts but only to its definable ones, in brief, if the form is to be first in the order of substance.

But how can a form thus have parts, even non-material ones, logical parts of some sort?[13] The ontological status of the definition answers this difficulty (Z 12); consider an example of definition by division: man = animal, walks upright, bipedal, etc. To speak of the ontological status of the definition is to ask how the genus of animal exists. Answer: animal is realized only in the pedestrian, the pedestrian in bipedal, etc.

In other words, what really exists is the *last difference*; the genus has reality only in its species, and these in their differences; Aristotle can thus say: "The definition is the statement (*logos*) formed beginning from differences alone" (1038a8) and: "The final difference will evidently be the substance itself of the thing and its definition" (*id.* a19-20); and, further on: "The definition is the statement (*logos*) formed starting from the differences and precisely from the last of the differences" (a28-29) (it suffices, in order to assure oneself, to look at the degrees of definition starting from the end: bipedal renders pedestrian superfluous, which renders animal superfluous). What makes for the unity of the definition therefore is the presence of the genus to the species and of the species to the last difference; Aristotle assimilates this presence of the genus to the last difference to the immanence of the

---

[13] We leave aside the question, debated at Z 10, on the universal character of the definition of the composite, and the singular or universal character of the definition of the form; we shall return to this in the chapter on individuation (PR).

matter to the form (the doublet H 6 nicely summarizes this move-ment of thought, 1045a29-35). One can no longer radically equate substance and determination, the genus being undetermined in relation to the more precise determination of the species, like the marble in relation to the statue. This extreme view of the ontologi-cal unity of the definition in one sense consolidates the theory of definition, which thereby finds the basis of its unity; but above all it makes the theory of substance the beneficiary of everything that has been acquired from the logic of the definition. At the same time the Platonic universal is definitely overturned, since it is the undetermined to which only the determined thing gives actuality, fully accomplished reality. The Platonic *eidos* has become the very form of the real. Has it become the individual? We have constantly bordered on this problem. Let us now take it up head on.

Chapter 18

Substance and the Individual

Introduction: situating the problem according to Aristotle

Before taking up Aristotle's difficulties and even contradictions, let us note that the problem is never broached directly by Aristotle himself: what makes an individual an individual distinct from another individual is an existential problem that does not interest Aristotle. What interests Aristotle is what *determines* reality, what gives it a stable and identifiable status. The entire reduction of substance to form is inspired by this concern. His anti-Platonism, which leads him to reimmerse forms in things, going so far as to identify them logically and physically with the things, does not go so far as to lead him to hunt down reality as far as its most singular existence. As a result, what we call the problem of individuation, that is, the *distinctive* constitution of one individual in relation to another, does not constitute a separate chapter in the work of Aristotle. It is up to us to look for the scattered elements in his work. It was Aristotle's successors who posed the problem and who projected it onto Aristotle's work, and first of all the neo-Platonism concerned to situate the individuality of souls in relation to the soul and in a system where all the individuals are souls. It is a question of knowing whether there are ideas of things (*Enn.* VII 7 begins thus: "Are there ideas of individual things? – Yes, since I, like every individual, raise myself to the intelligible, for my principle, like that of each one of us, is there."[1] One cannot put it any better than to say it is the problem of *personality* that imposes the problem of the individual in all its breadth. Beyond this, it would also be necessary to re-establish the Stoic phase of the problem: each thing is a "logos spermatikos" and hence a singular essence.) But it is above all the concern to individualize immortal souls that, in the Christian tradition of philosophy, will bring this problem to the fore. Aristotle, more a physicist than a moralist or a religious man, had no reason to give the problem of individuation such importance.

Nonetheless, this problem does impose itself on Aristotelianism for a series of reasons: 1) the problem of the "me" and 2) the problem of animal individuality necessarily impose themselves on a thought that culminates, on the one hand, in an ethics and, on the other, in a more pointed sense, in biological organisms rather than abstract mechanisms; 3) his system culminates in a form that is an individual: God; 4) but, above all, the struggle against Plato leads him to identify the ideas with things and consequently to connect the intelligibility of forms to the singularity of existents. All these reasons make the problem of the individual like a foreign country bordering on the properly Aristotelian analyses; it was natural that post-Aristotelian philosophy would try to extend the lines that converge toward this inevitable, albeit never systematically treated problem. So our approach will be as follows: to go from the properly Aristotelian way of posing the problem to the unresolved questions that constitute for us, though not for Aristotle, a residual problem.

1 The individual and reason

The individual, considered in relation to the theory of knowledge, is presented as the lower limit of the unchanging, certain, and unified knowledge that Aristotle calls *science*. One therefore speaks negatively of the individual, as that about which there is neither science nor demonstration. It is in this sense that *Categories* 5 and *Metaphysics* Z 15 speak about it. But we need to understand why it is that there is no science of the individual.

---

[1] The reference is of course to Plotinus, the neo-Platonist *par excellence*, and to his *Enneads*.

There is a simplistic interpretation that consists in repeating that the individual is the singular whereas science is about the universal. This is literally exact, but the meaning of such a formula is much more complex, otherwise Aristotelianism would split in two: on the one side a logic turned toward the universal, on the other an ontology turned toward the individual. Science and reality would thus be radically discordant. The interval can be partially filled if one considers that Aristotelian science extends toward the intelligible determinations closest to the individual and that, in return, the reality of the individual is not its singularity. Let us take up the matter in succession from the side of science and then from the side of the individual.

Aristotelian science is not a science of generalities.

It wants to stay close to the final species, immediately above individuals and in relation to which it is the genera that are undetermined. We saw earlier that the Aristotelian definition is the "final difference"; the genus is present to the species as an intelligible matter, as an undetermined field of signification which the last difference makes precise and resolves into a final core of meaning. It is this that the scientist, as Aristotle understands him, wants to know: not the most general, but the most determined. Thought's movement is not a flight toward the most universal, but rather an intelligible approximation of the real in the direction of what is most specific. Science is the science of "forms"; we shall see later on in what way these forms are still universals.

We arrive at the same result if we note with Rodier that the true object of science is the necessary, not the general;[2] in Aristotelian language it is the *kath'autou* (= καθ᾽ αὑτοῦ) and not the καθόλου[3] (universal). So it is necessary to return yet one more time to the problem of definition: its fulfillment lies in comprehension, not in extension; that is, that the bundle of determinations that necessarily belong to the thing, and ensure it is what it is, is[4] grasped in the thing before its belonging to a class. Universality, says Rodier, is an accidental outcome of necessity. So, if the individual is unknowable, it is because it escapes the definition's work of approximation, because its comprehension is infinite; it oversteps the *infima species*; not that it is opposed

---

[2] *La Théorie aristotélicienne de la substance, op. cit.*, pp. 173–174 (AC).
[3] *katholou.*
[4] The subject of this "is" is "the bundle."

as singular to universal, but rather as the contingent to the
necessary.

It is here that we must look at the question from the side of the
individual. Why is the individual beyond the sharpest determination of the definition? Why is it contingent? Z 15 answers this
way: the individual is the substance not as form (what has been
considered up to this point), but rather as form in some matter: a
composed substance. As Z 8 says,[5] it is only the composite that is
engendered, the form is unengendered: the smith makes a bronze
sphere, but does not make the roundness of the sphere. If the
composed is general, it is perishable; here is the true reason for
its indefinable character; for matter can be or not be; the precariousness of the composed object makes for the precariousness of
opinion (cf. 1039b27–1040a8; this text expressly links together
the chain of the following notions: individuality – matter – perishable – opinion, "opinion dealing solely with the contingent,"
1039b33). "Under these conditions," Aristotle concludes, "it is
evident that for individual sensible substances there can be neither
definition nor demonstration" (1039b27). The perishable at each
instant can disappear from actual sensation; and if the notion
subsists in memory, then it is in me that it subsists, it is me that
subsists, not the thing. One is struck by this "essential Platonism"
that survives the debacle of the Ideas and Universals; scientific
knowledge is always defined by its imperishability and the object
of science by its ungenerability: certainly the forms are immanent
and no longer transcendent; for all that they are no less entities
removed from time. So Aristotle is even more radical than this text
allows; one may well believe that opinion reaches the individual;
in reality the most elementary sensation has already gone beyond
the individual: "I perceive the man in Callias," says *Posterior
Analytics* I 31 87b30.[6] Sensation grasps a *toionde* = τοιόνδε (*quale*),
not a *tode* = τόδε (*hoc*); the senses already disengage the *act* from
the matter, just as the wax receives the form of the ring, not its
metal; that is why, on the very level of sensation, substance reveals
itself to be *form* and not the raw individual. This is why finally in

---

[5] Z 8 1033b16-19.

[6] This citation is not found as such in chapter 31 of the *Posterior Analytics*,
which Pellegrin titles "There is no demonstration through perception," but it
does correspond to Ricoeur's commentary. Cf. the translation of the *Seconds
Analytiques* by Pierre Pellegrin (Paris: GF-Flammarion, 2005), p. 221 and the
note on p. 390.

Aristotelianism the form is well named: *prote ousia* = πρώτη ουσία, first substance.

2 The status of the individual in Aristotelianism

In passing from the problem of the science of the individual to the problem of the nature of the individual and its ontological status in the philosophy of Aristotle, we pass from a specifically Aristotelian problem to a problem projected onto his philosophy by Aristotle's successors. In fact, the eighth aporia of Book B, which is the one that comes closest to the problem, and which Aristotle calls "the hardest of all," is still an epistemological aporia. It has to do not with the infinite number of individuals but with what is "outside" individuals. This eighth aporia is: if there is nothing outside individuals, and since individuals are infinite in number, science is impossible, for science supposes something unified and identical with itself and relates to the universal, which belongs to this principle. On the other hand, if science must be possible, there is an "outside," and we tumble back among the genera, outside the individuals, which is equally impossible. Everything that follows suggests that the aporia is oriented toward the determination of the notion of substance–form, which one can say is "outside" the form–matter composite. All that one can draw from this aporia concerning the status of the individual is that Aristotle is fundamentally in agreement with Plato in *Philebus* 15: one does not think the unlimited, but the intermediary between the "one" and the *apeiron*. The great difference between Plato and Aristotle has to do not with the question of the individual but with that of the form, which is no longer a transcendent universal, but an immanent quiddity. Yet the Aristotelian real is no less immutable than the Platonic real, although it is inherent in the things themselves. The eighth aporia points therefore toward a reinterpretation of the form in terms of the *Physics* and not toward an ontological determination of the individual as such. The eighth aporia aims to disengage, between the Platonic Idea which is a universal and individuals, the immanent forms that are *in* the sensible without being, for all that, *of* the sensible; that is how the eighth aporia connects up with the sixth and seventh aporias, which have to do with the "genera." In this sense, we may frankly say that there is no aporia of individuation in Aristotle.

To conclude, we shall look for the underlying reason why this is so.

We are therefore reduced to asking ourselves 1) up to what point the Aristotelian form individualizes reality; 2) what ultimate individuality matter introduces; 3) if the individuality eventuating from the form and that eventuating from the matter have the same meaning, and whether as a result there is not something equivocal in the very question that we are posing to Aristotle; 4) why finally the Aristotelian notion of being is indifferent to what we properly call existence and which we oppose to essence.

1) Up to what point does the Aristotelian form individualize things?

The fundamental motif that authorizes Aristotle's reader to seek in his work something like an individuation by the form is the conjunction of two fundamental theses: on the one hand, substance expresses what it is (its *ousia*) through its form, while, on the other hand, the universal cannot be substance. "It seems quite impossible that any universal term, whatever it might be, could be a substance" (*Metaphysics* Z 13 1038b9). Two arguments:

a) "The substance of an individual is that which is proper to it and that does not belong to another,"[7] whereas the universal is "common" to many. There is therefore opposition between the "proper" and the "common"; more precisely, substance is what confers a unity on a thing: "since the beings whose substance is one, in other words whose quiddity is one, are also one and the same being" (Z 13 1038b9-15). In the same sense: Z 8 1034a7; Z 11 1037a29-30.

b) Beyond that, predication excludes that the universal should be substance; for the universal is always attributed to another thing; whereas substance is never attributed to a substrate (Aristotle no longer alludes to the possibility of attributing substance to indeterminate matter as in Z 3 1029a23-25), Aristotle is really radical: one cannot even say (Z 13 1038b16-23) that the universal is "contained in the quiddity," under pain of introducing substances into substance and ruining the very

---

[7] Z 13 1038b9-15.

unity of the individual; there would be "in act" two substances immanent to the thing: for "the act separates."

This analysis of Z 13 permits us to tighten up our investigation: to ask if the form individualizes is to ask up to what point what is knowable and defined in a being, namely its quiddity, individualizes it. There is no doubt that a certain individuality attaches itself to the quiddity (to the *ti en einai*), since it is precisely what belongs to a being and has always belonged to it to be (Robin's translation); in other words: the quiddity represents the overall unity of the characters that constitute a nature at the interior of a genus.

A final confirmation, if there were need for one, would be to look in Book I devoted to the one and to unity. I 1 (which prolongs Δ 6) makes more precise what it is to be "numerically one" (ἓν ἀριθμῷ).[8] This, in some sense distributive, unity (one and then one and then one) has to be distinguished from being a part of unity in the sense of indivisibility (when I say that a closed chest has a unity or that an animal has a unity across the diversity of the organs); this unity of things unified because "continuous" (συνεχές) or "total" (ὅλον)[9] has to do with the indivisibility of the movement of the thing that one displaces as a whole (in the case of the "continuing" thing) or that has in itself the principle proper to its total displacement in the case of a living organism; the unity "in number" must to be distinguished for another thing from the intelligible unity (that of an understood notion); it is here that I 1 interests us: for numerical, distributive unity, which makes there to be an "each" (καθ' ἕκαστόν),[10] is expressly linked to the τόδε τί, to the "this" of composed substance. Consequently, the distributive unity coincides with the unity of the form–matter composite. But, our text asks, what is the unity of each thing, what makes "each" one the unity of its own form and matter? Answer: the form. There is no need to search for a principle of unity exterior to matter and form, for the immediate matter and the form are the same thing, except insofar as this thing is in potency on one side and in act on the other. "The thing in potency makes up just one thing in some way with the thing in act."[11] In other words, the form in positing

---

[8] *hen arithmo.*
[9] *suneches* and *holon.*
[10] *kath' hekaston.*
[11] Robin (AC).

itself posits the matter that fits it; conversely, the matter aspires to the form (*Physics* I 9 192a6-25).

This individuality that proceeds from the form and coincides with the *definite* is realized in God. Individual *par excellence*, he is individualized by the form alone, since he is without matter, that is, without the potency to become some other thing without indetermination. This individuality is further realized in the stars – with the reservation of an individuation that pertains to change of place – and finally, apart from a few differences which we shall look it in a little while, with human souls.

To deny a certain individuation by the form therefore would be to overturn the doctrine about God, the stars, and human souls.

2) What ultimate individuality does matter add?

And yet Aristotle does not stop affirming that the differentiation of things continues on beyond the *last difference*, the *atopon eidos*, which defines, which actualizes in a totally determined and precise signification the potentialities of the genus and the differentiating species, and which under this heading is a "principle" (seventh aporia). What does this individuation which is no longer that of quiddity indicate?

First aspect
In truth, what appears beyond the last difference no longer has to do with the order of "differentiation," which is why it is no longer intelligible. It is a diversification for which there is no longer a "logos," in any sense of the word: no discourse, no definition, no intelligible apprehension. B 4[12] (eighth aporia) alludes to this diversity, connected to Plato's *apeiron* in the *Philebus* ("being given that the individuals are infinite in number," 999a26). The first aspect of this individuality is therefore its character of unintelligible, not intellectually masterable plurality. This first aspect, like those that follow, is expressly linked to matter. *Metaphysics* Λ 8 1074a33: "everything that is numerically plural has to do with matter."

---

[12]   And not B 3, as written in the *Course*. The citation which follows, between parentheses, is to *Metaphysics* B 4 999a26 (and not to the *Philebus*, as the *Course* seems to indicate).

Second aspect
In each individual taken separately, the matter proper to it des-ignates its incompleteness, that is, its ability to become other (to perish, to be moved locally, to increase or decrease, to be changed). This aspect therefore lies at the opposite pole from the definite and refers to another character of matter: all imme-diate matter is *potency*, therefore incompleteness, a capacity to escape the net of determinisms attained *hic et nunc* in the *tode ti*.

Third aspect
Matter finally is the principle of contingency, as attested to by perversions and monstrosities. Form is not only the definite, but order. In this sense individuation is not only indetermination in the order of the definite, incompleteness in the order of actuality, but also imperfection in the order of finality.

It is therefore this triple function of matter (indefiniteness – potency – disorder) that prevents Aristotle from identifying the individual and the form. This is the threshold that Plotinus will attempt to cross in the 5th *Ennead* 7 – by positing an idea of Socrates in the *Nous*.

3) *The equivocations of individuality*

Having arrived at this point, we have to acknowledge that we are not speaking about the same thing when we say that the form confers a certain individuality and that the matter individualizes. In the second case, individuality means singularity, accidental vari-ation of a type. The very Greek words *tode ti* and *hekaston* harbor an ambiguity which Aristotle himself did not really bring to light.

Whence the interest of an attempt such as Robin's to dissociate the two senses and thereby to reconcile the two groups of texts. In the case of personality, the characters proper to the individual coincide with the last species, and reciprocally the last species is a *kath' hekaston* (Robin relies in particular on an important text: *Parts of Animals* I 4 644a23-b7, which calls Socrates a "final species," a "specifically undifferentiated species." He joins to this texts from *On the Soul* [περι Ψυχῆς = *peri Psyches*, II 2 414a and II 3] which say that the soul is defined not according to the genus, but "according to what is its own [οἰκεῖον] and according to

the undivided species [ἄτομον]";[13] whereas for plants and animals
there is no need in general to consider anything other than the
species, for man it is necessary to consider "such-and-such soul"
of "such-and-such body." In relation to this irrational singularity, the final species is just a type, an individualized type, if one
may put it this way, but just a type; it is the species that has a
personality, individuals are accidental variations of the type and
thought loses itself in the crowd of the *apeira*. Therefore there
would be two kinds of individuation, the one that *determines* and
the other that *indetermines*, the one that leads to what Kant will
call a "character" defined by its correlations and its own determinations, the other to an "accident" that escapes knowledge, as
regards its actuality as real and with respect to order: "Up to the
point where individuality merits being envisaged as an object for
thought, this is by the form that constitutes it," says Robin. "On
the contrary, far from individuating positively, matter founds only
a sort of negative individuality which thought bumps up against.")
     Two comments on this solution from Robin:
     It is necessary to acknowledge that this way of putting things in
order is not Aristotle's. Le Blond declares: "No doubt, here and
there in his work there are attachment points for a theory of individuation by the form, but Aristotle does not seem to have made
them perfectly clear." Le Blond grants that Robin's suggestions are
good ones: "One can, in developing these indicators, legitimate his
notion of substance and free it from a serious contradiction. But
we do not believe Aristotle himself had done so."[14] For that, it
would have been necessary that he be interested in the individual
as such, which was not the case for reasons we are going to discuss. In any case, this interpretation allows us retrospectively to
dissociate two readings of reality: according to the first one, reality
is a hierarchical unity of *personalized individuals*, from God to the
stars and souls: among these beings the connection is not generic
but analogical. This is the "psych-ic" reading of the real. We shall
come back to this problem when at the end of the course we will
examine in what sense God, the first example of substance, is the
answer to the problem of the unity of being as being. According
to a second reading, the forms are not fully individuals except

---

[13] *oikeion* and *atomon*.
[14] Le Blond, *op. cit.*, pp. 377 and 378 (AC).

through matter: substance is then the "composed" (σύνολον):[15] this is the "physic-al" reading of the real. Leibniz will rediscover this problem of the two "kingdoms" in his doctrine of the monads, which pose similar problems of individuation.

Second comment: the two senses of individuality, supposing they can be distinguished, are necessarily entangled, for, apart from God and the stars (with a reservation made for their "local motion"), personality is *also* singularity due to matter. The beings personalized by their form are also singularized by their matter: the "proper," the *itself-ness* [*par soi*], of Socrates does not contain "that which comes to him accidentally" (to be tall, small, reddish- or black-haired); between Socrates and Coriscos there are *proper* differences and an *accidental* diversity. So, the problem of individuation comes down to knowing whether one can distinguish what is specifically different due to the essence – or more exactly to the quiddity – and that which is accidentally diversified due to the matter. *Metaphysics* I 9 touches on this problem and distinguishes contrariety in essence, which institutes the intelligible differences (walks/flies), from contrariety in being, considered as associated with matter (white/black). "This is why neither the whiteness of the man nor his blackness constitute specific differences, and there is no specific difference between the white man and the black man, even if one were to impose a name on each" (I 9 1058b2-4). In this text, it does seem that the specific difference does not go very far in the direction of the individual: "The species man is the last and indivisible species" (1058b10). The case of sexuality is quite ambiguous, wavering between essential and accidental: the species is not affected by the sex, and yet "male and female are modifications proper to the animal, not substantial, but material and corporeal" (1058b22).

Every philosophy of "forms" leads to this separation of the of itself-ness and the accidental; perhaps this is the mortal difficulty that calls for a heartrending revision of this kind of philosophy. It is necessary therefore to guard ourselves against any enthusiasm about finding an overly clear solution to this paradox in a philosophy that had never reflected either on the original status of persons in connection to nature or on singularity as an event, as a novation, in nature itself. This leads us to the reasons why this problem is not an Aristotelian one.

---

[15] *sunolon.*

4) Why this problem is not Aristotelian

If Aristotle does not interest himself in individuation as such, and did not make it a distinct aporia, that depends on his conception not only of science, but of *reality*; both remain Platonic in spite of his taste for experience and his fondness for the spirit of the medical tradition. The real is the definite, the determined; the singularity is the undetermined; in this sense there is something unreal about the singularity. Robin is right: "For matter be capable of real individuation, it would be necessary, in the end, that it do so in the fashion of the form," that is, in the manner of that which determines. Something which, in Aristotelianism, is "contrary to the most essential principles of the doctrine."[16] We touch here on perhaps the most fundamental hesitation of Aristotelianism, which gets expressed in its theory of substance which, in opposition to the Platonic Idea, is a "subject"; a separate and individual existent is an "essence," "at the same time" an intelligible content. This is why substance is spoken of primarily under the rubric of form, even though what exists would be the form–matter composite. Le Blond, who speaks of an aporia of substance (an aporia for us, not for Aristotle), notes that Aristotle has indeed distinguished, but not really connected, two notions: "On one side the notion of intelligible content, of essence, on the other side the notion of the subject, of separate and individual existence."[17] To identify substance and subject would be to identify substance and matter (a temptation mentioned and set aside at Z 3). So Aristotle is driven back to the side of a philosophy of *quiddity* and not of the *individual*.

The equivocity of the substantive *ousia*, which the French [and English] word substance renders so poorly, is found again in the verb *to be* conjugated using a personal tense, for example in the distinction of the *ti esti* and the *ei esti*, wherein the Latin tradition has seen the distinction of essence and existence. Aristotle's logic, notes Le Blond, rightly distinguishes the two *questions*.[18] At the

---

[16] Robin, *op. cit.*, p. 95 (AC).

[17] Le Blond, *op. cit.*, p. 376 (AC).

[18] *Anal. Seconds* II I, 89b23 et seq. Four questions: the fact (τὸ ὅτι), the reason (τὸ διότι), the existence (εἰ ἐστιν), the essence (τί ἐστιν). The first two bear on complex facts; the last two, which interest us here, are about simple or at least unique beings. Although one might regroup them as 1 + 3 and 2 + 4: 1 + 3 belongs to the order of facts both as an attribution and as the positing of existence. The *ei estin* question is therefore the question of being taken absolutely (PR).

same time, Aristotle also distinguishes the copulative and existential use of the verb *to be*, as for example: Does God exist?, What *is* God? "But this distinction is not firmly maintained."[19] And why not? Because Aristotelian existence does not correspond exactly to what we call existence and which would be precisely the singularity of individuals. If it is indeed true that the use of the verb *to be* in the absolute sense (different from the copulative usage) implies a positing of existence and that Aristotle, before Kant, had indeed seen that existence adds nothing to essence (*An. Part.* II, 7; 92b13),[20] it remains that the usage he makes of it is entirely different: Aristotle thinks so little about being as the positing of existence that the reason that he gives for the essence–existence distinction falls away: "The *einai*," he says, "is not a genus," not as a positing of existence, but as an overly vague characteristic. (Le Blond notes how, by his very vocabulary, Aristotle dodges the problem of existence: after having said: the *to einai* is in no way the "essence," he states: for *to on* is not a genus. One has run up against a conceptual problem.)[21] Elsewhere Suzanne Mansion takes *ousia* and *to on* as synonyms. We are thereby brought back to the theory of being as the "analogue" of all its significations and for that reason different from a genus (*Metaphysics* E 2). The existential order is so unfamiliar to Aristotle that he even speaks of the *ei esti* of the triangle. Here *to exist* means: not to be fictional, not to be invented, in brief, to be "objective" in the modern sense of the word. Le Blond notes moreover that, in return, the essence is envisaged quite concretely as soon as one refuses the generalities so as to grasp more closely the "quiddities." Essence and existence then tend to coincide in the philosophy of quiddity. In the same sense, Suzanne Mansion writes: "If Aristotle's system is to be understood, it must be considered as a development and a perfecting of the conceptual philosophy established by Socrates and enriched by Plato."[22] Hence she does not think Aristotle reached the concrete positing of existence in the *ei esti* question: "The

---

[19] Le Blond, *op. cit.*, p. 378 (AC).

[20] It is Avicenna and then the Thomists who have drawn all the consequences. With Avicenna, existence is added on accidentally, with St Thomas, existence and essence are distinct but not separate (regarding this, cf. Le Blond, p. 173 notes 2 and 3) (PR). [The Aristotle reference is to the work *Parts of Animals*.]

[21] Le Blond, *op. cit.*, p. 174 (AC).

[22] Suzanne Mansion, *Le Jugement d'existence chez Aristote* (Louvain: Institut supérieur de philosophie, 1946; Peeters, 1998), p. 11.

existence intended in the *ei esti* question is therefore the concrete existence, that which the individuals that surround us possess. Aristotle does not know of any other kind. But it is this existence taken in an abstract and undetermined state . . ."[23] "Aristotle did not dream of separating the possibility of essences from their existence, because he does not possess a precise idea of metaphysical contingency."[24]

Conclusion

It is in the theory of quiddity (τό τί ἤν εἶναι)[25] that the two personalities which struggle in Aristotle find their equilibrium: the Platonic and the Asclepian; on the one side "the secret sympathy and fight for Democritus," on the other the profound sense of the reality of the form, that is, of the idea (Le Blond here cites Brémond, *Le Dilemme aristotélicien:*[26] "The essence or the idea is what is most real in the individual. And that certainly seems to call for a transcendence of the idea that Aristotle obstinately denies").[27] But to defend Aristotle we must say that what compensates and rebalances Aristotle is the key idea of the whole *Physics*, namely, the most brilliant distinction of the system, that of act and potency. It ends up interfering with the essential Platonism of his philosophy of quiddity. There is in nature a margin of incompleteness, of the indefinite, which is the lower limit of knowledge; if "nature" were actuality, the forms would be individuals, and everything real would be intelligible. His philosophy of *ousia*, of *beingness*,[28] of *etance*, oscillates between a Platonic philosophy of the Form and an empiricist philosophy of the concrete understood as an "act" mixed with potentiality. It is this latter philosophy that a Leibniz will retrieve in order to oppose Cartesian mathematicism.

---

[23] *Id.*, p. 261 (AC).
[24] *Id.*, p. 273 (AC).
[25] *to ti en einai.*
[26] André Brémond, *Le Dilemme aristotélicien* (Paris: Beauchesne, 1933).
[27] Le Blond, *op. cit.*, p. 378, note 1 (AC).
[28] In English in the *Course.*

Chapter 19

"Separate" Substance

Introduction: The problem of "separate substance" in the economy of the Metaphysics

The central books[1] devoted to sensible substance (Z Θ I)[2] have been inserted in this place as a way of setting up the investigation of supra-sensible substance. But, in the very texture of these books, there is nothing to justify the existence of such substances: all that is shown is that form is the "first example" of substance. The principle that renders the thing knowable is indiscernible from the thing itself; what is more, Z Θ I were not written to resolve the aporias of A [to] E 1.[3] They have an independent base and are the prolongation of Δ. They would ultimately have been connected through the "tenon" (E 2–4). Whatever the chronological order may be, at the end of group Z Θ I all that has been analyzed is, in the language of E 2, the substance of "second philosophy": that is, the sensible substances that are the "second" examples of substance; the problem of "first substance," the object of "first philosophy" or theology, remains in suspense. In this sense, a *scientific* treatment of sensible substance still remains a dialectical

---

[1] In what follows the references will always be to the *Metaphysics*, whose books are designated by capital Greek letters.

[2] Zeta, Theta, Iota.

[3] *Alpha* to *Epsilon*, chapter 1.

treatment, an aporematic approach to the central problem of the
Metaphysics. At most one has set aside the Platonic way of the
Ideas by putting the forms back in things, thanks to physics and
logic; the problem of first philosophy remains intact.

The group of books Λ M N[4] as a block constitutes an answer to
this problem. But already M 1–9 must be set aside (it is true that
the first lines of M 1 connect the book to the central problem: does
there exist or not, apart from sensible substances, an unmoving
and eternal substance? And, if this substance exists, what is its
nature?). But right off Aristotle indicates that M 1–9 will once
again be a preparatory detour: it is necessary first to study the
doctrines of the other philosophers, for if they are mistaken . . .,
etc. Whence the long discussion about the mathematical objects
and the Ideas, which is placed on the ground of the fifth aporia
(*Metaphysics* B 2 997a34 et seq.). Book M 1–9 therefore has as
its task to clear the field of supra-sensible numbers, figures, Ideas,
which are not separate substances through themselves but just for
the mathematician; these are therefore still not the causes sought
for by wisdom, since the cause of being ought to be "separate"
(Z 1 1028a20-b2); so M 1–9 simply frees up the horizon of the
doctrine of substance.

It is only at Λ 6 that Aristotle's theology begins (Λ 1–5 is a reca-
pitulation of the theory of substance, which appears here as a propaedeutic to theology). Λ 6 links up directly with the conception of
philosophy set out in E 1: three sciences arranged as a function of
the three modalities of substance (physics, mathematics, theology).
It is, therefore, in this second part of Λ that one must search for the
answers to the two questions posed by E 1:

1. In what sense is the *separate* substance the *first* example of
   substance?
2. How are the other substances connected to it, in such a manner
   as to constitute, together with it, the analogical unity of being?

The first question receives an explicit answer: this is the classic
part of Aristotelian theology; we will lay it out quite schemati-
cally, since it is elsewhere the object of a detailed *explication de
textes*. In contrast, the second question barely receives an answer;
this incomplete aspect of Aristotle's theology has repercussions

---

[4] Lambda, Mu, Nu.

throughout the whole system; as we have seen, the very coherence of a philosophy that identifies general ontology with a theology, that is, the ontological with the ontics of the divine, depends on the answer to the second question.

1 The unmoving mover: structure of the argument

The two steps of Aristotle's demonstration concern, first, the *existence* and, second, the *essence* of the supreme substance; one goes therefore from the εἰ ἐστίν to the ἐστίν (here we jump over the difficult chapter 7 devoted to the manner by which the unmoved mover moves; this *motion through desire* is in effect the answer, or the beginning of an answer, to the second question, that of the unity of beings in being. We shall therefore connect directly Λ 9 to Λ 6, which makes the progress of the thought from the one to the other even more arresting. We jump over chapter 8 as well, which is a quite late interpolation and constitutes a revision of the theology: in place of the "god" in Λ 6, 7, 9 it substitutes or adds the multiplicity of the unmoving spheres, which are as much realizations of substantiality in its eminent state).

The two moments in Aristotle's theology are in reality much more than a determination of existence then of essence; from the one to the other, the overall conception of the divine is enriched and deepened. One begins with a somehow "physical" god that supports the movement of the world and is the root of eternity, and rises to a spiritual god who thinks, and thinks itself thinking. What is in question is therefore much more than a progress from existence to essence; for *that which* exists, according to the first moment, is much poorer than *that which* is determined by analogy with the thought of the wise man, according to the second moment.

Let us consider, therefore, the two moments of this progression.

a) The "physical" God

How to prove that "there must necessarily exist some eternal, unmoving substance"? (setting aside a reservation as to whether this substance is one or many).

The starting point of the argument is furnished by the *eternity of movement*. This is itself a consequence of the eternity of time, since time is "something of movement"; as for the eternity of time, it is known directly through simple inspection of the notion: a time before time is still a time (*Physics* VIII 1 250b23–251b13 establishes the eternity of movement directly, without going through that of time). What movement is eternal? A continuous movement (*Physics* VIII 6 259a16); but there is no continuous movement other than local movement, and the only continuous local movement is circular movement (*Metaphysics* Λ 6 1071b12).

Next one establishes that both eternities – the eternity of movement and that of time – reside in a substance without matter and without potency: otherwise the movement *could* cease; the shadow of a contingency, of a nothingness, has to be kept apart from the first substance to avoid affecting the perdurability of movement.

This is how eternal substance presents itself: it is pure Act, Act without potentiality; it in this sense that it is called "unmoving."

So we have, if not the complete answer to the first question, at least one element of that answer; the substance that is most substance is the one that is only form, that is just Act, that is, without indetermination. It is obviously toward this outcome that the theory of sensible substance was already oriented; it is form that makes for the substantiality of substance.

We see in what sense the god this argument reveals is "physical," this is a god that is inseparable from a cosmological structure, the *eternity of movement*. The eternity of the world and the eternity of God adhere to each other. Aristotle's theology is thus, at least on this first level, in the line that runs from the world soul according to Platonism (cf. the αὐτοκινοῦν of *Phaedrus* 246c)[5] to that of Stoicism and Plotinus. But, even at this first level, Aristotle's originality is great: it has to do entirely with his metaphysical analysis of the real that ends in the distinction of potency and act; his whole argument rests on the priority of act over potency; it is the perfect that makes sense of the imperfect; that which becomes, is on the way, does not of itself suffice; being, as determined, fulfilled, arrived at plenitude is the principle of indeterminate, unfulfilled being, on the march toward the maturity of some form. Therein lies Aristotle's philosophical legacy.

---

[5] *autokinoun. Phaedrus* 295c indicated in the *Course* does not exist. The reference should have been to *Metaphysics* Λ 6 1072a1.

b) The "spiritual" god

The meditation on the pure act makes a second leap at Λ 9: the unmoving mover reveals itself as "thought thinking itself."[6] How is this possible? Through a procedure that one could call an analogical extrapolation. We have, so to speak, a figure approximating the pure act in the experience of one "kind of life" (βίος = *bios*), the contemplative life. It is therefore the *ethical* doctrine of kinds of life that furnishes the principle for this new step. In this sense one can say we have an experience analogous to that of the pure act in the *unmoving activity of theoria*. What we do rarely and with fatigue, God does unceasingly. Book X 7 of the *Nicomachean Ethics* is thus on the path which leads from the "physical" god to the "spiritual" god of *Metaphysics* Λ.

But what is it to "contemplate"? A second link in the argument is furnished by the *De anima* III 4: contemplation is the perfect knowledge of causes and principles; in this knowing, our intelligence – that "part" of the soul which is *capable* of principles and causes – is in the same position as the sensitive soul with regard to the sensibles; it becomes what it looks at; just as sensation is the common act of the sensor and the sensed, the intelligence in act is the common act of the subject and the object. One can say the same thing in another way: since the Intelligence *is* the Intelligibles that it contemplates, it is itself that it thinks in thinking all things in their principle. We have formed in this way the idea of a Pure Act that is at the same time Pure Thought, namely, "Thought which itself thinks itself in grasping the intelligible." It is this idea of a Thinking–Thought–Thinking ITSELF which is at the center of this page (*Metaphysics* Λ 7 1072b14-30) that Plotinus will admire so much and in which he will find the principle of his second hypostasis, the Intelligence (this will be only the second hypostasis, subordinated to the One, because thought that thinks itself in

---

[6] It is worth noting that the simplicity and the immateriality of the divine leaves the question of its unity intact. The "divine" is the foundation of things, but its notion does not allow us to decide whether it is one or many. The sole question Aristotle looks at is that of the order or hierarchy of perfection. The opposition between monotheism and polytheism, essential in a Hebraic context, is secondary in Greek philosophy. It is necessary to keep in mind this difference between problematics in order to put Aristotle's variations on the *number* of unmoving movers in their true place; it is in this perspective that it is necessary to approach Λ 8 (which seems to contradict Λ 7 1072b13) (PR).

thinking the Intelligibles already contains the duality of reflection and the multiplicity of the Intelligibles).

Hence Aristotle's God is our contemplation – at least if we are "wise" – our contemplation and its joy, but continual and undisturbed.

What makes for the unity of these two moments – the eternity of movement and the eternity of contemplation – is therefore the notion of a pure Act; it is what allows integrating *the analogy of wisdom* into the determination of the first substance; without it theology splits into the eternity of the world and that of wisdom. But the former alone furnishes a starting point and the second an analogy: Pure Act furnishes the principle.

2 The operation of the unmoved mover

We are at the threshold of the greatest difficulty of the *Metaphysics*. How does the first of beings make for the unity of being? or, to speak as E 1 does, how is it "universal because first"?

We have a rough sketch of an answer in chapter 7 of the book, where Aristotle lays out how the pure, "unmoving" Act can be said *to move* all the rest.

We left aside this difficult text; it is, however, there that the "moving" role of the pure Act is revealed; without this analysis one can speak of an unmoved Act, but not of an unmoved mover. What therefore is the *motion* that proceeds from this immobility?

Aristotle attempts to elucidate it by an analogy: that of the *desirable*. We are going to consider this analogy from the point of view of the problem that interests us here, namely, the unity of the chain of beings, attached to the first being:[7] "It is in this fashion

---

[7] In the progress of this meditation, this page is situated between the theory of the eternity of the world (which serves as the base of departure for the determination of pure Act) and that of the Thought that thinks itself; therefore between the "physical" god and the "spiritual" god. It plays therefore a role of mediation between the two fundamental moments of his theology; turned on the one side toward the movement of the first heaven, on the other toward the immobility of meditation, that sovereign attraction – and sovereign in repose – of the First desirable assures the decisive transition from one phase to the other of the meditation. It is *still* physical and *already* "spiritual." Thus it is necessary to read these pages as a spiral movement that goes more deeply into the idea of a separate substance: the principle for the eternity of movement,

that the desirable and the intelligible move: they move without being moved" (*Metaphysics* Λ 7 1072a26; one refers here to the psychological experience of desire: its object arouses the movement of desire and of knowledge without being itself affected by this movement).

This analogy is incomprehensible unless one keeps in mind the *schema* of the Aristotelian universe; it is a hierarchy of realities whose key is given by the metaphysical analysis of the real in terms of form and matter, act and potency; in effect the hierarchical order is assured by the *relational* character of each of these notions; the same thing is form relative to one thing and matter relative to another. The sequence of the realms of nature gives an idea of this hierarchical order (the human is constructed on the living, the living on the inorganic, etc.). But this scheme of the universe remains empirical and is explored by the sciences only in its "middle terms," which are all "movers-moved" (the first heaven and the series of concentric circles of the supra-lunar level, the permutation of elements in the great infra-lunar exchanges, humanity, living beings, things, etc.). Only a metaphysical analysis bearing on the radical enchainment of all the "movers-moved," therefore on the "extreme term" of the series of the "middle terms," can lift this representation of the Cosmos to the level of rational necessity that "the Science which we seek" requires.

It is here that the analogy of aspiring through desire comes in.

The demonstration is quite laborious. It is necessary first of all to establish that the *first* desirable is also the *first* intelligible: it is necessary to justify this co-incidence which is true only for the first in each series; the apparently good object of empirical desires is not always rationally good; but the Good in itself, to which all the apparent goods refer, and which is the term aimed at by the movement of willing, cannot not be the first intelligible. We thus have a first series of synonyms: First desirable, Good in itself, First Intelligible.

It remains to show that the First Intelligible is the simple substance, the pure act; Aristotle establishes this by putting in one column the positive terms and in the other the negative terms; the positives are first with respect to the negatives and the first intelligible is the first of the positives.

God becomes the Loved who draws everything to him, finally the supreme Meditator (PR).

What is it? "In this series, substance is first and in substance that which is simple is first" (*Metaphysics* Λ 7 1072a32). A striking summation of Aristotle's whole substantialist ontology: the group A–E establishes the first proposition: "substance is first"; as for the second, it is true that Z H Θ do not know about simple substance, but rather composed substances; but, in establishing the primacy of form as the principle both of the intelligibility and of the reality of substance, this group of analyses prepares for the second proposition: "in substance, that which is simple is first"; but it only prepares for it; the intuition by Intelligence of an uncomposed substance is the intuition of the fundamental and foundational role of the pure Act in relation to all the operations tainted by unfulfillment, by potentialities; in brief, this second proposition is the metaphysical positing of the primacy of being over becoming, of pure act over potency.

So the series of synonyms begun above is complete: First desirable, Good in itself, First Intelligible, simple and immaterial Substance. Then, reading this series in the reverse direction, we say that simple and immaterial substance (the last term of this chain of identifications) moves just like the first desirable (the initial term of the series).

In what way does this identification of the movement of God with that of a "desirable" contribute to resolving the fundamental problem of the unity of the beings within being? One point has been acquired: the accent has been shifted from *efficiency* to *finality*. To move without being moved, we have said, is the privileged of the Beloved; for "the final cause moves like the object of love, and all other things move by the fact that they are themselves moved" (Λ 7 1072b3); and, further on: "both heaven and nature hang on such a principle" (1072b14). The relation of final causality, according to this text, seems indeed to be not only *a* way, but *the only* way that Aristotelianism offers to account for the analogical bond that unites the first substance and the other substances under the same "equivocal" rubric of being. Unfortunately the *Metaphysics* stops short at the threshold of the difficulty. Let us attempt to pinpoint this partial defeat (§3) and discern the motive for it (§4).

3 The incompletion of the Metaphysics

To be proved, the analogical unity of beings within being requires that the first being has to be the *foundation of the analogy*. But while this is sketchily indicated, it is not really developed. Let us look at the principal features of this sketch.

First step: substance is form

We have seen that the entire philosophy of *ousia* comes together around the *ti en einai* (quiddity), which is the core both of reality and of intelligibility; it is the thing *itself* and it is the *knowable* thing. It was there that Aristotle originally abandoned Plato. No doubt, Platonism is "retained" in the sense that the quiddity is a determined, necessary, and unchangeable content of signification; each quiddity is an ultimate difference, an ultimate term in the investigation of things; so Aristotle like Plato clings expressly to the level of the many, of the "differences." But the Platonic many is taken to lie at the level of thought-out significations, whereas the Aristotelian many are the realities produced by nature or human arts. The Parmenidean problem of the One is eluded as "archaic," and therefore the problem of the genesis of the many from the One as well. There will be neither "procession" nor "genesis" in Aristotelian thought, but at best a *hierarchization* of forms, all of them unengendered.

Second step: form is act

The inspired idea of Aristotelianism is to have identified form and act; the knowable in the form is the actuality, reality's coming to fulfillment of its proper signification. As a result, the form–matter connection has nothing to do with the connection of a fullness and an emptiness, or the connection of a unifying operation with a diversity, as with Leibniz and Kant. The form is the fullness of the real and of meaning. The split between the fulfilled and the unfulfilled, between act and potency, is the foundation of the *Physics*; one has seen that the definition of movement depends on it. It is furthermore the doctrine of the principle of movement that completes Aristotle's break with Platonism; for the "Universals" are finally in potency, in the sense that the genera are a field of possibilities of which just one is realized by means of the specific difference and the "last differences." Finally, and above all, the distinction of act and potency is the key to the ontological problem of the hierarchization of the real. For beings are more or less being depending on whether they are more or less act, that is, without indetermination, without the threat of destruction, of change.

Third step: the pure act is the supreme intelligible

If the form is what one understands in the real, this will be (according to 7)[8] the "simple" substance, what is only act, which will realize the height of intelligibility. For the first time, Aristotle's theology links up with his great design: and it is necessary to say that Aristotle has not *substituted* his unmoved mover for the Platonic Idea in the region (common to Aristotle and Plato) of the suprasensible; this is not a substitution on the same level, but an innovation; the "pure act" is a novel metaphysical dimension, because this notion presupposes the double revolution of form and act; in this sense 7 is no longer anything like a Platonic residue, more or less well integrated into a new metaphysics, but already a notion built on Aristotelian soil; it is an analysis not of language and its significations, but of the real as form and as act that supports the reflection on separate substance.[9]

Fourth step: the pure act is repeated in sensible things

We are therefore at the litigious point: how is separate substance the source of being? The *Metaphysics* contains only a few lines responding to this question: θ 8 1050b28: "Corruptible things *imitate* the incorruptible." Cf. Λ 7 1072b13-14: "All things depend on the separate entity as their final cause."[10] So it is therefore in the exclusive direction of final causality that Aristotle sought the foundation of analogy that allows founding a single science of being as being on the basis of a science of first being.

This bond of imitation and dependence in relation to a *terminus ad quem* is never treated systematically by Aristotle, even though it is there that the unity of ontology and theology plays out; one finds only sparse allusions to this grand principle of the unification of beings. Owens cites:

---

[8] *Metaphysics* Λ 7 1072a33-34.
[9] Cf. Étienne Gilson, *L'Être et l'essence* (Paris: Vrin, 1948), p. 47 (AC).
[10] The reference is imprecise.

1) *De Anima* II 4 415a26-27: to create a being similar to oneself is "to participate in the eternal and in the divine, in the measure possible, for such is the object of desire of all beings, the end of their natural activity." The living individual cannot remain the same and numerically one, it is the species that through its perpetuation imitates the divine unchangeability.
2) *De Caelo*[11] I 9 279a17-30: "From the immortal and divine duration derives the being and the life which the other things enjoy, some in a manner more or less articulated, the others feebly."
3) *De Gen. et Corr.*[12] II 10, 336b27–337a7, where final causality and imitation are explained by each other. Owens notes that it is a real struggle for the best that constitutes the imitation of being by beings:[13] circular movement, the perpetuity of generation, the cycle of the elements, and even linear movement; for it is "by imitation of circular movement that the linear movement is continuous."

What character of the pure Act is thereby repeated? Essentially permanence in an activity that is not undergone, not received, not "moved": that permanence of an active repose that Aristotle calls thought thinking itself. What is imitated is not so much an intelligible universal as a singular intelligence. The act that perpetuates life, the act that perpetuates the cycle of the physical elements, the act above all by which the wise person is established in the contemplative life (according to the portrait in the *Nicomachean Ethics*) are different approximations of this analogical unity of being; and this analogical unity of beings within being, in turn, founds an analogical unity in the science of being. But these categories of pure imitation, of the struggle for the proximate best or the distant imitation, for a degree of being, etc., are not really elaborated by Aristotle but dealt with allusively: in order to elaborate them rigorously it would be necessary to draw closer together the fundamental difference between Platonic participation which goes from intelligible to sensible and Aristotelian imitation which goes from the pure act to the mixed act, from the real form to the unreal form, from the divine intelligence to human contemplation,

---

[11] *On the Heavens.*
[12] *On Generation and Corruption.*
[13] Owens, *op. cit.*, p. 420, n. 35 (AC).

to a life and a natural movement as the unfulfilled act of potency. Then one could catch sight of in what sense the Individuality of first Being is the principle of the universality of being as being, and one would understand why there is no separate ontology in Aristotle, why the father of ontology did not even invent the word. Aristotle did not explicitly realize it; this is why his sketch is coherent, but his working it out remains in suspense.

4 The limit of a philosophy of form: form and existence

If Aristotle did not complete his program, it was no doubt because of his indifference about what it is that makes for the *existence of a being*. We have noted several times[14] that his philosophy remains a philosophy of *quiddities*, of forms. This is why, between God and beings, Aristotle did not look for a relation that posits existence, but rather for a similarity of form; also, his philosophy rests on *final causality* and not on efficient production.

It is the encounter with the God of Israel – who "creates" things, rather than allowing them to imitate his serene thought thinking thought – that will provoke the renewal of Aristotelianism. The sole question that interests us here is knowing whether this shift of accent from final causality to productive causality was in conformity with Aristotle's genial insight or if it was not instead an overturning of the Aristotelian problematic.

Aristotelian *ousia* is indeed "that which is," it is fully a subject in relation to what happens to it, for example a man or a particular horse, as he says in *Categories* V; it is even an energy, a source of action. But recent commentators (Ross, Tricot, Owens, Gilson) agree in saying that Aristotle remained halfway between the universal and the concrete and that his notion of *ousia* suffers from an irreducible ambiguity, which gets expressed in the difficulties of translation: *ousia* is substance *and* essence (Ravaisson translates essence, Tricot translates substance, Owens translates *entity*. It is he who seems to me to respect the lack of differentiation of essence and existence in *ousia*; it is necessary to find a word that remains intact in relation to the medieval distinctions).

---

[14] Note: cf. the reduction of causality to identity of the form: the omission of singularity to the profit of quiddity in the "final differences" (PR).

Gilson can speak of a "subtle elimination of problems linked to the fundamental fact of existence."[15] Cf. his entire analysis,[16] which ends as follows: "This whole philosophy, which in fact is only interested in that which exists, always approaches it in such a way that the problem of its existence need not be posed." He sees in this the fundamental reason why the question of the "origin of the world" makes no sense in Aristotelianism; in the final analysis Aristotle ignores the real distinction between essence and existence, but this is what it is necessary to posit in order to understand his *ousia*, his "be-ingness." So, the cause of a thing is its form, and "to seek why a thing is, is to seek why it is itself, therefore really not to seek anything at all."[17] It is in virtue of one and the same principle that a being is and that it is a cause[18] (we have already cited that extraordinary text of Aristotle's: "In this way therefore, in every production, as with every syllogism, the principle is the essence (*ousia*); for it is beginning from the quiddity that syllogisms are made and it is beginning from there too that the generations occur," Z 9 1034a30-32). The relation of God to the world cannot therefore be *existential*; God is the cause of "that which" the world is; he is not the cause why the world "should be" ("Aristotle's de-existentialized *ousia* does not allow resolving the problems of existence and, to the degree that efficient causality implies a problem of existence, it does not allow offering an adequate interpretation of this kind of causality").[19] It was the "theologies of the Old Testament," as Gilson says, that introduced a problematic of existence distinct from that of *ousia*, and above all the Muslim Arabs. It is here that a retrospective analysis starting from Averroes, Avicenna, St Thomas, would allow confirmation of what a direct analysis of Aristotle has allowed us to discover.

Had Aristotle known a story of creation, he undoubtedly would have placed it on the side of tall tales, for creation would have appeared to him to bring philosophical knowledge back to the level of being by accident, and therefore outside the field of science. What is more, as Owens forcefully puts it, the pure act cannot do anything outside itself because it is entirely determined and its

---

[15] Gilson, *L'Être et l'Essence, op. cit.*, p. 58 (AC).
[16] *Id.*, pp. 46–58, *cit.* p. 58 (AC).
[17] *Id.*, p. 59 (AC).
[18] *Id.*, p. 60 (AC). [Above, p. 219, Ricoeur cites a different translation.]
[19] Gilson, *op. cit.*, p. 62 (AC).

"actuality" would then be placed in the patient who receives its action (Θ 8 1050a30-31); Owens even speaks of a "finitude" of the separate entity, something that would be equivocal when it came to stating the *definition* of a perfect form; a "Potency of God" would be a crippled potentiality; moreover, there is no place for efficient causality in the source of being.[20]

This is the reason that the derivation of plurality starting from unity is not an Aristotelian problem, but just the setting in order, by the path of final causality, of a hierarchical series of forms. The eternity of the world is thus the leitmotif that gets maintained from Parmenides to the Atomists, to Plato, to Aristotle, to the Stoics, to Plotinus. But, given this common scheme, it is radically discontinuous philosophies that spring up in history. It is through a discontinuity more important than the one that separates Aristotle from Plato that a medieval problematic of the radical origin of existence will spring up from the non-philosophy of the Old Testament.

Conclusion of the second part

The moment has come to take an overall look at the *Metaphysics* and to ask whether Aristotle has fulfilled his own program.

1 Chronological sequence and logical sequence

First we have to show how the two readings of the *Metaphysics* fit together, that of Werner Jaeger, who seeks to find the order of discovery, the chronological order of the theses, starting from a Platonizing *Urmetaphysik* moving toward a properly Aristotelian stage, and the order of exposition, the one Aristotle wanted the reader to follow in giving this ultimate arrangement to writings from quite different periods and mentalities.

According to the probable chronological order, the theology of Λ would represent an earlier state; the objective of the *Metaphysics* would still be, in the Platonic manner, to determine a supra-sensible reality; the ontology of Book E would represent the final stage: the objective of the *Metaphysics* would be to order the meaning of being in a such a way as to encompass and overcome

---

[20] Owens, *op. cit.*, p. 297 (AC).

the duality of sensible substances (for which the group Z H Θ, introduced late, would have demonstrated its reality and ontological dignity) and the unmoving substances inherited from the first period.

Let us suppose this chronological schema to be true. How can we make use of it to understand Aristotle? It is necessary to maintain strongly that this understanding of Aristotle would be the best and even the only one possible if the contradiction of the two designs – that of doing a theology or a doctrine of divine being and that of being as being – were a radical contradiction; all that would in fact be left to us would be to divide these two enterprises into two psychological periods in Aristotle's fateful life and to seek the equally psychological motivation that presided over this substitution. But if Aristotle did believe he could give this final arrangement to his work (which places the theology at the end and the doctrine of being as being in the middle as a sort of "tenon" between the diaporematic investigation of A–E 1, the preparatory explanation of sensible *ousia* in Z H Θ, and the theory of separate substances in Λ M N), it was that he thought that the two plans were coherent and that the older thesis of metaphysics as theology was the partial realization of the program, maybe glimpsed *last*, of metaphysics as ontology, but placed *before* the theology. The search for this logical coherence is independent of the search for the chronological succession: only if it fails is it that the psychological explanation remains the sole one possible. Still, many authors have begun from the postulate that the tension between ontology and theology was untenable and hence the chronological explanation which is a psychological explanation dispenses with having to *understand* the work as it is, as it was finally intended.

2 Recapitulation of the problem of being and beings

Let us recall the propositions that map out the *Metaphysics*.

1. Wisdom is the search for the causes and first principles of things (A): philosophy is etiology.
2. "There is a science that studies being as being and the attributes that belong to it essentially." Thus begins Γ 1: philosophy is ontology.
3. It is in terms of substances (*ousia*) that philosophy ought to

apprehend the principles and causes (Λ 1 1069a18);[21] philosophy is ousiology.

4. "If an unmoving substance exists, the science of this subject
   must be prior and must be first philosophy" (E 1 1026a30);
   philosophy is theology.

From the cause to being, from being to *ousia*, from first *ousia* to
separate *ousia*, such is the Aristotelian *way*. What is it that makes
for the unity of this reasoning? The fundamental thesis that being
is not a genus that is divided into species, but rather the analogical unity of a series of accepted meanings that arrange themselves
around a first signification taken as a reference; the meanings of
the word are not equivocal, but equivocal *pros hen* (relative to a
basic meaning). This is the methodological thread of the whole
Metaphysics. In effect, if *ousia* is the meaning of being as being,
in turn the meaning of *ousia* is ordered following a sequence of
examples, for which the separate substance is the first example.

All this is quite coherent; what Werner Jaeger has established is
that the overall meaning appeared last and culminates in the final
words of E 1: "If there were no other substances than those that
are constituted by nature, physics would be the first science. But if
there exists an unmoving substance, the science of this substance[22]
must be prior and must be first philosophy; and it is universal in
this way because it is first: and it will be for it to consider Being
as being, that is both its essence and the attributes that belong to
it as being."

Except this plan remains quite muddled. First of all, Aristotle
was led to discern in the word being not one series of meanings,
but four: 1) the series that constitutes being according to the categories (substance, quality, quantity, place, time, and all the other
analogous modes of significations of being); 2) being as accident;
3) Being in the sense of truth; 4) Being as act and as potency.
An elucidation of the meanings of being develops in a tree-like
manner, along the axis *on – ousia – ousia prote* (W. Jaeger also
speaks of a "phenomenology of being" developed starting from
the conviction that being is not a genus but a bundle of related
significations); this phenomenology of being represents the final
state of Aristotle's thought about being (E 2–4). On its side, the

---

[21] "Λ 2" in the *Course*.

[22] In the *Course*, "substance" was erroneously replaced by "sublime."

word *ousia* is also a source for proliferations of meaning: it is the first in an ordered series of examples, but it is so in many ways; it is the substrate of the accidents (Z 1),[23] it is matter, it is form, it is the concrete composition; by analogy, it is the accident functioning as substrate. It is even the universal substance as secondary substance. Above all, *ousia* is "first" in a double sense, first as form taken without its matter (Z 7 1032b1-4), and finally the form denuded by itself of all matter (Γ 3 1005a35; E 1 1026a10-31; Λ 7 1072a32), which in turn designates the thinking God of Λ 7, the unmoving movers of Λ 8, and the agent intellect, "separate" from the body, of *De anima* III 4.

Thus the *Metaphysics* is a book overloaded with annexed investigations; the central line is marked by crossroads explored in all directions. All this is, if not simple, at least coherent.

But beyond the question of the coherence of the design lies the question of its complete fulfillment. Aristotle would have made it all the way to the end of his task if he had shown in what way "first philosophy is universal because first"; he has only indicated the direction, in positing that the universality of being consists in the "dependence" of every being on the most excellent among them; but the connection to finality – to final attraction – in which this dependence consists in turn remains a connection of extrinsic imitation of the most perfect by the least perfect. Aristotle entirely ignores an initial giving of existence.

So the unity of beings within being remains precarious, even more than does the unity of accepted meanings of being in the sequence of the categories. Aristotle's whole ontology rests on these two "transitions": from being as being to substance, from perfect substance to second substances; these two transitions indicate the two moments wherein everything in Aristotelianism is won or lost.

---

[23] Rather, Z 3.

Index

Albert the Great, 155
Alexander the Great, 152, 155
anankê, 78
Anaxagoras, 81, 120, 123, 125, 126, 127, 128, 138, 155, 165, 166, 167
Anaximander, 118, 119, 122, 123, 124, 125, 127, 128, 135
Anaximenes, 120
Andronicus, 151, 153
Anselm, 53
Antisthenes, 81, 171, 180
Apelt, Otto, 64
Aquinas, Thomas, 155, 170, 235, 249
archê, 106, 107, 115, 118, 119, 120, 123, 129, 130, 132, 133, 204, 214, 230
Aristotelianism, 73, 156, 157, 180, 224, 225, 227, 234, 245, 248, 249, 253
Aristotle, 35, 40, 65, 72, 73, 76, 79, 96, 98, 115, 119, 121, 123, 125, 126, 127
Augustine, 153
Averroes, 249
Avicenna, 23, 245, 249

Beautiful, idea of, 35, 56, 77, 104, 137

being
    as accident, 252
    analogical, 185, 191, 195, 206, 232, 235, 238, 244, 247
    aporia of, 71–3, 78
    appearing, 18, 131
    becoming, 15, 18, 129, 244
    as being, 121, 146, 147, 148, 157, 159, 164, 174, 177, 179, 182, 183, 184, 190, 192, 195, 196, 232, 248, 251, 253
    being-known, 135
    beingness, 145, 184, 236, 249
    beings, 71, 122, 184
    concrete, 236, 248
    as copula, 10
    corporeal, 91
    definition of, 94, 135
    dialectic of, 48, 82, 173
    divine, 251
    doctrine of, 145
    eternal, 159
    as existence, 10
    first, 164, 196, 242, 246, 248
    as idea, of ideas, 188
    kinds, 64, 66, 68, 134, 173–4
    language, 15
    many, 90
    material, 91
    meaning of, 156, 157, 250, 253
    motionless, 177, 196

movement, 93
   multiple meanings of, 173–4, 185,
      186, 188, 191, 195, 198, 207,
      253
   non-being, 17, 81, 82, 86, 88, 89,
      90, 93, 95, 122, 173, 186, 208,
      209
   one, 76, 83, 84, 86, 87, 90, 91, 92,
      128, 173, 174
   immanence of, 87
   reality of, 85
   theology of, 84, 87
   transcendence of, 87, 133
   unity of, 85
   otherness, 88
   ousia, 10, 17, 23, 35, 36, 71, 92,
      100, 145, 185–6, 187, 191, 195,
      236, 245, 249
   perfect, 192
   presence, 26
   problem of, 73, 74, 92, 93–5, 156,
      188
   pseudo-idea of, 174
   as pure act, 192
   question of, 9, 187
   reality, 232–3, 234
   reciprocity of being and non-being,
      89
   rest, 94
   seeming, 129
   third, 94, 95, 187
   total, 137
   transcendental, 64
   true being, 1, 129, 146, 177,
      183
   truth of, 26, 122, 252
   unfulfilled, 212
   unity of, 232, 238, 242, 244, 247,
      253
   universal, 253
   unmoved, 159
Bergson, Henri, 52, 163, 216
Bonitz, Hermann, 151, 155
Bosch, Hieronymus, 141
Brémond, André, 236
Brisson, Luc, 106
Brochard, Victor, 75, 84, 85, 86, 97,
   98, 136
Brueghel, Pieter, 141
Brunschvicg, Léon, 201
Bureau, Stéphane, viii
Burnet, John, 119, 123
Burnyeat, Miles F., 26, 131, 163

categories, 35, 174, 177, 179, 186,
   199, 203, 211, 252, 253
Categories, 201, 224, 248
causality, causes, 32, 38, 45, 60, 77,
   78, 103, 105–8, 109, 133, 134,
   138, 139, 158, 163, 165, 168–9,
   176, 178, 180, 184, 204, 207,
   217, 218, 219, 220, 238, 249,
   252
   becoming, 103
   efficient, 177, 218, 249, 250
   exemplary, 138
   final, 38, 135, 177, 244, 246, 247,
      248, 250
   first, 162, 164
   formal, 135, 177, 181
   personalized, 138
   productive, 248, 249
   reason, 218, 219
   workman-like, 137
cave, allegory of, 37, 45, 52
Chambry, Émile, 14, 26, 52, 86, 99,
   100, 107, 131, 163
change, 165, 187, 200–1, 210, 211,
   213, 217, 230
chôra, 97–8, 102, 109
Cicero, 153
contemplation, 47, 55, 58, 60, 61,
   67
Cornford, F. M., 26, 86, 94, 100, 131,
   163
Cratylus, 167
Cratylus, 13–19, 34, 57, 110, 130
Croiset, Alfred, 10
courage, 36

Damascenus, Damascius, 59
De Anima, 164, 189, 207, 231, 241,
   247, 253
De Caelo, 189, 247
death, 22, 28, 48, 52–3, 54, 57, 58,
   68, 131, 132, 142
definition, 11–12, 23, 129, 171,
   178, 216, 220–1, 222, 225, 230,
   250
   verbal, 23
Deichgräber, Karl, 125
demiurge, 99, 102, 105, 106, 107,
   108, 109, 125, 126, 127, 128,
   137, 138, 139, 142
Democritus, 120, 186, 205, 236
Descartes, René, 17, 20, 40, 52, 187,
   202, 220

desire, 52, 54, 110, 192, 207, 209, 239, 243
  analogy of, 242–3
diairésis, 62, 81, 88
dialectic, 14, 42, 48, 49, 56–7, 58, 59, 61, 62, 64, 67, 68, 76, 80, 81, 82, 84, 88, 89, 92, 95, 97, 98, 102, 146, 153, 174, 175, 176
  ascending, 60, 62, 64, 67, 91
  of beings, 82
  descending, 62, 64, 67
  eristic, 80, 86, 92, 131
  fragmented, 134
  of great kinds, 96
  of idea of being, 68, 82, 173
  of ideas, 81, 134
  of intelligible and sensible, 84, 107, 108
  movement and rest, 100
  reflective, 88–9
  of same and other, 96
  same–other, 93
  of sensible, 80
  of the one, 93
  total, 132
Diels, Hermann Alexander, 120
Diès, Auguste, 9, 17, 26, 54, 63, 68, 71, 72, 97, 115, 128, 129, 136
Diogenes, 43, 120, 126, 127, 138
Dionysius of Syracuse, 22
Diotima, 48–9, 61, 68, 108
divided line, 39–44, 46
divine, 115, 119, 126, 128, 139, 142, 163, 189, 196, 239, 251
  immanent, 133–4
  personalized, 126, 138
  philosophy of, 127
  precedes God, 133, 138
  proportional to being, 129
  science of, 163, 196
  transcendent, 133
Dumont, Jean-Paul, 105, 125

Empedocles, 120, 123, 165, 166
empiricism, 24, 25, 41
Epicurus, 123, 153
Epinomis, 153, 154
essence, 8, 14–19, 23, 171, 179, 183, 188, 216, 228, 233, 235, 239, 248, 249
  inherence, 10
  ontology of, 15
  participation, 11

quiddity, 171, 172, 181, 187, 198, 204, 216, 217, 218, 219, 227, 228, 229, 230, 233, 234, 235, 236, 245, 248, 249
Euclid, 43, 81
evil, 108, 109, 110
  theodicy, 109
existence, 168, 188, 228, 234, 235, 236, 239, 248, 250, 253
  individual, 217, 228
explanation, 204–5

Faust, 52
Festugière, Paul, 26, 54, 56, 59, 60, 61, 63, 64, 67–8, 173
form, 145, 171, 192, 209, 213, 215, 216, 219, 228, 231, 237, 245, 247–50
  definition, 220
  eternal, 219
  non-sensible, 219
  ousia, 178
  pure, 215
  see also substance
forms, *see* idea(s)
Fouillé, 52
Frede, Dorothea, 52, 99, 107

Gaye, R. K., 118, 125, 209
genus–species, 12, 178, 181, 185, 191, 205, 221, 229, 230, 245, 253
Gill, Mary Louise, 86
Gilson, Étienne, 10, 192, 247, 248, 249
God, gods, 37, 107, 109, 110, 115, 116, 117, 119, 120, 121, 122, 127, 128, 133, 135, 138, 139, 140, 142, 164, 189, 192, 219, 224, 230, 232, 233, 235, 239, 242, 243, 247, 253
  Hebrew, 248
  physical, 239–40, 241
  spiritual, 239, 241–42
  see also divine
Goethe, Johann Wolfgang von, 155
Goldschmidt, Victor, 25, 110, 115, 122, 129, 132, 134, 141
good, idea of, 34, 35, 37, 38, 42, 43, 44, 45, 48, 50, 56, 58–61, 64, 67, 77, 84, 87, 91–2, 110, 111, 116,

123, 127, 128, 131, 132, 133, 134, 135, 136, 137, 139, 173, 174, 177, 243
Gorgias, 81
Gorgias, 33, 110, 111, 140, 141
Grube, G. M. A., 38, 56
Guéroult, Martial, 53, 55

Hackforth, R., 52, 99, 107
Hamelin, Octave, 191, 218
Hardie, R. P., 118, 125, 209
Hegel, G. W. F., 53, 134
Heidegger, Martin, 94, 120
Heraclitus, 18, 22, 24, 34, 87, 93, 105, 120, 123, 124, 125, 127, 128, 130, 135, 167, 168, 180, 187, 201
Herodotus, 163
Hesiod, 153
Hippias Major, 35
Hume, David, 220
Husserl, Edmund, 15, 24, 25

idea(s)
  articulated plurality, 11
  attribute of things, 7
  being of, 56, 64, 80, 81, 86, 94, 103, 180
  cause, 102
  compossibility, 36, 44, 57, 60, 85, 88
  dialectically related, 51, 81
  distinction determination of, 36, 37, 38, 51, 58, 133, 137
  divine, 115, 116
  enumerable, 8, 36, 92
  eternal, 140, 180
  hierarchy of, 46
  highest kinds, 60, 63, 64, 66, 68, 86, 88, 92, 94, 96, 98, 100, 134, 170
  infinite, 118, 119, 123
  intermediate, 92
  mathematical, 35
  movement–rest, 73, 93, 100
  non-being, 86, 88, 98, 109, 110, 111, 115
  one, 44, 48, 59, 61, 66, 67, 75, 80, 82, 83, 86, 91, 111, 115, 116, 122, 123, 128, 132, 134, 135, 138, 241, 245
  one and many, 48, 62, 75, 77, 90, 92, 93, 104, 125

one and other, 93
ontology of, 7, 71, 116
order of, 36
origin, 77
other, 76, 88, 93, 95, 98, 109, 115, 146, 177
participation, 71, 77
philosophy of, 97, 139
platonic, 216–17, 222, 227, 234, 238, 246
principle of existence, 171
principle of unity, 132
real, 77, 170
religious function of, 115
rule-governed multiplicity, 65
same–other, 73, 93
separate reality, 47
similar–dissimilar, 76
things, 103
totality, all, 104, 107–8, 136, 140
unit of signification, 171
value, 45–6
world, 140
see also good, idea of
imitation, 10–11, 15–16, 35, 40, 168, 246, 253
  copy, 15
  model, 15, 35
  pre-empirical, 52
infinite, 66, 118, 119, 123, 125, 128
intersubjectivity, 16
intuition, 28, 48, 49, 52, 57, 58, 59, 60, 62, 131
  beyond discourse, 59
  mythic, 68
  synoptic, 57, 61–62, 67
  unifying, 62

Jaeger, Werner, 120, 122, 125, 146, 147, 151, 152, 154, 155, 156, 157, 158, 176, 179, 180, 190, 192, 196, 204, 250, 253
Jesus, 58
Job, 109
Jowett, Benjamin, 14, 106
justice, 35, 45

Kant, Immanuel, 17, 21, 23, 25, 27, 40, 51, 52, 60, 88, 104, 121, 135, 186, 220, 232, 235, 245
  schematization, 135, 136, 137
Kirk, G. S., 105, 119, 120, 125

knowledge, 26, 71, 87, 99, 100, 101, 162, 217, 224, 232, 236, 241, 243
  degrees of, 23, 37, 39, 49, 53
  good as foundation, 136
  migration, 130
  ontology of 23
  right opinion, 29, 30–3, 40, 47, 53–4, 108, 131, 142
  scientific, 226

language, 12, 13, 48, 50, 71, 109, 111, 129, 145, 169, 186, 199, 200, 201, 203, 206, 212, 246
  attribution, 89, 96, 187
  discourse, 36, 61–2, 87, 92, 97, 99
  equivocity of, 14
  naming, 16, 25, 36, 88, 91, 92, 99, 110, 132, 216
  ontology of, 115
  philosophical, 97
  philosophy of, 92
  predication, 228
  signification(s), 13, 17, 88, 92, 104, 129, 146, 156, 171, 183, 197, 246
Laws, 134, 135, 153
Le Blond, Jean Marie, 148, 199, 200, 204, 205, 206, 211, 232, 234, 235, 236
Leibniz, Gottfried, 64, 187, 233, 236, 245
Letter VII, 36, 131
Levett, 26, 131, 163
logic, 179, 180, 187, 196, 215–16, 234, 238
logical positivism, 25–6
logos, 123–4, 135, 220

Malebranche, Nicolas, 40
Mansion, Auguste, 148, 159, 205
Mansion, Suzanne, 235
mathematics, 11, 21, 31, 32, 36, 40, 42, 44, 45, 47, 49, 52, 55, 66, 77, 82, 159, 182, 188, 238
  intermediary function of, 34, 40, 45, 46
  objects of, 35, 41, 42, 46
matter, 148, 165, 166, 171, 183, 189, 192, 199, 201, 202, 204, 205, 206, 207, 208–9, 212–14, 215, 217, 221, 226, 227, 228, 230, 231, 233, 234, 253

generation, 208
  privation, 208–9
measure, 44–5, 99, 124, 134, 135, 137, 203
  just measure, 44–5, 66, 134
memory, 162, 226
Meno, 29, 30, 33, 41, 43, 164
métanoia, 130
metaphysics, 147, 157, 158–9
  of ideas, 153
  object of, 183
Metaphysics, 2, 40, 98
Meyerson, Émile, 218
mimêsis, see imitation
Moreau, Joseph, 35, 154
movement, 206, 209, 210, 211, 212, 217, 220, 229, 239–40, 242, 245
  eternity of, 239, 240, 242
Mugler, Charles, 41, 42, 43
Mugnier, René, 129, 132, 139
myth, 47–8, 50, 52, 54, 57, 68, 97, 101, 105–6, 119, 127, 139, 140, 142, 163
  eschatological, 129, 140, 141–2
  generation of sensible, 97
  judgment and retribution, 140–1

Natorp, Paul, 179
nature, 209–10, 236, 243
Neo-Kantianism, 84, 139
Neo-Platonism 29, 47, 49, 60–1, 84, 155, 223
Newton, Isaac, 104
Nicomachean Ethics, 152, 173, 241, 247
Nietzsche, Friedrich, 120, 167
noûs, 123, 124, 125, 126, 138, 157, 165, 167, 189, 231
Nuyens, Franciscus, 154, 159, 160

Olympiodorus, 59
On Generation and Corruption, 247
On Philosophy, 153, 157
ontology, 95, 111, 115, 123, 145, 146, 148, 157, 160, 188, 190, 210, 225, 239, 248, 250, 251, 253
  Aristotelian, 2, 156, 180, 184, 186, 190, 253
  critical, 2
  essentially discontinuous, 17
  first-degree, 1, 71, 146

general, 147
of knowledge, 23
limits of, 111
Platonic, 17, 116
second-degree, 1, 71, 88, 89, 173, 174
theology, 115, 127, 246, 251
see also being
ousia, see being, form, substance
Owens, Joseph, 148, 191, 192, 196, 203, 220, 246–47, 248, 249–50

Pachet, Pierre, 38, 56
Parian, Brice, 12
Parmenides, 17, 23, 55, 71, 72, 74, 75, 77, 80, 81, 93, 105, 120, 121, 122–3, 124, 125, 127, 128, 130, 146, 167, 202, 245, 250
Parmenides, 1, 44, 68, 72–89, 90, 91, 92, 93, 96–101, 102, 116, 128, 137, 152, 153, 167, 168, 168, 179
participation, 77, 84, 86, 87, 93, 94–5, 96, 98, 108, 110, 111, 168, 169, 172, 179, 247
analogical representation, 78
hypothesis of, 78
impossible, 79, 84
intelligible in intelligible, 77, 86, 88, 96, 97, 137, 177
intelligible to sensible, 138
intentional representation, 79
lateral, 80, 102
material representation, 78, 97
non-participation, 85
possible, 84
resemblance, 78, 96
sensible in intelligible, 77, 88, 96, 97–100, 102, 137
unthinkable, 78–9
vertical, 80, 102
Parts of Animals, 206, 231, 235
Pascal, Blaise, 31
Pelligrin, Pierre, 118, 125
Pericles, 32
Phaedo, 35, 44, 52–4, 56, 57, 60, 77, 81, 98, 100, 103, 110, 125, 129, 130, 133, 134, 136, 140, 141, 152, 165, 167, 172
Phaedrus, 49, 50–1, 55, 80, 81, 88, 97, 103, 106, 107, 129, 130, 131, 132, 134, 138, 140, 240
Philebus, 37, 45, 48, 52, 59, 60, 61,

65–7, 84, 87, 91, 92, 97, 98, 103, 104, 107, 108, 116, 125, 133, 134, 135, 138, 139, 174, 227, 230
Philo, 127
philosophy, 21–2, 54, 68, 98, 161, 164, 176, 195, 196, 251–2
aporia of, 87
ascent, 27
evasion, 27
failure, 29
first, 147, 155, 157, 158, 176, 180, 188, 189, 190, 237–8, 252, 253
history of, 72, 90, 93, 94, 153–4, 161,164, 182, 187
immediate, 23–4
inevitable defeat of, 27
Ionian, 165
myth of, 68
object of, 196, 200
reflection on religion, 53
religion, 120, 132
second, 237
Socratic, 93
theology, 184, 200
physics, 2, 159, 169, 179, 180, 188, 189, 197, 208, 210, 215–16, 217, 238, 253
Physics, 118, 164, 168, 169, 186, 189, 190, 196, 200, 201, 204, 206, 207, 208, 209, 210, 211, 212, 227, 230, 236, 240, 245
Physis, 117, 119, 120, 121, 122
phronêsis, 54
Plato, 145, 146, 148, 151, 152, 153, 154, 156, 158, 162, 164, 165, 166, 167, 168, 169, 170, 171, 172, 173, 175, 180, 186, 187, 197, 208, 220, 224, 227, 235, 245, 250
Platonism, 1, 10, 11, 14, 16, 17, 18, 19, 29, 34, 35, 47, 58, 64, 67, 71, 80, 87, 90, 91, 101, 103, 106, 107, 110, 111, 116, 117, 128, 132, 134, 139, 145, 152, 153, 156, 161, 162, 167, 168, 169, 170, 171, 172, 173, 174, 176, 179, 201, 219, 223, 226, 236, 240, 245
Plotinus, 58, 111, 123, 124, 133, 223–4, 231, 240, 241, 250
politics, 32, 33, 37, 45
Posterior Analytics, 226, 234, 235

Pradines, Maurice, 51
praxis, 16
Proclus, 43, 82, 83
Protagoras, 18, 24, 27, 28, 34, 81, 85,
   124, 155, 180, 187
Protrepticus, 153
Pythagoras, Pythagoreans, 22, 65,
   104, 123, 166, 168

Ravaisson, Félix, 170, 248
Raven, J. E., 105, 119, 120
Reeve, C. D. C., 14, 38, 56, 125
Reinhardt, Karl, 121
religion, 115, 117, 118, 119, 139
   Orphic, 53, 54, 57, 103, 122, 130,
      132, 153
   philosophy, 120
   rational, 115, 117, 121, 128
reminiscence, 11, 30, 31, 41–2, 49,
   52, 68, 121
Republic, 34, 35, 36–44, 45, 48, 49,
   50, 52, 54, 55, 56, 59, 60, 61,
   63, 64, 80, 81, 84, 87, 91, 92,
   116, 120, 129, 130, 131, 133,
   134, 135, 136, 137, 138, 139,
   140, 173
Ricoeur archive, vii
Robin, Léon, 32, 52, 148, 169, 171,
   172, 173, 228, 231, 232, 234
Rodier, Georges, 43, 44, 63, 64, 65,
   67, 195, 199, 213, 225
Rohde, Erwin, 120
Ross, W. D., 9, 15, 100, 120, 148,
   166, 172, 186, 189, 213, 220,
   248
Ryan, Paul, 86

Schofield, M., 105, 119, 120, 125
Schopenhauer, Arthur, 154
science, 20–1, 22, 23, 31, 32, 33, 37,
   47, 62, 108, 129, 131, 162, 164,
   170, 176–7, 178, 182, 183, 189,
   190, 195, 201, 204, 224, 225,
   227, 234, 243, 246, 247, 249
   approximate, 23
   Aristotelian, 225
   beginning of, 49
   divine, 129–30
   first causes, 195
   hierarchy of, 37
   object of, 226
   sciences, 188
   unity of, 20, 37, 133

second immediacy, 28
Shorey, Paul, 37, 56, 129
Simplicius, 118, 119, 200
Socrates, 13, 29–30, 31, 33, 41, 42,
   57–8, 61, 62, 68, 72, 74–5, 76,
   77, 78, 81, 120, 136, 138, 154,
   155, 167, 168, 202, 231, 233,
   235
Socratic philosophy, 93, 125
Solon, 32
Sophist, 37, 44, 57, 58, 63–5, 67, 72,
   73, 74, 78, 80, 82, 84, 85, 86,
   87, 88, 89, 90–101, 102, 128,
   134, 135, 136, 137, 138, 145,
   146, 168, 172, 174, 179, 187,
   201
Sophists, sophism, 22, 27, 71, 80, 81,
   109, 124, 129, 202
soul, 31, 32, 35, 38, 41, 52, 53, 55,
   98, 99–100, 101, 106, 107, 110,
   111, 131, 135, 136, 138, 140,
   142, 164, 223, 224, 230, 231,
   241
   becoming of, 52
   fall of, 103, 107
   just, 141
   noûs, 58
   Orphic, 132
   pre-existence, 47, 132
   purified, 57
   resembles idea, 55
   unjust, 111, 141
   world soul, 240
Speusippus, 152
Spinoza, Baruch, 22, 26, 53, 131,
   187, 220
Statesman, 44, 57, 66, 72, 87, 138
Stevens, Annick, 209
Stoics, Stoicism, 124, 126, 153, 154,
   224, 240, 250
substance, 145, 156, 157, 164, 170,
   171, 172, 173, 177, 178, 181,
   184, 186, 187, 188–9, 198, 215,
   220, 221, 222, 223, 226, 228,
   232, 234, 237, 252
   composed, 226, 227, 229, 233,
      234, 244
   concrete, 203, 248
   eternal, 238, 239, 240
   finality, 192, 244, 253
   first, 127, 189, 196–7, 201, 202,
      227, 237, 240, 242
   form, 192, 202, 204, 205, 209,

210, 213–14, 215, 219, 221,
223, 226, 228, 229, 230, 234,
240, 253
formal, 189
genus, 198, 225, 245
hupokeimenon, 198, 202
immaterial, 244
imperfect, 210
individual, 170, 201, 203, 206, 211
last difference, 221–2, 225, 231–2,
245, 248
ousia, 145, 177, 179, 183, 195,
198, 210, 227, 228, 234, 235,
248, 249, 251, 252, 253
potency–act, 204, 205, 207–14,
215, 229, 231, 236, 240, 243,
244, 245, 247, 252
primacy of, 187
pure act, 240, 241, 242, 243, 244,
246–8, 249
secondary, 189, 253
sensible, 2, 11, 148, 156, 158, 177,
189, 196, 197, 198, 215, 226,
237, 238, 240, 251
separate, 147, 184, 246, 251, 253
simple, 246
subject, 198, 199, 203, 208, 234,
248
substances, 188
substrate, 198–204, 212, 228, 253
supra-sensible, 158–9, 177, 237,
250
supreme, 2
uncomposed, 244
universal, 198
unmoving, 184, 190, 191, 192,
200, 238, 239, 251, 252
sunagôgê, 62–3
Symposium, 49, 51, 58, 59, 60, 61,
108, 130, 131, 152

Taylor, 9
testimony, 27
Thales, 117
Theaetetus, 24, 153

Theaetetus, 34, 35–6, 37, 43, 54, 57,
71, 72, 73, 87, 92, 96, 111, 125,
129, 131, 163, 187, 201
theology, 115, 127, 146–7, 148, 153,
156–7, 159, 160, 184, 188, 189,
190, 192, 196, 197, 200, 215,
237, 238, 239, 240, 242, 246,
250, 251
astral, 153, 154, 157
Stoic, 154
théôria, 48, 52, 56, 57, 61, 131, 241
Timaeus, 55, 67, 77, 78, 97, 98, 102,
108, 109, 134, 137, 153
time, 43, 48, 51, 239–40
tragedy, 81, 108, 110
Tricot, Jules, x, 148, 162, 167, 170,
186, 189, 191, 192, 199, 203,
213, 219, 220, 248
truth, 10, 23, 24, 26, 31, 32, 40, 52,
61, 62, 88, 100, 103, 121, 123
alêtheia, 130
growth of, 30
mathematical, 33
moment of, 42
recognition of, 30
time of, 22

unmoved mover(s), 239–44, 246, 253

virtue, 20, 32, 33
vision, 9, 47
Volkmann-Schluck, Karl-Heinz, 58

Wahl, Jean, 81, 82, 83, 84, 86
White, Nicholas P., 100
wisdom, 177, 184, 188, 195, 238,
242, 251
analogy of, 242

Xenophon, 126, 127, 138
Xenophanes, 120

Zeller, Eduard, 64
Zeno, 72, 74, 75, 76, 80, 82
Zeyl, Donald J., 106

Index of Passages Cited in Plato and Aristotle

Plato

Cratylus
383d, 15
385c, 15
386a-c, 15
386c, 129
386e, 15, 17
387c, 16, 17
388b, 16
388c, 16
389d, 15, 129
390c, 14
401c, 10
439a, 14, 15, 16
439b, 16
439c, 14, 110
439d-e, 18
440d, 18
Euthyphro
5d, 9
11a, 15
Gorgias
522a, 141
522c–527e, 140
526d, 141
527d, 141
Hippias Major
288a, 9
292c, 10

Laches
190c, 8
191d, 8
191e, 8, 9
192a, 10
192b, 11
Laws
283a–285a, 134
893, 107
894b, 107
895e, 107
899b, 117
Letter VII
341a, 59
341c-d, 59
342a–344d, 23
Meno
72a, 11
72c, 11, 29
74a, 10, 29
77a, 10, 29
80d, 30
81d, 30, 41
82b, 31
82e, 31
84a-b, 31
85c, 32
85d, 31
86b-c, 31, 41
86c–87a, 42
96c 32

97a-b, 32
98a, 20, 33
98c, 32
99b, 32
99c, 33
100b, 33
Parmenides
127e–130a, 74
128c–130a, 76
129c, 76
129d-e, 96
130a–135c, 75, 76
130d, 78
130e1-4, 78
133b, 79
135a-b, 79
136b, 86
137b, 80
139b-e, 93
140a-e, 93
141e, 91
142b-c, 83
146a, 93
146b–147a, 93
166c, 85
Phaedo
64a, 53, 54
64e, 54
66a, 20
66b, 110
66e, 54
66a–67b, 20
66c, 129
67a, 110
67b, 54
72c, 56
73a, 56
74a-b, 56
75c-d, 35
76c–77a, 56
76d, 35
77a, 56
77b-c, 56
78b, 54
78d, 17, 35
80a-b, 54
80b, 129
82e, 110
92c-e, 56
97b–99a, 125
98a, 20
99b, 133
99c–100b, 56

100b, 35
100b-c, 56
101c, 81
101d, 56
101e, 41
107a, 57
107b, 56
107c-d, 141
107d–115a, 140
110d, 103
Phaedrus
245d, 106
246a–257b, 140
246b, 106
246c, 240
246d, 129
247c, 129
247c-d, 107
247c-e, 50
247d, 132
249c, 138
249e, 132
288b-c, 107
248c, 51
249c, 51
250b, 51, 107
254b, 107
261c, 81
265d–266c, 62, 134
266b, 62
270a–272c, 62
277b, 62
Philebus
13c–27e, 59
16c, 67
16d, 98
16e, 97
16c–17a, 65, 134
16c–18d, 92
17, 66
17a, 98
17c, 99
23c–27e, 91
27b, 97, 107
28d, 125
28e, 125
58a, 60
64b, 52
64c–65a, 45
64e–65a, 134
65a, 53
66a-b, 45
66b, 45, 134

Republic
379b-c, 111
476a, 17, 129
476c, 129
477b, 129
477d, 21
490b, 17, 129
502d, 36
504e, 36
505a, 37
505d, 37
505e, 38, 133
506a, 38
506d, 60
506e, 38, 133
507b, 38
507c, 138
507e, 38
508c–509b, 133
508e, 38, 130, 136
508e–509c, 59
509a, 38
509b, 38
509d, 37, 46
510b, 40, 56, 82
510c, 40
510c-d, 42
510d-e, 42
511a, 63
511b, 44, 56, 82
511d, 40
514a, 37
517a-c, 45
517b, 133
517b-c, 60, 139
517c, 137
521e, 41
526c, 41
526e, 46
527a, 41
532a, 17, 63, 129
532a-d, 45
533a–535a, 43
533c, 44
534c, 44
535d, 44
537c, 61, 134
546a, 110
614a–621d, 140
617c, 109
617e, 111
Sophist
218a, 91

242c, 90
243d-e, 91
244b, 91
244b-c, 91
244d, 91
246a, 10
248a, 100
248e–249a, 135
249a, 100
249b, 100
249d, 136, 137
251d–252e, 85
252a-b, 73
253b–254b, 63, 134
253d, 68, 96
253d5-9, 63
254a, 64
255b, 95
255e, 95
256c, 92
256e, 95
259a-b, 95
259c, 95
262c, 19
265c-d, 138
Statesman
269e, 111
270a, 138
273b-c, 111
283c–285a, 44
283e, 66
284b, 72
284c, 44
284d, 45
Symposium
203e, 49
210c–211, 49, 59
211, 50
Theaetetus
146d, 20
146e, 129
151e, 24
155d, 163
172c–177c, 27
177c–179d, 25
181c–183c, 25
183c, 71
185a–187a, 26
185c, 35
185e, 53
186a-b, 35
187a, 53, 131

Timaeus
  27d–28, 107
  28a-b, 106
  28c, 106
  29a, 104, 108
  29c, 108
  30a, 109
  30b-c, 108
  31a-b, 104
  33a, 104
  34a, 104
  34a-b, 137
  41e, 111
  42d, 111
  47a, 104
  48a, 109
  49a, 109
  51a, 97
  53c, 109
  68e, 140
  92b, 137

Aristotle

De Anima
  407a32, 164
  412b18, 207
  414a, 231
  415a26-27, 247
De Caelo
  279a17-30, 247
Metaphysics
  981b24, 163
  981b27, 162
  982b12, 163
  982b17-20, 163
  983a5-7, 164
  984a18, 165
  984b8-11, 152
  984b15, 126
  984b18, 165
  985a17, 126
  986a12-15, 166
  986b5-7, 166
  986b13, 167
  986b15, 182
  986b16-17, 166
  986b31, 167
  987a30, 16
  987a33-34, 167
  987b1-5, 167
  987b12-13, 168
  987b15, 46

  988a20-22, 169
  990b1, 168
  993a10-12, 169
  993b13, 177
  996b13-16, 177
  996b31, 178
  997a14, 178
  997a34, 238
  999a26, 230
  1003a7-13, 170
  1003b17-18, 188
  1003b18, 187
  1004a3-10, 199
  1004a10-16, 186
  1005a11, 191
  1005a35, 253
  1017b10, 200
  1017b23, 201
  1019a15, 210
  1019a19, 213
  1019b27, 212
  1026a6, 189
  1026a10-31, 253
  1026a13, 159
  1026a14, 189
  1026a16, 189
  1028a20-b2, 238
  1031a12, 171
  1031a15-28, 172
  1026a23, 191
  1026a28-32, 191
  1026a30, 252
  1028a23, 199
  1028a26, 199
  1028a27, 203
  1028b2-3, 195
  1029a1, 201
  1029a7, 202
  1029a10, 202
  1029a19-20, 202
  1029a23, 202
  1029a23-25, 228
  1029b15, 216
  1031b3-18, 171
  1031b6, 217
  1031b15-18, 219
  1031b31–1032a, 172
  1032b1-4, 253
  1032b3-6, 186
  1032b22, 218
  1033b16-19, 226
  1033b17-19, 218
  1033b20-31, 219

Metaphysics (cont.)
1034a7, 228
1034a30, 219
1034a30-32, 249
1035a7-9, 217
1035b27-31, 172
1036a28-30, 221
1037a29-30, 228
1038a8, 221
1038a19-20, 221
1038a28-29, 221
1038b9, 228
1038b9-15, 228
1038b16-23, 228
1039a3, 219
1039b27, 226
1039b27-1040a8, 226
1039b33, 226
1041a4, 201
1042a25, 207
1042b9-10, 208
1043a14, 207
1043a-1043b2, 208
1045a23-24, 208
1045a29-30, 208
1045a29-35, 222
1045b18-19, 208
1046a1, 210
1050a15, 213
1050a30-31, 250
1050b28, 246
1051a22, 40
1058b2-4, 233
1058b10, 233
1058b22, 233
1060b21, 170
1064–1065, 158
1069a18, 252
1072a32, 253
1072a33-34, 246
1072a26, 243
1072a32, 244
1072b3, 244
1072b13, 241
1072b13-14, 246
1072b14, 244

1072b14-30, 241
1074a33, 230
1086a21, 159
1086b21, 170
1086b32-35, 170
1088b–1089a, 72
1096a17-23, 173
1096b8-25, 173
Nicomachean Ethics
1096a13-17, 152
On Generation and Corruption
336b27–337a7, 247
Parts of Animals
644a23-b7, 231
Physics
184a12–184b15, 204
186a9ff., 200
190a6-12, 200
190a15-24, 200
192a6, 209
192a10-11, 208
192a22-24, 209
192a23, 207
192b21-22, 209
192b33, 209
193a10-13, 209
193a28, 209
193b18, 210
200a3, 207
200a24, 207
200b5, 207
200b26-27, 211
201a10, 211
201b25, 212
201b30–202a2, 212
203b1-15, 118
207a18, 125
247b13, 164
250b23–251b13, 240
259a16, 240
Posterior Analytics
73b26, 183
74a3, 183
87b30, 226
89b23, 234
92b13, 235

Printed in the USA
CPSIA information can be obtained
at www.ICGtesting.com
LVHW021220221223
766828LV00023B/89